Library of
Davidson College

INNOVATIVE TEACHING STRATEGIES

Michael J. Rockler
Rutgers University

Gorsuch Scarisbrick, Publishers
Scottsdale, Arizona

Cover Design by Formaz

Gorsuch Scarisbrick, Publishers
8233 Via Paseo del Norte, Suite F-400
Scottsdale, Arizona 85258

10 9 8 7 6 5 4 3 2 1

ISBN 0-89787-523-0

Copyright © 1988 by Gorsuch Scarisbrick, Publishers

All rights reserved. No part of this publication may be reproduced, stored in a retrieval system, or transmitted, in any form or by any means, electronic, mechanical, photocopy, recording or otherwise, without the prior written permission of the Publisher.

Printed in the United States of America.

PREFACE

This book serves as an introductory text on innovative teaching strategies for those who are learning to be teachers. It has been my experience, as a professor of pre-service and in-service education, that teachers learn best when theory and practice are balanced. Concrete applications of theories help educators understand the nature of effective instruction. The bringing together of theoretical scholarship with hands-on activity becomes more necessary as greater emphasis is placed on the role of field experience in teacher training. Today, fieldwork is introduced earlier and with increased intensity in most education programs. Teachers must understand the rationale for specific methods and learn to translate this comprehension into actual practice. The many complete exercises found in this volume offer support to the reader who is going to enter the classroom for the first time.

Throughout my teaching of many courses on strategy, curriculum, and methods, I have combined abstract ideas with hands-on activities. This text continues that practice. Ideas that support the use of innovative teaching strategies are reinforced by many types of examples; these examples provide creativity exercises, simulation/games, and future studies techniques. Those who use this book will understand why a theory or technique applies, will know how to apply it, and will be able to choose from a variety of good procedures. The exercises included in this volume have all been tried by students in my classes; the reader can use them with the assurance that they work.

Because this is a book about teaching strategies, it includes all the topics which must be considered in a general methods course:

- The process of choosing objectives is introduced in Chapter 2.
- Thinking skills are discussed in Chapter 4.

- Organization of instruction—short term and long term—is discussed and demonstrated in Chapter 2.
- Chapter 2 also examines the process of conceptualization.
- An in-depth examination of classroom management can be found in Chapter 12, which discusses a variety of perspectives and offers advice from practitioners about limit setting.
- Discovery learning is analyzed in the chapters on simulation/gaming and creativity. Techniques for facilitating discovery teaching can be found in Chapters 5, 8, and 10.
- Questioning as part of instruction and as it relates to evaluation is discussed in Chapter 2.
- Information about teaching the gifted and talented is included in Chapter 11.

Innovative Teaching Strategies is more than a standard textbook on teaching methodology. It provides the teacher with techniques designed to prepare pupils for life in the twenty-first century. The first chapter presents the need for innovative teaching strategies and offers an overview of them. Chapter 2 describes methods for effective organization of instruction. Chapters 3 and 4 are theoretical examinations of the process of creativity while Chapter 5 presents the reader with a great variety of techniques for facilitating creative behavior. Chapters 6 and 7 examine theories of simulation/gaming while Chapter 8 indicates ways to use the process in the classroom. Chapters 9 and 10 address future studies both theoretically and in terms of teaching procedures. The use of innovative teaching strategies with gifted and talented students is examined in Chapter 11. Chapter 12 provides alternative perspectives on classroom management. An epilogue discusses conclusions that may be drawn from the material in this volume.

A developing concept in education is the notion of brain compatible teaching, which suggests that understanding the brain can lead to teaching techniques consistent with human learning. The strategies described in this volume are brain compatible; they may be used in ways that maximize pupil achievement.

As a result of using this book, the reader will learn how to prepare for teaching, how to use innovative teaching strategies, and how to create a context in which teaching can be effective.

Acknowledgments

My greatest debt is to my wife, Linda DiDesidero, who has served unselfishly as the editor of all of my writings. Her perspectives on creativity, gaming, and future studies have influenced me in immeasurable ways. *Innovative Teaching Strategies* is dedicated to her with love.

Several of my colleagues at Rutgers University have been helpful to me over the years and their support has made this work possible. Specifically, I acknowledge the friendship and help of J. J. Chambliss, Miriam Chaplin, Sidney Katz, Ed Mauger, and Abe Mencer. I also wish to acknowledge the support and encouragement of my friend Richard Bergman, whose insights have added much to the development of this book.

I would like to thank the following publishers for their permission to reprint material used in this volume:

Chapter 1, pp. 2–3: Excerpts from *The Dance of Life* by Edward T. Hall. Copyright © 1983 by Edward T. Hall. Reprinted by permission of Doubleday & Co., Inc.

Chapter 4, pp. 55–56: From J. P. Guilford, "The Structure of the Intellect." Copyright © by J. P. Guilford. Reprinted with permission.

Chapter 4, pp. 62–65: From William J. J. Gordon, *The New Art of the Possible.* Copyright © by SES Associates, 121 Brattle Street, Cambridge, MA 02138. Reprinted with permission.

Chapter 5, pp. 83–84: From *Turn-ons* by Stephen K. Smuin, copyright © 1978 by David S. Lake Publishers, Belmont, CA 94002. Reprinted with permission.

Chapter 5, pp. 87–88: From William J. J. Gordon, *Strange and Familiar* (Book Six). Copyright © by SES Associates, 121 Brattle Street, Cambridge, MA 02138. Reprinted with permission.

Chapter 7, pp. 111–113: From *An Inventory of Hunches* by Hall Sprague and Garry Shirts. Reprinted by permission of Simile II, P.O. Box 910, Del Mar, CA 92014.

Chapter 7, p. 123: From *Games for Growth* by Alice Kaplan Gordon. Copyright © 1970, Science Research Associates, Inc. Reprinted by permission of the publisher.

Chapter 8, pp. 131–133: From *Freeway Planning Game* by Michael Chester. Reprinted by permission of Simile II, P.O. Box 910, Del Mar, CA 92014.

Chapter 8, pp. 133–138: From P. Douglas McConatha, *Quick City.* Copyright © by P. Douglas McConatha. Reprinted with permission.

Chapter 9, pp. 158–159: From Draper L. Kaufman, *Teaching the Future.* Copyright © by ETC Publications, Palm Springs, CA 92263. Reprinted with permission.

Chapter 10, pp. 174–177: From William C. Miller, *The Third Wave and Education's Futures.* Copyright © by Phi Delta Kappa Educational Foundation, Bloomington, IN 47402. Reprinted with permission.

Chapter 10, pp. 182–183: From *Turn-Ons* by Stephen K. Smuin. Copyright © 1978 by David S. Lake Publishers, Belmont, CA 94002. Reprinted with permission.

Chapter 10, p. 185: From Doris Shallcross in Jack Canfield and Harold C. Wells, *100 Ways to Enhance Self-Concept in the Classroom: A Handbook for Teachers and Parents,* copyright © 1976, p. 173. Reprinted by permission of Prentice-Hall, Inc., Englewood Cliffs, NJ.

Chapter 10, p. 186: From Martha Crampton and George Brown in Jack Canfield and Harold C. Wells, *100 Ways to Enhance Self-Concept in the Classroom: A Handbook for Teachers and Parents,* copyright © 1976, p. 175. Reprinted by permission of Prentice-Hall, Inc., Englewood Cliffs, NJ.

Chapter 11, pp. 214–215: From Carol Carpenter, "Who Are the Gifted?" *Curriculum Review,* April, 1981. Copyright © *Curriculum Review,* Chicago, IL. Reprinted with permission.

CONTENTS

1 Introduction   1
Introduction   1
Hall's Perspectives on Time: Micro Time and Sync Time   2
Time, Culture, and Learning   4
The Three Strategies   6
Summary   12

2 Organization of Instruction   13
Introduction   13
The Components of Instruction   15
Organization: A Behavioral Perspective   18
Organization: A Conceptual Perspective   20
Sample Lesson Plans   23
Asking Questions   29
Long-Range Planning   32
Summary   33

3 The Process of Creativity   35
Introduction   35
Definitions of Creativity   36
Person, Product, Process, Environment   39
Creative Ways of Knowing: Endocepts and Janusian Thinking   42
Some Questions   44
Components of Creativity   45
Conscious and Unconscious Aspects of the Process of Creativity   46
Facilitating Creative Behavior   48
Summary   49

4 Theories of Creativity 51
Introduction 51
Theories Based on the Study of Consciousness 52
Theories Based on the Study of the Unconscious 59
Summary 67

5 Techniques for Facilitating Creative Behavior 69
Introduction: John Dewey and the Use of Activity in Education 69
Planning: A Psychodrama Model 70
Activities 71
Summary 92

6 The Process of Simulation/Gaming 93
Introduction 93
Definitions 94
The Nature of the Process 95
The History of Simulation/Gaming 97
Facilitating Learning 99
Gaming as Interdisciplinary Learning 101
Gaming and Creativity 102
Game as Creative Environment 104
Simulation/Gaming and Group Process 106
Computer Gaming 107
Summary 108

7 Theories of Simulation and Gaming 111
Introduction 111
John Dewey and Simulation/Gaming 114
Abraham Maslow and Self-Actualization 116
Simulation/Gaming and Human Potential 118
Psychological Aspects of Gaming 119
Simulation/Gaming as Future's Language 121
Summary 123

8 Using Simulation/Games 125
Introduction 125
Using Games 126
Three Games 130
An Annotated List of Simulation/Games 138
Summary 147

9 Future Studies   149
Prologue   149
Introduction: The Need for Future Studies   151
The Nature of Future Studies   156
Conceptualizing the Future   158
Creativity Theorists and Future Studies   163
Summary   168

10 Techniques for Studying the Future   171
Introduction   171
Curricular Considerations   171
Curriculum and Third Wave Society   174
The World Future Society   178
Activities for Teaching Future Studies   179
Simulations   187
Summary   195

11 Giftedness and Innovative Teaching Strategies   197
Introduction   197
Definitions   199
Components of the Gifted and Talented   201
Characteristics of Gifted and Talented Students   202
Characteristics of Teachers   205
Design of Programs   206
Theorists of Gifted and Talented Education   208
The Three Strategies and Giftedness   211
Summary   214

12 Classroom Management   217
Introduction   217
Behavior Modification   219
William Glasser: Reality Therapy and Control Theory   221
Humanistic Psychology and Classroom Management   225
Advice from Practitioners   227
Conclusions   230

Epilogue: Implications and Conclusions   233

Additional Reading   240

Index   241

CHAPTER

1

Introduction

INTRODUCTION

Students today, like students in the past, need to be equipped by their education for the challenges of their lives. They must learn and practice skills; they must have access to information and know how to find it and use it; they must acquire a sense of the interrelatedness of past, current, and future events. But, in addition, the growing problems of the late twentieth century require students to learn in ways that maximize their ability to become *problem solvers.*

Alvin Toffler, the noted futurist, speaks of "future shock"—a sense of malaise, a feeling that nothing can ever go right. It arises, Toffler argues, because the present era is a transitional one ("between waves") in which the rate of change has so accelerated that people are left feeling overwhelmed by a future that intrudes on the present in a way never before experienced.

Change comes in many forms, and offers problems as well as solutions. Change confronts people in the form of new technological devices and procedures that may bring displacement and intimidation as often as they offer convenience and improvement. Governments grow larger and yet may become less responsive, leading to a sense of frustration in their citizens. The increasing world population has had a profoundly negative effect on the planet and its resources. The temporary abatement of the energy crisis has removed some of the urgency from this issue, but the issue itself is still with us. And of course the most significant problem facing mankind is the threat of destruction by nuclear war or accident.

The solutions to the major difficulties facing this planet will require cooperation, foresight, and creativity. Today's students' must become effective problem-solvers, and education must facilitate this aspect of their growth. The strategies in this book include the facilitation of creative behavior, simulation/gaming, and future studies.

HALL'S PERSPECTIVES ON TIME: MICRO TIME AND SYNC TIME

An understanding of anthropologist Edward T. Hall's perspectives on time, synchrony, and communication can improve instruction by helping educators facilitate different learning styles. Hall describes these constructs in two books: *Beyond Culture* (1976) and *The Dance of Life* (1983).

Time, Hall argues, is inseparable from culture—is a part of its core. He views time as a language that serves as a primary organizer for all activities. Time is a way of handling priorities and categorizing experience. In effect, people must learn the language of time as well as the spoken language in order to communicate.

Hall identifies several kinds of time, including *physical time,* based on the rotation of the earth and its movement around the sun; *biological time,* the cycles of life and death experienced by all things in nature; and *personal time,* the subjective feeling within all people that their time is either flying or crawling.

Hall describes two kinds of time that have particular relevance for facilitating learning; these are *micro time* and *sync time*. Micro time is a system that is congruent with and a product of *primary level culture* (PLC), or the "hidden cultural grammar" that defines the way in which people view the world. PLC determines values and establishes the basic tempos and rhythms of life. Micro time is one of the building blocks of culture.

Two subtypes exist within micro time: *monochronic* (or M-time) and *polychronic* (or P-time) (see Figure 1.1). Hall explains the difference between the two as follows:

> Years of exposure to other cultures demonstrated that complex societies organize time in at least two different ways: events scheduled as separate items—one thing at a time—as in North Europe, or following the Mediterranean model of involvement in several things at once.... I have termed doing many things at once polychronic, P-time. The North European system—doing one thing at a time—is

monochronic, M-time. P-time stresses involvement of people and completion of transactions rather than adherence to present schedules. Appointments are not taken as seriously and as a consequence are frequently broken. P-time is treated as less tangible than M-time. For polychronic people, time is seldom experienced as "wasted," and is apt to be considered a point rather than a ribbon or a road.

Though M-time cultures tend to make a fetish out of management, there are points at which M-time doesn't make as much sense as it might. Life in general is at times unpredictable; and who can tell how long a particular client, patient, or set of transactions will take. These are imponderables in the chemistry of human transactions. What can be accomplished one day in ten minutes may take twenty minutes on the next. Some days people will be rushed and can't finish; on others there is time to spare, so they "waste" the remaining time.

MICRO TIME	SYNC TIME
Monochronic Time Polychronic Time	

FIGURE 1.1

People in the United States and northern Europe tend to view micro time as exclusively monochronic; but, Hall argues, M-time is arbitrary and imposed—a learned perception that "is *not* inherent in man's biological rhythms or his creative drives." Yet M-time has become so thoroughly integrated into Western culture that it is treated as the only logical and natural way of organizing life. Many of the conflicts in the modern world may be identified as conflicts between cultures that are primarily monochronic and those that are polychronic.

Hall's concept of *sync time* relates to the rhythms of relations between people. When people achieve interpersonal synchrony—when they are in sync—they are able to communicate and function together in ways that enhance mutual achievement. Communication and learning require that people be in sync with each other. Hall believes that people find better synchronization, and thus better communication, in P-time because polychronic life requires group interaction, whereas M-time culture emphasizes individual relationships.

Hall uses the term *entrainment* to define the situation that exists when people are in sync; that is, when two or more people are operating with the same rhythms. In general, as culture approaches the polychronic end of the spectrum, it requires a greater degree of entrainment because the intensity of group interaction increases. Hence, an attempt to balance monochronic behavior with polychronic behavior also involves the need to increase entrainment.

Before relating this discussion of time and its different forms to the process of education, one additional term needs to be defined. Hall discusses the concept of *extensions,* saying that "extensions are a particular kind of tool that not only speeds up work and makes it easier but also separates people from their work. Extensions are a kind of amplifier."

The telephone is an example of an extension of the human voice, the crane extends human strength, and computers extend human memory and mental capacity.

Extensions are sometimes confused with the *process* of being extended. Hall calls this *extension transference.* For example, words, which are extensions of communication, can come to be seen as real in and of themselves rather than as symbols extending the things and processes of the world. The clock and the calendar are also prime examples of extension transference. They extend the human ability to measure time, but can lead to the imposition of artificial schedules on people. The inventions of the clock and the calendar are mainly responsible for the creation of monochronic time and for the tendency of Western peoples to run their lives by schedules. However, polychronic activity can redress the balance between natural time and time measured by the clock and calendar.

TIME, CULTURE, AND LEARNING

Since each classroom is a product of the overall culture, and is itself a culture, the teacher who can understand and apply the constructs of *micro time* (including polychronic and monochronic emphasis), *sync time* (including the concept of entrainment), and *extension,* can facilitate instruction. Such a teacher can enrich and consciously shape the learning environment.

The need for the kinds of behavior described by Hall that would balance natural time and measured time increases in a world where complexity and limitless extensions make polychronic life difficult to achieve. The strategies described in this book provide experience with polychronic culture and with interpersonal synchrony. They offer ways to facilitate alternative learning styles. For example, simulation/gaming—one of the strategies described in this book—fosters polychronic development because its central focus is usually the group. A major difference between P-time and M-time involves the perceptions of individuals and groups. Monochronic culture and monochronic people prefer one-on-one relationships just as they tend to live one minute at a time. Polychronic people seek to relate simultaneously to large numbers of people just as they perceive time in greater, less precisely scheduled segments. Games can increase polychronic behavior because they usually take place in groups and because many good games require polychronic behavior as they proceed.

Many simulation/games (described in considerable detail in Chapter 8) are able to achieve this. *Culture Contact* (designed by Abt Associates) is one example. This game brings two different cultures together—one polychronic and the other monochronic. Polychronic behavior must be developed by both teams in order for the game to end in a satisfactory manner. Each side must be able to evaluate aspects of the other culture while simultaneously pursuing its own goals. Simile II's *Bafa Bafa,* another game that involves competing cultures, and *Starpower,* an exercise that builds a three-tiered society, are other games in which polychronic values and behaviors are developed. *Freeway Planning,* a game by Michael Chester, involves a variety of group interactions that can bring about polychronic behavior.

Games can also develop interpersonal synchrony. Because of their group nature, players must develop rhythm between each other if the process is to be effective. Games such as the High School Geography Project's *Metfab,* in which players must find a site for a factory, and Robert Horn's *Participative Decision Making,* a simulation that examines the process of creating a school budget, have this quality as players work together to solve problems and make compromises. A game written by the author—*Interdepartmental Decision Making*—demonstrates the problems that arise when people are not in sync and are not able to engage in polychronic behavior. Another exercise that involves polychronic skills and demands interpersonal synchrony is one called *Parcoes* in which teams must work together to create a product that is to be sold in a market.

Most simulations that involve group decision making and those which require the completion of a task by a group (and there are hundreds that do both) are games that can foster polychronic values and synchrony.

Hall's construct of the use and control of extensions (which are valuable human tools so long as they do not lead to extension transference) can also be facilitated by the use of the simulation process. Any good game is an extension, extending human experience by providing a vicarious, simulated experience. Games extend the ability to understand, communicate, and experience; we can avoid extension transference by maintaining appropriate reality orientation—the balance between too little and too much detail.

Improved balance between monochronic and polychronic behavior, improved interpersonal synchrony, and the appropriate use of extensions can all improve problem-solving ability. The strategies described in this book can facilitate all of these outcomes. As these kinds of strategies improve polychronic behavior and facilitate interpersonal synchrony, they increase the teacher's ability to provide for the variety of learning styles found among students.

THE THREE STRATEGIES

The purpose of this book is to demonstrate how three strategies—facilitating creative behavior, simulation/gaming, and the study of the future can be used to meet the needs of alternative learning styles and increase problem-solving capability among students. In this section, these three techniques are introduced and defined.

Facilitating Creative Behavior

Defining creativity seems simple: *Creativity is a means by which a person obtains a new perspective and, as a result, brings something new to consciousness.*

This ostensibly clear definition is, however, laden with complexities: Is "means" a process or a quality? When does the creative act begin and when does it end? How does it begin? Does it progress through stages? Must it always culminate in a tangible product? Is this "something new" novel for the person or new to the universe?

Many creativity theorists deal with these complexities in defining the creative act. Although each has a different conceptualization and model of the creative process, the theorists operate basically within a paradigm of accepted beliefs. That is, the definitions they offer seem to be complementary rather than contradictory.

Creativity theory derives from at least two separate sources: the study of intelligence and the development of psychoanalysis. The study of intelligence began with the work of the psychologist Sir Francis Galton, who was interested in how heredity and environment each contribute to the development of mental ability. Galton also investigated the relationship between motor skills and intelligence, which he believed were significantly related. Both issues remain controversial and unresolved.

The relationship between intelligence theory and education originated with Alfred Binet, who wished to predict the potential school success of children. Binet created age-referenced norms for a variety of ability tests (memory, mental imagery, imagination, and so on) and obtained a composite average score for children at various school levels. He reasoned that children who scored above the norm for their age would do well in school and those who achieved below the mean would have difficulties. Binet's logic was correct; however, his work was soon transformed by those who equated achievement at an age norm with *mental age*—leading to the concept of *intelligence quotient* or IQ (mental age divided by chronological age times 100).

The concept of IQ has created enormous problems. In working with gifted and talented students, for example, one must be careful that IQ not be the only criterion for selection. Even when other measures are used, the IQ score often becomes a major determinant. This leads to the rejection of some children who could gain from a gifted and talented program. At times IQ has been misused by encouraging a belief that small differences in IQ are significant when they are, in fact, not. Another abuse of the concept of IQ results from the argument that some racial or ethnic groups have better IQs because of superior gene pools—a total misunderstanding of the concept. Perhaps the most damaging effect has been the tendency to assume that mental ability is unidimensional—that intellectual skill can be equated with the size of IQ.

Psychologist J. P. Guilford reacted against this single measure of intelligence by developing a multidimensional model called "the structure of intellect." In this paradigm (obtained by mathematical factoring based on correlations) Guilford demonstrated that persons are able to create a variety of products from any kinds of content using five types of mental operations: memory, cognition, evaluation, and convergent and divergent production.

It is the operation of divergent production—innovative, experimental thought patterns turning "outward" to examine all possibilities—leading to a transformation or discovery that defines creativity. This conceptualization makes it possible to understand creative behavior as a quality that can be improved by direct intervention. Divergent production can be taught and creativity is thus increased.

In the early 1970s E. Paul Torrance converted Guilford's sophisticated psychological theory into procedures that were suitable for classroom use. In his writings, Torrance describes methods for encouraging creative behavior by improving specific attributes including sensitivity to problems, fluency, flexibility, originality, elaboration, and redefinition.

These traits can be improved with practice. Teachers, for example, can provide students with an object with traditional uses (e.g., a tin can) and help them formulate new ways to view the object (cans are usually used to hold vegetables but string could transform them into walkie-talkies). Torrance created many exercises to facilitate creative behavior.

These result in a greater curiosity, a desire to meet challenges, and a willingness to attempt difficult tasks. The development of all these traits lead to greater individuality and more innovative activity.

The attempt to foster creative behavior also has its roots in psychoanalysis. For Sigmund Freud, creativity arose from the need to resolve conflict; it incorporated childhood fantasy into adult life. Although it was controversial, Freud's view led to a better understanding of the importance of the unconscious in the creative act. Simply put, a censorlike mechanism represses most innovative activity, and does not allow persons to associate apparently unrelated events in their unconscious; this prevents the creation of a new synthesis in the conscious domain. In order to increase input from the unconscious it becomes necessary to weaken (but not destroy) the censor. For many who have sought to unlock their creativity, this increased flow from the unconscious can result from the use of metaphor.

Just as Torrance developed specific materials for the application of Guilford's model in the classroom, so William J. J. Gordon described procedures for teaching the process of metaphor. Gordon calls his approach "synectics"—an extended process for applying analogy to problem-solving. Although Gordon began his career by using synectics in industry, he later turned to its application in education. We turn to a discussion of Gordon's work later in the book.

Simulation/Gaming

> Time was running out; the tension in the Cabinet Room mounted. For the first time since the advent of the crisis there appeared to be cracks in President Briody's outward calm. The President bit her lip as she received the latest set of options sent to her by teletype.
>
> She could launch a full-scale attack on the Soviet Union and hope they'd be caught off-guard. The second option was to put all United States forces on stand-down status; this might convince the Soviets that the Bombers which had already passed their failsafe points on their way to the Soviet Union were there because of an error. Her third option was to call the Soviet President to set up a hotline call between the Strategic Air Command (SAC) in the U.S. and the Russian forces; in this way, the U.S. would help the Soviets intercept the bombers. If she took no action, the bombers would continue on their way to the Soviet Union. This could result in war and/or the destruction of the world.
>
> The President's previous attempt to reestablish radio contact with the bombers had failed. National Security advisers and a group of

advisers from SAC worked with the President to attempt to solve this dilemma and avoid world destruction.

The SAC group had advised the President to surprise the Soviets with a full-scale attack. National Security advisers argued for placing U.S. forces on stand-down status to let the Soviets know there had been a mistake. The President took the advice of neither group. Instead, she called the Soviet leader on the hotline to set up communication between SAC and the Russian air command. Both countries would work together to intercept the bombers. But ... would the Soviets trust her?

Yes! Using the information provided for them, the Soviets intercepted the approaching bombers. As the President announced the result, cheers went up in the Cabinet Room. Mingled with the elation was a genuine sense of relief.

This narrative describes a group of students playing the computer simulation/game *Failsafe* (an adaptation for the computer of Burdick and Wheeler's book). Often a group of players will choose a strategy that results in a peaceful solution to the crisis; just as often, however, the game results in war and world destruction. The challenge of this game, and many other games available for instruction purposes (both computer- and non-computer-based) for students is immense. Whatever the outcome, certain things are always true.

Players become totally involved with the crisis, even though it is a simulation and nothing real is at stake. The game becomes real for the participants and the atmosphere is always charged with tension. Players learn about executive decision making, and in the post-game discussion, they achieve a degree of empathy for each of the decision makers. Participants also learn how to use a computer. The screen provides the scenario, time up-dates, and a set of options following each decision. Finally, playing the game is not only fun, it also provides students with motivation to learn.

Because many people think of games as simply fun, they underestimate their value. Teachers tend to deny the validity of games as teaching techniques, and, for many, viewing games as integral part of living seem preposterous.

Actually, simulation/gaming has its roots in war games, which continue to be used extensively by the military in training officers and soldiers to understand martial conflict and to deal with these conflicts strategically. Presently, simulation/games are also used in the training of lawyers, all types of administrators, and corporate executives and employees. The technique has also found its way into schools, although not to the extent that its success might indicate. The process of simulation/

gaming has many applications, most of which do not require a computer. However, with the growing availability of microcomputers both in schools and in many homes, computer-based simulation/gaming is growing quickly. In this text, the process is addressed in a general way with attention to computer gaming as well.

A game is basically a contest between two or more players that proceeds in accordance with a set of rules. A simulation/game, such as *Failsafe,* attempts to emulate a real world event in a realistic, but simulated setting. Participants have goals they try to achieve; their behavior is governed by a set of rules and their actions lead to a variety of outcomes.

The commercial game, *Monopoly,* requires players to attempt to obtain property as they move around a board. Role-play simulations assign players specific parts in order to solve a problem or make a decision. Their choices may affect several other players as well. Both kinds of game come under the category simulation/game: those played on boards (many instructional ones as well as commercial types) and those involving role-play. Hybrids also exist: these assign roles to board players. It is also possible to use commercial games in an educational way. Computer games are an additional category and some computer games (such as *Failsafe*) require role-play.

Games and simulations have much value for students. They can be used to teach content, concepts, skills, and attitudes. *Failsafe,* for instance, teaches the content of world military powers. It develops the concept of decision making and instructs in computer techniques and also teaches interpersonal skills. It provides students with an opportunity to examine their own attitudes concerning the issues of war and power.

Games also provide players with an understanding of human behavior, of overt as well as covert actions and motives. Games may be used as tools of socialization; players learn how to win, how to lose, how to accept the role of chance in life, and how to take risks. Owing to their sociodramatic quality, games may also be used to improve mental health. All of these themes, and others, are developed in the chapters on simulation/gaming.

Future Studies

The discipline of future studies has arisen, in part, as a result of the difficulties that persons experience with regard to contemplating tomorrow. Professional futurists (persons who make careers of attempting to anticipate the time to come) seek to use an interdisciplinary focus in order to comprehend coming eras. The interdisciplinary approach fits in well with strategies designed to provide for alternative learning styles.

One approach to the future involves prediction, or attempts to extrapolate the potential future from current happenings. A prediction may be a statement that begins, "If current trends continue..." Unfortunately, they rarely do. Many examples of this can be seen in a book by Paul Dickson entitled *The Future File*.[1] In it the author includes the following quotation, "Aerial flight is one of that great class of problems with which man can never cope..." This prediction was made by astronomer Simon Newcomb in October, 1903—two months before Wilbur and Orville opened the modern age of aviation! Other erroneous predictions from *The Future File:*

- The automobile will never replace the bicycle as a primary source of transportation. (1899)
- Commercial television is unlikely to be successful. (1926)
- The construction of a highway system is impossible. (1902)

In August, 1948, *Science Digest* correctly predicted that man would land on the moon... in the year 2148!

Dickson's book contains correct forecasts as well, although they are not as much fun to describe as the erroneous ones. His collection of false predictions conveys an important message: humankind has a limited ability to correctly anticipate the future.

One way in which people attempt to cope with this frustrating inability to see tomorrow is through the ancient art of prophecy. Prophets often attract well-paying customers. Those who have (or claim to have) the ability to foretell events earn good livings. Astrologers write in most daily newspapers, palm readers are found in every major city. Ouija boards and magic eight balls may often be sold as toys, but many people regard them with serious superstition.

A certain genre of science fiction stories also illustrates this theme. In these tales, sophisticated artificial intelligence is employed to predict the future. The computer forecasts a tragic event, perhaps even death. The customer obtains the prediction and alters his or her behavior accordingly. S/he avoids the fatal rocket ship to Venus and survives the galactic collision in hyperspace. The computer has erred, a correct forecast would have been possible only if the machine could have taken the modified action into account. But this would lead to an infinite regress—an impossible situation. These stories end with a familiar realization: It is immensely difficult to discern future events.

The incorrect forecasts described by Dickson and the failure of computer predictions in science fiction stories are metaphoric ways of describing the issues analyzed by Toffler that were discussed in the introduction. They demonstrate the difficulty of planning alternative courses of action. These conundrums by their very nature attract the interest of many students.

Computer projections, the examination of alternative futures, and the extrapolation from current trends remain valid but limited means of attempting to adjust to rapid change.

The discipline of future studies also suggests another strategy for preparing persons for life in the time to come, and it represents a central theme of this book. It is an approach that seeks the full development of human potential as it aids persons in using their creative and spontaneous selves.

The evidence strongly suggests that tomorrow is basically unknowable. Whereas the past is a closed system, the future remains open. Instead of computers to extrapolate the coming era from current trends, tomorrow requires flexible human beings who are capable of adjusting to rapidly changing circumstances. The study of the future can support this. Helping students become futurists provides them with intellectual challenges and gives society the benefits of persons who can cope with the transition to the third wave and with future shock.

SUMMARY

This chapter has introduced three innovative strategies for use by teachers who wish to improve classroom instruction—the facilitation of creative behavior, simulation/gaming, and the study of the future.

The chapter began with an examination of the need for innovative strategies in a world facing enormous problems and beset by future shock. It described the work of anthropologist Edward T. Hall, whose writings demonstrate the existence of alternative learning styles. It argued that the three strategies described in this text can help meet the needs of a variety of learning styles.

Finally, the chapter offered a brief overview of the process of facilitating creative behavior, simulation/gaming, and future studies. Subsequent chapters will develop these techniques theoretically and with specific examples of how to apply them in the classroom.

NOTES

1. Paul Dickson, *The Future File* (New York: Rawson Associates, 1977).

CHAPTER

2

Organization of Instruction

INTRODUCTION

Competent instruction demands careful planning. Without thoughtful organization of lessons, the most committed teachers will fail and the most effective strategies, no matter how innovative, will not work. Careful planning remains the foundation of teaching. Furthermore, quality preparation and competent instructional organization can liberate teachers. A new teacher spends an enormous amount of time preparing for day-to-day instruction; once s/he masters the process of short-term and long-range planning, s/he can design quality lessons in less time.

The first step of learning to plan is to develop an understanding of the nature of objectives. Desired outcomes can be global or specific; both types are important and both are parts of the process of organizing instruction.

Global objectives are goals that reflect the needs of society. "The achievement of effective citizenship" is an example of a global goal—an outcome desired in a democratic society. It requires specific behaviors, including being well informed about issues and being willing and able to engage in discussion about the nature of the society. It calls for participation in the political process as an informed and intelligent voter.

This very broad outcome cannot be achieved in a short-term instructional plan. Nonetheless, day-to-day instruction must mirror the larger goals of the society in ways that help bring them about. A process must exist to translate the global needs of the society into objectives that can be achieved by teachers in a single lesson, in a long-term unit, and over a school year.

On a given day, when the social studies instructor teaches students how to detect bias as part of a unit on propaganda techniques (a single objective for a particular lesson), s/he is also helping to achieve the societal goal of preparing effective citizens.

Similar relationships exist in other subjects as well. The English teacher may use a synectics exercise (described in Chapter 5) to improve writing and to facilitate creative behavior. At the same time s/he is also working toward the global goal of improving literacy in the society. The physics teacher who uses a simulation/game to teach the concept of energy use and conservation is also achieving the societal objective of understanding the nature of limited resources and the need to conserve them. When the math teacher enables students to understand computers, s/he is also helping them to accommodate to the future and minimize future shock—a global outcome desired by the society.

This chapter focuses on the process of organizing instruction for both short-term and long-term outcomes. Learning how to achieve global goals from specific objectives cannot be taught in a brief discussion in a textbook about teaching strategies. How each teacher and each district achieves this is a policy decision beyond the scope of learning innovative teaching techniques. The purpose of this introduction, however, is to indicate that planning for instruction takes place in a broad context and the teacher who wishes to use innovative teaching strategies in his or her instruction must know that a connection exists between his or her daily planning and the global outcomes desired by the society.

Another important issue must be addressed in introducing the topic of planning. Sometimes teachers view the organization of instruction as the filling of time. This leads to the following kind of lesson plan:

8:30 to 8:35:   Take attendance
8:35 to 8:41:   Return yesterday's work
8:41 to 8:55:   Have students read pages 25 to 30 in the textbook
8:55 to 9:05:   Review reading
9:05 to 9:10:   Assign homework due tomorrow
9:10 to 9:12:   Answer questions
9:12:   CLASS DISMISSED!

Many teachers use this kind of planning and they are often reinforced by school administrators who provide teacher lesson books in which teachers are asked to provide plans that can be made available for substitute teachers. Although this approach to *scheduling* time has some

value and must often be done for the school, it is neither effective planning nor genuine organization of instruction.
Organization of instruction must be based on objectives. The purpose of planning is to achieve outcomes. Step one in organizing instruction is the identification of objectives. These cannot precisely relate to a time period. A teacher may find one of his or her classes quick and receptive, and s/he can complete a lesson in two days. Another group of students during a later period in the day may be slower and have more difficulty; the same lesson requires three days with these pupils. Planning is based on objectives and the amount of time needed depends, at least in part, on the ability of students to learn. Therefore, the accomplishment of objectives should be the central focus of teaching rather than the simple filling of time.

THE COMPONENTS OF INSTRUCTION

An effective plan for organizing instruction always contains the following components:

1. objectives
2. content
3. instructional techniques
4. methods of evaluation
5. materials of instruction
6. reference material for teachers

Objectives, which can be behavioral or conceptual, identify three kinds of outcomes. The first type concerns understanding; that is, cognitive outcomes or knowledge. The second type of objective is aimed at skills; these vary from discipline to discipline and consist of specific behaviors necessary to master the discipline. The ability to use a Bunsen burner is an example of a skill necessary for learning chemistry; the ability to use correct punctuation is necessary for learning English. The third includes objectives about attitudes and values or the affective part of life. In an academic setting, they are often the perspectives necessary for the pursuit of knowledge. In social studies, for example, a desired attitude is the rejection of simple single-cause explanations of complex phenomena. In science one learns to value the careful collection and recording of data in conducting experiments.

Skills and attitudes exist for all teaching fields, though some overlap subjects. Many attitudes about the nature of knowledge, for example, are desired in every teaching field (e.g., knowledge is tentative; it is achieved through rational inquiry). Skills also overlap disciplines. The sciences and the social sciences share certain data-gathering procedures. Learning English and history requires similar intellectual skills. Generally, however, the understandings of any teaching field tend to be unique—cognitive structures differentiating one field from another. (The process of future studies, however, suggests that the uniqueness of subject areas is changing as interdisciplinary perspectives come to supplant the traditional division of knowledge by disciplines.)

Content is the second component necessary to the organization of instruction. It represents the data base from which learning occurs. Teachers need to identify content to achieve their objectives. Having students learn the data, however, must not become the *only* objective. This sometimes occurs when teachers confuse the use of content with the achievement of objectives. Specific information in any teaching field quickly becomes outdated. The most effective use of content is as factual material for achieving objectives. The relationship between content and objectives is illustrated by the specific lesson plans described later in this chapter.

Instructional techniques are the teaching procedures of a lesson plan. They describe what pupils will be doing and how the lesson will proceed. An effective plan will include three types of instructional techniques.

The first type, *initiatory activity,* begins the lesson. Its purpose is to introduce the lesson to students; this procedure generates interest and poses the problem of the lesson in ways that motivate student learning. Initiatory activities are fun for the teacher and the students because they are involving and produce a high level of interest. A simulation/game, for example, often serves as an excellent initiatory activity because it quickly involves the student in the learning process and it leads to a high level of interest. It is an activity that simultaneously provides for many ability levels. These and other aspects of the simulation/game will be discussed in more detail in Chapters 6 and 7.

The second kind of instructional technique, *developmental activity,* moves the lesson along. This is the part of the lesson in which concepts are presented, hypotheses created, and explanations given. The student is introduced to skills and has an opportunity to practice them. The class discusses attitudes and values. The developmental section of a lesson is its essential part.

Culminating activity is the third type of instructional technique. These procedures bring the lesson together and provide for closure. Teachers can use many kinds of activity to finish the lesson, from student debates, to such nonverbal activities as students drawing pictures to demonstrate what they have learned. A typical culminating activity is an examination—a perfectly appropriate option but not the only way to conclude an instructional unit.

Evaluation of instruction is a fourth component of the lesson plan. It can be *formative;* that is, ongoing evaluations that provide feedback to pupils while the lesson is being taught. Formative evaluation can be formal (a written quiz part way through a lesson) or informal (a word from the teacher on an exercise the student has completed). This kind of feedback is useful because it provides a student with information about how s/he is doing before the end of the lesson. Evaluation can also be *summative;* that is, testing that occurs at the end of the lesson, most often in the form of a written examination.

Teachers have a wide variety of options in conducting summative evaluations: true–false tests (though these are of limited value because they contain a 50 percent probability for guessing), multiple-choice tests, short answer tests, essay examinations, and tests using a combination of these types of questions. The kind of instrument used should depend on the type of the material taught; no single form of testing is superior. In recent years, however, educators have overrelied on objective testing (particularly on multiple-choice); this has contributed to the problem of decreased skill in student writing. However, if teachers provide a variety of kinds of summative evaluation, many opportunities for writing exist as part of the examination process.

A fifth component of a lesson plan is the **materials of instruction.** In this section the teacher identifies the readings, games, charts, films, and other materials s/he will be using. This provides the teacher with a checklist so that s/he can be sure the materials have been gathered prior to the teaching of the lesson.

The final component of a lesson plan is the **reference material for teachers.** This section should contain one or two sources that the teacher has consulted for background information. While this is often not included in the lesson, its existence makes the lesson plan self-contained since another teacher with the same general training could read the reference material and be able to teach the lesson plan written by the instructor.

The components of a lesson plan are interrelated. The objectives are achieved through the use of the instructional techniques; the content provides the teacher with data for use with the teaching procedures; the evaluation process determines the extent to which the objectives have been accomplished; and the materials section provides sources for the students and the teacher.

Lessons may be complex (requiring several days to teach) or simple (requiring less than one classroom period to complete) but all should contain the components described in this section.

ORGANIZATION: A BEHAVIORAL PERSPECTIVE

Behavioral psychology has been a major source for the development of the theories of discipline in education, resulting sometimes in too narrow a focus for teaching. In many parts of the world, other schools of psychology have more influence than they do in the United States. However, because of the strong behavioral influence on American education, educators here have relied heavily on "performance" objectives in lesson planning.

Behavioral psychology began with the work of the Russian psychologist Ivan P. Pavlov (1849–1936) who created a paradigm of classical conditioning, based on the connection of stimulus and response in his experiments with dogs. He presented a hungry animal with food; this caused salivation. Pavlov labeled the food the *unconditioned stimulus* and the salivation the *unconditioned response*. He then paired a bell with the food and taught the dog to salivate at the sound of the bell even when the food was not present. Pavlov called the bell the *conditioned stimulus* and the salivation at the sound of the bell the *conditioned response*.

Psychologist B. F. Skinner (1904–) refined Pavlov's model to create *instrumental conditioning*. Skinner, who used pigeons in his experiments, required the bird to press a lever in a "Skinner Box." He then rewarded the animal with food. In his model, the response (pressing the lever) came first and was followed by the stimulus.

Many other psychologists have also contributed to behavioral psychology. However sophisticated their constructs, the basis of the model lies in the stimulus-and-response bond. Behaviorism holds that action can be shaped, and that rewards, which are called reinforcers, can increase the frequency of some behaviors and diminish the occurrence of others. Through a variety of techniques, they claim, responses can be predicted and controlled. The S-R psychologists reject terminology related to the existence of the unconscious because for them all behavior is objective and measurable. They define learning as a relatively permanent change in behavior.

Behavioral objectives and behavioral lesson planning come directly from these constructs of S-R psychology. The advocates of this approach seek visible outcomes as evidence that learning has taken place. They have difficulty with arguments that learning has other dimensions that can be inferred from other visible signs.

Contemporary psychologist Robert Mager has been the major proponent of behavioral objectives. His book *Preparing Instructional Objectives* (Pitman Learning, Inc., California, 1975) has become the standard reference for the writing of behavioral objectives.

Behavioral or performance objectives usually contain three major elements: first, they identify observable performance on the part of the learner; second, they define the conditions under which the behavior is to take place; and finally, they indicate the criteria of minimal acceptance. This is the level of performance by the student that demonstrates that learning has, in fact, occurred.

The following are some examples of performance objectives that meet Mager's criteria:

- *History*
  Given a map of Western Europe, the student will be able to identify those countries that supported the Reformation and those countries that remained in the Catholic Church. The student will be able to do this with 80 percent accuracy in a class period.

- *Government*
  Given the concept of political socialization, the student will be able to list at least eight of ten devices used by the schools to achieve it in a thirty-minute period of time.

- *Foreign Language*
  Given a list of ten Spanish verbs, the student will be able to correctly conjugate nine of them within a twenty-minute period.

- *Mathematics*
  Given five sets of triangles, the student will be able to prove them congruent using three different theorems. The student must accurately prove at least three of the sets congruent within the allotted time of one hour.

- *English*
  Given an unpunctuated paragraph, the student will be able to correctly supply the punctuation with 80 percent accuracy in a twenty-minute period.

In summary, a behavioral objective is a statement that describes an outcome desired by the teacher. It communicates the instructor's intent and indicates what the learner will be doing when demonstrating his or her achievement. It also describes the criteria for judging adequate performance. Performance objectives should be written for every aspect of a lesson and each educational intent specified in a single instructional objective.

Behavioral objectives dominate the organization of instruction. They appeal to administrators and supervisors because they allow for easy measurement and are relatively simple to create. Anyone who wishes to teach in contemporary schools must learn to write them. Nevertheless, performance objectives do have their limitations. Their most significant deficiency is that they tend to limit outcomes to those actions that are most readily made into behavioral objectives. Some kinds of achievements are not so easily adaptable to behavioral objectives (e.g., music appreciation or the acceptance of alternative perspectives). The next section of this chapter presents an alternative to performance objectives.

ORGANIZATION: A CONCEPTUAL PERSPECTIVE

Reality is always perceived by human beings in discrete instances; that is, things in the real world occur one at a time, each representing a perception separate from any other. This is by no means obvious. If one is asked, "What do you see?" the answer is never a report of a discrete experience. Rather the answer is a response such as, "I see a chair," or "I smell a rose." The step from what is actually perceived to the report of that perception using a general term is one of the most remarkable of all human phenomena—the process of conceptualization.

Human social life—anchored in communication—could not exist without it. The process by which we conceptualize contains the following steps:

1. Certain characteristics are abstracted from objects. This abstracting is somewhat arbitrary. For example, a plow horse and a race horse are considerably different, yet they have enough common elements for us to call them both *horses*.
2. Once these common elements have been abstracted, we create categories into which individual objects are placed. All things that "moo," give milk, and eat grass we place in a single category.
3. The category is given a name. For example, we have labeled those things that "moo," give milk, and eat grass as *cows*.

The process of conceptualization, the movement from categorical abstraction to the creation of a concept, must contain all three steps. Learning the names associated with things or processes is not the same as learning to conceptualize. When teachers simply give students definitions of terms, they have not allowed students to discover concepts for themselves but have short-circuited the process. Sometimes, of course, this is necessary. But the effective way to learn most concepts is to engage in the process by which a teacher provides data to students so that they can learn concepts inductively.

Teachers do not have to teach children to conceptualize; it is a natural process engaged in by all human beings from the time they are infants. Parents can see their child make increasingly sophisticated conceptualizations. The child begins by calling all solid foods "num-num." All liquids may be "wah-wah." Later these notions are refined so that "num-num" becomes pizza, cookies, and ice cream whereas "wah-wah" becomes milk, juice, and soda.

We have concepts for the world of material things (cows, horses, snow, etc.), and for intangibles as well. The same categorical abstraction that creates concepts for objects also produces them for nonmaterial ideas. Thus we have concepts for *love, justice,* and *freedom.*

The importance of conceptualization is that it makes sense out of discrete reality. Our ability to conceptualize results in the ordering of reality so that interaction between human beings can occur. Communication between people breaks down whenever they have different labels for their categorical abstractions—for instance, when two people speak different languages. Even people who ostensibly speak the same language may experience a failure of communication when the labels that they have given their concepts do not coincide. This often occurs between subcultures who speak the same language differently. Teachers can unwittingly entertain a class by using a word that means one thing to them and another to their students.

Communication occurs not only through concepts but also from their interrelationship. The concept of *grass* denotes green herbiage consisting of narrow-leafed plants affording pasture for grazing animals. The concept *cow* may be interrelated with the concept of *grass* to form a generalization: *Cows eat grass.* A generalization is the interrelationship of two or more concepts. We also generalize from nonmaterial concepts. The political concept of *power* is used to form the following generalization: *Power is unevenly divided in any political system.*

The study of the nature of concepts has been a major interest of the school of cognitive-field psychology. An early advocate of this position (who called himself a Gestalt psychologist) was Wolfgang Kohler (1887-1967). He did a series of famous experiments with apes in which the animals were required to form insights for problem solving. In one case an ape received three sections of a stick and learned to put the parts together to reach a banana outside of his cage.

The fundamental tenet of cognitive-field psychology is the development of insight. Whereas S-R psychologists tend to focus on parts of behavior, the emphasis in cognitive-field theory is on behavioral wholes. Field psychologists believe that learners come to a point at which a new insight is formed that leads to a general understanding of a situation. This general perspective occurs all at once (the "aha experience").

Cognitivie-field theory emphasizes the learning of principles to a greater extent than does the S-R position which focuses on parts of behavior. The cognitive-field psychologist accepts the existence of a subconscious that can achieve new awareness without external behavioral evidence. For field psychologists, learning is defined as a change in insight or a gain in insight.

Hilda Taba, a major curriculum theorist, based her work on the cognitive-field theory of psychology. She influenced curriculum development greatly, being in fact the first person to use the term "teaching strategy." It is primarily from Taba's work that the process of creating conceptual lesson plans evolved.

Taba stated three postulates about thinking. First, thinking can be taught. Debate exists about this but Taba gathered evidence to support the notion that using a conceptual approach to teaching could bring about an increase in thinking skills. Second, thinking is an active transaction between the individual and data. It comes about as a result of the process of conceptualization when students use data in the particular subject matter being studied to make categorical abstractions and discover relevant concepts and generalizations. Third, thought progresses through a lawful sequence, which means that in order to master more complex concepts and generalizations, simpler ones must first be learned. Thus Taba saw conceptualization as a sequential process in which later learning builds on earlier knowledge.

Taba developed the teaching strategy *concept formation* (which was also facilitated by the work of Jerome Bruner, another psychologist who studied the role of conceptualization in curriculum development). For Taba, concept formation involves identifying and enumerating data that is relevant to a particular problem, grouping the data according to some basis of similarity, and developing categories and labels for the groups.

In her later years, Taba identified other teaching strategies that evolved from her work in concept formation. The inductive method of teaching is now strongly identified with her work.

The following are examples of generalizations that can serve as conceptual objectives for lesson plans:

- *English*
  The theme of a work of literature is a function of the thoughts and actions of its characters; it attempts to persuade the reader to a point of view by alluding to a doctrine or thesis.
- *Geography*
  The character of a place is the product of the past as well as an interim phase in an ever-changing existence.
- *Government*
  Groups with power in any political system tend to maintain it and only come to share it reluctantly.
- *History*
  Revolutions occur when oppressed groups within a society come to believe that there is no hope for peaceful change.

- *Math*
  If $A = B$, and $B = C$, then $A = C$.
- *Science*
  Matter has mass, occupies space, has inertia, and appears everywhere.
- *Social Studies*
  Subcultures that dominate a society in terms of power may define other subcultures as deviant.

A number of principles about the process of conceptualization have been supported by research. These can serve to summarize this section.

First, it is generally agreed that the acquisition of concepts is what makes learning possible. Second, concept learning liberates individuals from the control of specific stimuli. This means that they can be freed from dealing with discrete data and learn to understand the world in greater depth. Third, principles and concepts show marked resistance to forgetting and are frequently remembered over periods of months and years. This can be contrasted to the study of discrete data which are often forgotten in a brief period of time. Fourth, most curriculum theorists agree that understanding concepts and generalizations makes a subject more comprehensible.

Theorists also believe that learning is facilitated by the development of various types of thinking processes. These processes rather than rote learning constitute the most important outcomes. Furthermore, material that is meaningful is remembered longer than material that is not. Meaningfulness consists of the relationships of facts, concepts, generalizations, rules, and principles for which students see some use.

Furnishing learners with information in the form of underlying principles promotes *transfer* and facilitates future discovery of new principles. In general, understanding fundamental principles and ideas appears to be the most successful way to achieve transfer of learning.

SAMPLE LESSON PLANS

A Conceptual Plan

The following is an example of a lesson plan based on a conceptual approach to objectives and learning. It can serve as a model for those who wish to use this approach to planning. It contains all the components described in the first part of the chapter.

Subject Matter: Geography
Topic: The Nature of Change in Urban Environments
Grade Level: Eleven

Objectives

Understanding. The character of a place is the product of the past as well as an interim phase in an ever-changing existence.

Skill. The ability to draw and use simple sketch maps of an area.

Attitude. Rejects simple, single-cause explanations of behavior and seeks evidence to support explanations.

Content

The character of a place is the product of the past, as well as an interim phase in an ever-changing existence.

A. The character of the city of Camden, New Jersey, is a product of its past.
 1. Camden was settled in part in order to maximize its proximity to the Delaware River.
 2. The nearness of Camden to Philadelphia has affected Camden's development.
B. The character of Camden is an interim phase in its ever-changing existence.
 1. Many industries have left Camden and they must be replaced with new kinds of development.
 2. Camden's center city is being rebuilt with the development of government offices as well as with private investment.
C. The character of Duluth, Minnesota, is the product of the past as well as an interim phase in an ever-changing existence.
 1. Duluth was once important because of the mining of iron ore in its vicinity.
 2. The end of the mining industry left Duluth economically depressed.
 3. Duluth's recovery came with the building of the St. Lawrence Seaway.
D. The characters of most major cities of the world are products of the past as well as interim phases in ever-changing existences.

Instructional Techniques

Initiatory activity.
1. As an introduction to community development, have students play the future studies game, *Building the Future's Community*. As part

of the debriefing, ask students to discuss elements needed in any community in order for it to function effectively. Also use the game to initiate a discussion of how communities develop.

Developmental activities.
2. Show students several examples of sketch maps. Using an overhead projector, prepare a sketch map of the neighborhood where the school is located. Then have students use paper and pencil to do the same for their own neighborhoods.
3. Present a lecture to students on the history of Camden. Illustrate the talk with slides available from the New Jersey Historical Society.
4. Using history and geography texts, have students draw sketch maps of Camden as it appeared at the beginning of the nineteenth century. Discuss the role of the Delaware River and the proximity of Camden to Philadelphia. ASK: How have these phenomena affected life in Camden?
5. Have a group of students do research on the current status of industry in Camden and report on it to the class.
6. Invite a guest speaker to discuss current developments in Camden's center city.
7. Hold a brainstorming session: How can Camden be made a better place in the future? Perhaps use the nonverbal brainstorming activity described in Chapter 5.
8. Discuss ways in which the character of Camden has changed. Do other cities change as well?
9. Ask another group of students to read about Duluth, Minnesota, and report on how it has changed from an iron ore center to a shipping center with the development of the St. Lawrence Seaway.
10. Play the simulation/game *Metfab* to demonstrate how decisions are made for locating industry. In the debriefing, analyze how cities like Camden and Duluth are affected by events like those portrayed in *Metfab*.
11. Have still another group of students choose several cities from around the world and report on how they have changed over time.

Culminating activity.
12. Hold a summarizing discussion on the way in which the character of a place is the product of the past as well as an interim phase in an ever-changing existence. Use the data gathered to illustrate this conceptual objective.

13. Discuss the process of explanation. Ask students how many causes they can identify with regard to the changing nature of cities. Use this discussion to teach the attitude objective of the lesson.
14. Have students take a written examination.

Materials of Instruction

- Simulation Games: *Building the Future's Community* and *Metfab*
- Overhead projector and blank transparencies
- Slides on the history of Camden, New Jersey
- Pamphlet on the history of Duluth, Minnesota

References

Gabler, Robert E., et al. *Essentials of Physical Geography.* Philadelphia: Saunders Publishing, 1987.

Gay, Kathlyn. *Cities Under Stress.* New York: Watts Publishing Company, 1985.

Hanmer, Trudy. *The Growth of Cities.* New York: Watts Publishing Company, 1985.

Note: In teaching a conceptual lesson, the teacher begins with the instructional techniques, which are concrete, and uses them to teach the objectives, which are abstract. In planning, the opposite holds true. The instructor chooses the objectives (perhaps together with a supervisor), which are abstract, and from them plans the content and instructional techniques, which are concrete.

Behavioral Lesson Plans

Behavioral plans involve smaller amounts of time and work. Hence, plans using this orientation will tend to focus on a single objective rather than on multiple ones as in the conceptual approach. The several plans included attempt to achieve outcomes similar to those in the lesson outlined previously, but do so with behavioral objectives. The format used is a typical one for performance learning.

Behavioral Lesson One

Objective. Given information about Camden, New Jersey, and Duluth, Minnesota, the student will be able to state that the character of a place is the product of the past as well as an interim phase of an ever-changing existence. S/he will do so in his or her own words in a culminating essay assigned by the instructor. The student will be allowed forty minutes to compose the essay.

Materials.
- Slides depicting the history of Camden, New Jersey
- Pamphlet on the history of Duluth, Minnesota
- Simulation/game: *Building the Future's Community*

Procedures.
1. Students will play the simulation/game, *Building the Future's Community*. As part of the debriefing, ask students to discuss elements that are needed in any community in order for it to function effectively. Also use the game for a discussion of how communities develop.
2. Present a lecture to students on the history of Camden. Illustrate it with slides available from the New Jersey Historical Society.
3. Have a group of students do research on the current status of industry in Camden and report on it to the class.
4. Invite a guest speaker to discuss current developments in Camden's city center.
5. Hold a brainstorming session: How can Camden be made a better place in the future? (Perhaps use the nonverbal brainstorming activity described in Chapter 5.)
6. Ask another group of students to read about Duluth, Minnesota, and report on how it has changed from an iron ore center to a shipping center with the development of the St. Lawrence Seaway.

Evaluation. Students will write an essay in which they compare Camden, New Jersey, with Duluth, Minnesota. The topic for the essay will be: How are cities' characters products of their past as well as interim phases in ever-changing existences?

Behavioral Lesson Two

Objective. The student will be able to draw simple sketch maps and use these maps to interpret data. Given information from history and geography texts, s/he will be able to draw more complex sketch maps that accurately portray the area being mapped. The student will have forty minutes to complete his or her drawing.

Materials.
- Overhead projector
- Transparencies
- Drawing materials

Procedures.
1. Show students several examples of sketch maps. Using an overhead projector, draw a sketch map of the neighborhood where the school is located.
2. Have students prepare sketch maps of their own neighborhoods.
3. Using history and geography texts, ask students to draw sketch maps of Camden as it appeared at the beginning of the nineteenth century.

Evaluation. Using the material about Duluth, Minnesota, which the students read in lesson plan one, have students prepare a sketch map of the city today, noting its position in relation to the St. Lawrence Seaway.

Behavioral Plan Three

Objective. In an essay of not more than 250 words, the student will demonstrate his or her ability to reject simple, single-cause explanations of behavior. Students will have thirty minutes to complete the essay.

Materials. The materials for this lesson will consist of all the materials used in behavioral lessons one and two.

Procedures.
1. The teacher will conduct a discussion with students that is based on lessons one and two. In it s/he will review the understanding that the character of a place is a product of the past as well as an interim phase of an ever-changing existence.
2. Students will list as many factors as they can to explain the current nature of Camden, New Jersey, and Duluth, Minnesota.
3. The teacher will then describe the process of explanation in a more general way. S/he can draw on students' experiences in their own lives to illustrate the point.

Evaluation. Each student will write an essay of not more than 250 words to demonstrate his or her understanding of the limits of single-cause explanation of complex phenomena.

This section of the chapter has illustrated both conceptual and behavioral lesson planning by offering examples. These samples serve to demonstrate how similar ideas can be taught using two very different orientations. The conceptual approach has the advantage of teaching several objectives at the same time. It lends itself to better integration of objectives since it is based on cognitive-field psychology that deals with wholes more effectively than does behavioral psychology. The behavioral approach offers the advantage of approaching ideas in smaller segments, reflecting the ability of behavioral psychology to deal with parts of behavior. Furthermore, the behavioral approach is favored by many school administrators and supervisors.

Which approach to planning should be adopted? Part of the answer to this question depends on the preference of the teacher and on school district policy. A compromise also exists. Long-term planning is discussed in the last section of this chapter. It is possible for this kind of organization to be exclusively conceptual in nature whereas short-term planning is behavioral. The teacher can develop his or her long-term plans and then translate them into short-term ones which are behavioral. These examples of lesson plans indicate how this can be done; the three behavioral lesson plans were restatements of the more complex, conceptual one.

ASKING QUESTIONS

Levels of Questioning

The nature of questioning relates to the process of organizing instruction. Questioning is part of teaching—in conducting classroom discussions and in composing examinations. Both of these must be done carefully in order to achieve the lesson's objectives. Discussion enables students to move from the specific data to more abstract concepts and generalizations. Effective examinations help students focus their studies on objectives rather than on trivia. No matter what the teacher says about his or her objectives, students will study for the kinds of questions the instructor typically uses on examinations.

In 1956, psychologist Benjamin Bloom and several of his colleagues published a taxonomy of educational objectives.[1] It is a standard reference work for questioning. The taxonomy identified six levels of objectives. Questions, whether for classroom discussion or for examinations, can be related to this taxonomy. The higher on the taxonomy the question, the more significant it is.

Bloom's classifications include the following:

- **Knowledge**
  This category includes questions that emphasize the remembering, either by recognition or recall, of ideas, material, or phenomena.
  Example:
  What is the definition of matter given in the textbook?

- **Comprehension**
  Comprehension questions lead to responses demonstrating an understanding of the literal message contained in a communication.
  Example:
  Indicate your understanding of the Preamble to the Constitution by stating it in your own words.
- **Application**
  This occurs when the student solves a problem and uses the solution in a new situation on his or her own initiative.
  Example:
  A student correctly punctuates a paragraph that s/he has not seen before as a result of practice with other paragraphs.
- **Analysis**
  Analysis emphasizes the examination of material in terms of its component parts. The student demonstrates the relationship between the parts and how they are organized.
  Example:
  After reading major addresses by Dwight Eisenhower and Adlai Stevenson during the 1952 presidential campaign, list several ways in which the two candidates differed.
- **Synthesis**
  Combining elements to form a whole or to constitute a pattern or structure not clearly there before indicates that synthesis has occurred.
  Example:
  How might society best deal with the problems of the homeless? Suggest some solutions to this problem and then defend your answer with arguments.
- **Evaluation**
  This category involves the making of judgments about the value, for some purpose, of ideas, products, or processes.
  Example:
  Which contemporary mystery writer that you have read this semester can be called the true successor to Dashiell Hammett? Give reasons for your answer.

The importance of Bloom's taxonomy is that it enables teachers to recognize the level (on examinations as well as in classroom discussion) of the questions they ask. Whereas all levels of questioning occur and are necessary during instruction, teachers tend to focus on the lower end of the taxonomy more than on the higher-level questions. Students need experience at all levels; understanding Bloom's categories can help sensitive teachers to the differences and raise the level of their questioning. It can enable instructors to seek a balance among the questions that are being asked.

Facilitating Discussion

A significant way to improve discussion is to ask students questions from a variety of levels on Bloom's taxonomy. Teachers can also facilitate discussion by keeping the following points in mind:

1. *Use good key or pivotal questions.* A good question is one that allows for differing opinions. Recall questions require a correct answer but once given, there is no possibility of continuing. These questions are appropriate if a recitation is being conducted. To have a discussion, an issue with at least two sides must be raised.

2. *Ask clear questions.* If pupils do not understand what is being asked, they cannot respond. Sometimes what seems perfectly clear to the teacher has left the students totally confused. Clear questions require thought.

3. *After asking a question, wait for response.* Students need time to think. Sometimes teachers answer their own questions if students have not responded immediately. Waiting a bit increases student participation. If the teacher gets into the habit of responding to his or her own questions, the pupils will never participate because they know that eventually the instructor will provide the answer.

4. *Seek widespread participation.* Often classroom discussion involves only a few students who are the first to raise their hands. Other students come to expect this pattern and let the most eager students do the work. The teacher can increase involvement by waiting for other students to volunteer and by occasionally calling on a student who has not volunteered, especially when the question asks for an opinion rather than a specific fact.

5. *Move the discussion toward some end.* The teacher must have a clear objective in mind when conducting a discussion and this purpose should eventually be apparent to the students. This occurs most often when the questions being asked are related and orderly.

6. *Summarize when needed.* The facilitator's role requires summarizing from time to time in order to keep the discussion moving and on track, and also requires providing clarification when it is needed. The amount of summary and clarification need not be excessive and should not make the discussion leader the dominant speaker.

7. *Keep the discussion moving.* Do not let the discussion drag on with undue attention to specific points.
8. *Turn questions raised by students back to the class.* Encourage students to interact among themselves.
9. *Finally, provide an open atmosphere.* Know the correct names of students and call on them. Give credit for good responses and avoid negative remarks about poor replies (including negative nonverbal feedback). In an open discussion atmosphere, avoid cutting students off in the middle of a remark. Listen carefully to what is being said by each student and avoid paraphrasing what each participant offers.

Conducting an effective discussion is one of the most difficult tasks facing any teacher. Being aware of the levels of questioning and seeking to effectively facilitate the process can make the task more effective and more pleasant for both students and teachers.

LONG-RANGE PLANNING

Long-range planning involves the construction of teaching units for periods of from four to six weeks. This kind of organization of instruction frees the teacher from a daily focus on lesson planning, allowing him or her time to read and study, and to relax from the demands of teaching.

Long-range planning requires the selection of a topic that can be appropriately studied for four to six weeks. In science this might be a unit on matter, in mathematics a unit on proving triangles congruent, or in social studies, one about westward expansion.

As in a lesson plan, the objectives of a unit consist of understandings, skills, and attitudes and values. A unit, however, contains many more objectives than a lesson plan. The content is more extensive as well. In writing this portion of a unit, formal outlining procedures should be used. Each understanding will become a Roman numeral in the outline. Hence, *understanding one* will be *Roman numeral one, understanding two* will become *Roman numeral two,* and so on. Under each understanding, examples should be provided in appropriate outline form. For every "A" in an outline, a balancing "B" exists. This means that each understanding will be demonstrated by at least two examples. More than two are preferable since students learn best when they have a number of examples to consider.

The instructional techniques section of the unit should include activities to teach all the understandings, content skills, and attitudes and values. Care should be taken to see that activities exist for each objective. A wide variety of kinds of activities should be included so that the unit does not depend only on lecture, recitation, and discussion.

The *materials of instruction* section contains an alphabetical list of all the materials to be used by the students in the unit. A section listing *appropriate reference material* for the teacher is also included. Unit plans also include appendices that consist of original material written by the teacher for use with students.

The long-term plan described here is an extension of the conceptual lesson plan described earlier. As suggested before, long-term plans can be translated into short-term behavioral plans, and they provide the teacher with flexibility in organizing instruction.

SUMMARY

The purpose of this chapter is to prepare students for using innovative teaching strategies by focusing on the organization of instruction. It began by describing the general nature of objectives and then examined the components of instruction. Next, it introduced behavioral and conceptual perspectives for planning and described sample lesson plans from each perspective. Teachers were also offered suggestions for asking questions and facilitating discussion. Finally, the chapter discussed the process of long-term planning.

NOTES

1. Benjamin Bloom et al., *Taxonomy of Educational Objectives. The Classification of Educational Goals. Handbook I: The Cognitive Domain* (New York: David McKay, 1956).

CHAPTER

3

The Process of Creativity

INTRODUCTION

This chapter explores the process of creativity and seeks to help readers understand the general nature of innovation. It proceeds from a central premise: *Human beings have within them the capacity to establish new perspectives.* This ability is neither mysterious nor rare; we use it at its simplest level to understand the world, and at a higher level to express that understanding.

As children become adults, the educational process can cause them to lose touch with their creativity, their ability to make things new. They may learn to say, "I'm not creative," or "It's not good to be different." Students can develop preferences for safely conventional ways of living and become frightened of and resistant to change.

This chapter and the two that follow are designed to help teachers find and support the creative, spontaneous qualities of students. This material explores the creative person and the creative process in depth. Understanding these basic concepts is necessary before we can explore theorists of creativity and their techniques in subsequent chapters.

Creative expression occurs in many ways; it ranges from a clay doll constructed by a young child to the immortal plays of Shakespeare. It appears in the humor of Jack Benny and in Einstein's view of the universe. It surfaces at one level in Plato's dialogues and in another in the househusband's substitution of cooking oil for butter in his favorite recipe. It exists in the sculpture of Michelangelo and in the drama of Arthur

Miller. What is creativity? What causes it? How can persons be helped to become more creative?

The various roles of creativity are illustrated in the following anecdotes, the first of which is from Abraham Maslow's *Toward a Psychology of Being:*

> Unconsciously, I had assumed that creativeness was the prerogative solely of certain professionals. But these expectations were broken up by various of my subjects. For instance, one woman, uneducated, poor, a full-time housewife and mother, did none of these [professional] things and yet was a marvelous cook, mother, wife, and homemaker. With little money, her home was somehow always beautiful. She was a perfect hostess. Her meals were banquets. Her taste in linens, silver, glass, crockery, and furniture was impeccable. She was in all these areas original, novel, ingenious, unexpected, inventive. I just *had* to call her creative. I learned from her and others like her that a first-rate soup is more creative than a second-rate painting, and that generally, cooking or parenthood or making a home could be creative while poetry need not be; it could be uncreative![1]

The second is an anecdote about a French clothes designer who is approached by a wealthy woman. She demands that he create a hat of unique design for her.

> "Of course, Madame," he agrees. He then proceeds to cut a long piece of orange ribbon from a nearby spool. He twists, turns, and shapes the material. Without glue, thread or any other fasteners, he creates a special bonnet for the woman.
>
> "Oh, Pierre!" she exclaims. "It is magnificent! I love it! How much will you charge me for it?"
>
> "400 Francs, Madame."
>
> "400? Outlandish, for what is, after all, a piece of ribbon!"
>
> Pierre then takes back the hat and reverses all that he has done to it, returning it to its original form. Handing it to the woman, he says, "Madame, the ribbon is free."

DEFINITIONS OF CREATIVITY

In Chapter 1, *creativity* was defined as a means by which a person obtains a new perspective and, as a result, brings something new to consciousness. This definition contains many complexities; it raises questions about the beginning of the creative act and its end, about whether or not creativity progresses through stages, and whether or not it culminates in a tangible product. By this definition, is the "something new" novel for the person or is it rather new to the universe? Many creativity theorists deal with these complexities in defining the *creative act* and the next chapter examines the works of several. Whereas some theorists are alluded to in this chapter, the focus is on the creative process itself in general terms.

The psychotherapy treatment called *transactional analysis* (TA) provides one definition of creativity. TA describes three separate ego-states within a person's psyche: Parent, Adult, and Child. The Parent ego-state contains ideas learned from one's parents and maintained in rote fashion. This encompasses many uncritical biases (e.g., "all niggers are lazy," "all Jews are money-hungry," or "women are weaker than men.") However, this ego-state, repository of many survival techniques, can provide nurturance as well. The Adult ego-state is the data-gathering portion of the personality; it provides an objective perspective for understanding the world. The Child ego-state houses the spontaneous self which, for TA theorists, serves as the source of creativity. In a definition based on transactional analysis, creativity comes about when the nurturing Parent allows the Child to exist.

This definition has implications for teaching. It also has particular relevance for instruction that comes from the parents but relates to classroom teachers as well. The role of *Parent tapes,* that is, the replaying by the individual of Parental precepts, as negative forces in inhibiting creativity has been well established by the TA therapists. Parents need to help their offspring legitimize their creative behavior at an early age. Parents must literally provide children with the right to exist as creative beings. When youngsters reach school, the teacher—in the role of parent-surrogate—must also provide this legitimization.

Definitions of creativity also come from the writings of human potential psychologists, scholars who investigate the search for *self-actualization.* Three major figures in this field, Abraham Maslow, Carl Rogers, and Rollo May, consider the relationship of creativity to the movement toward self-actualization.

For Maslow, self-actualization can be achieved when persons are redesigned to become creative, to develop the characteristics found in innovative people—humility, openness, a willingness to make mistakes, and the ability to be spontaneous. Maslow calls for freedom from prejudice and wants the creative person to be as uninhibited as a naive child. Maslow shares Dewey's perspective that children grow up to be responsible adults whereas grown-ups need occasionally to be as uninhibited as children.

Carl Rogers views creativity as growth, as an effort to reach individual potential. The urge to create, he says, is a natural tendency of all organisms. Although it may "become deeply buried under layer after layer of encrusted psychological defenses . . . it exists in every individual and awaits only the proper conditions to be released and expressed." Rogers sees innovation as the interaction of several forces:

> My definition, then, of the creative process is that it is the emergence in action of novel, relational production, growing out of the uniqueness of the individual on the one hand, and the materials, events, people, or circumstances of his life on the other.[2]

Rollo May also offers a definition of the creative process. Like Rogers, May explains creativity as "the expression of normal people in the act of actualizing themselves." May contends that the drive to create comes from the human awareness of death and the ensuing desire to leave something behind. (Dramatist Arthur Miller calls this a need "to leave a thumbprint upon the world.") In addition, for May a creative act involves an encounter of great intensity and total absorption. This conscious act of creating comes from the ongoing struggle between a person's spontaneity and all the real limits that exist in the world. "A continual dialectical process goes on between world and self and self and world," writes May, "one implies the other and neither can be understood without the other."[3]

The work of writer Arthur Koestler, whose many interests included the creative process, can also help provide a definition of creativity. Koestler, an iconoclastic thinker, who stood in opposition to many traditional views of learning, approached the process from an aesthetic, nonbehavioral, nonempirical point of view. He writes in *The Act of Creation:*

> I have coined the term "bisociation" in order to make a distinction between the routine skills of thinking on a single 'plane,' as it were, and the creative act, which as I shall try to show always operates on more than one plane. The former may be called single-minded, the latter a double-minded transitory state of unequal equilibrium where the balance of both emotion and thought is disturbed.[4]

Koestler maintains that thoughts and actions exist in separate matrices of existence stored in the psyche's unconscious. They have arrived there as a result of the person's activities in the world during his or her day-to-day life. Each matrix is governed by a code of rules in order to respond to environmental needs. A creative act occurs when two previously separate matrices interact—or are "bisociated." The integration of experience results in science, their juxtaposition leads to art, and the collision of matrices produces humor. Any creative act has the potential to enter into any of these three realms. Thus the bisociation of the matrix of *drawing* with the matrix of *visual reception* can produce a humorous caricature, an aesthetically pleasing portrait, or a scientific diagram.

Creative persons accomplish the bisociation of matrices more easily than others. These individuals seem to have less strongly developed censor-mechanisms that allow them to be less inhibited in combining their experiences in novel ways. This partly accounts for their tendency to be divergent thinkers and is what helps them make the familiar strange. Koestler sees the process of creativity as similar whether it occurs in science, in art, or in humor. Educators need to remember that when gifted and talented students are allowed to participate in many kinds of activities and experiences, these students accrue a fund of matrices for use in their future creative endeavors. Educators should also consider the implications for average and below average students.

From these definitions of creativity, we can formulate some useful generalizations.

1. Creativity is present to a larger or smaller degree in everyone.
2. Creativity requires the attainment of a new perspective—new at least to the person.
3. This new perspective is achieved by bringing together previously unrelated experiences.
4. Creativity demands intensity.
5. A person must approach his or her environment in a holistic manner.
6. Creative persons must assume childlike states with regard to fantasy, play, and thought.
7. Creative persons are spontaneous, flexible, and open to experiences.
8. Human spontaneity is a source of creativity.

PERSON, PRODUCT, PROCESS, ENVIRONMENT

Creative behavior can be understood by examining studies of creative people, processes, products, and environments.

Studying what creative people have to say about their experiences offers one approach to understanding the nature of innovation. The following letter, written by Mozart, is his description of the creative act. Consider how many of the above generalizations about creativity apply here.

> When I am, as it were, completely myself, entirely alone, and of good cheer—say traveling in a carriage, or walking after a good meal, or during the night when I cannot sleep; it is on such occasions that my ideas flow best and most abundantly. *Whence* and how they come, I

know not; nor can I force them. Those pleasures that please me I retain in my memory, and am accustomed as I have been told, to hum them to myself. If I continue in this way, it soon occurs to me how I may turn this or that morsel to account, so as to make a good dish of it, that is to say, agreeably to the rules of counterpoint, to the peculiarities of the various instruments, etc.

All this fires my soul, and provided I am not disturbed, my subject enlarges itself, becomes methodized and defined, and the whole, though it be long, stands almost complete and finished in my mind, so that I can survey it, like a fine picture or a beautiful statue, at a glance. Nor do I hear in my imagination the parts *successively,* but I hear them, as it were, all at once *(gleich zusammen).* What a delight this is, I cannot tell! All inventing, this producing, takes place in a pleasing lively dream. Still the actual hearing of the *tout ensemble* is after all the best. What has been thus produced I do not easily forget, and this is perhaps the best gift I have my Divine Maker to thank for.

When I proceed to write down my ideas, I take out of the bag of my memory, if I may use that phrase, what has been previously collected into it in the way I have mentioned. For this reason the committing to paper is done quickly enough, for everything is, as I have said before, already finished; and it rarely differs on paper from what it was in my imagination. At this occupation I can therefore suffer myself to be disturbed; for whatever may be going on around me, I write, and even talk, but only of fowls and geese, or of Gretel or Barbel, or some such matters. But why my productions take from my hand that particular form and style that makes them Mozartish, and different from the works of other composers, is probably owing to the same cause which renders my nose so large or so acquiline, or in short, makes it Mozart's and different from those people. For I really do not study or aim at any originality.

Other examples of writings on creative persons can be found in such collections as *The Creativity Question* by Albert Rothenberg and Carl R. Hausman, which includes works by Plato, Aristotle, and Immanuel Kant.

Scholars have also made studies of creative persons. One example is D. W. MacKinnon's study of architects in which the author describes the characteristics of creative architects. MacKinnon indicates that these architects are effectively intelligent, open to experience, and free from petty restraints. Creative architects, according to MacKinnon, also demonstrate aesthetic sensitivity, cognitive flexibility, and independence in their thought and action. MacKinnon further found that architects exhibit high levels of energy, an unquestioning commitment to creative endeavor, and an unceasing striving for innovative solutions.

Another interesting study of gifted and innovative persons is Victor and Mildred Goertzel's *Cradles of Eminence*. These authors studied well-known creative people and identified their common traits. Eminent persons are usually loners as children; they generally do not like school and tend to have conflicts with their parents.

Psychologist Frank Barron studied Ph.D. candidates in the sciences at the University of California, particularly with regard to the originality of their work and thoughts. Barron's work indicates that original persons prefer complexity, make independent judgments, are self-assertive, and suppress few impulses. He concludes that creative people are more observant than most; can deal with several ideas simultaneously; are motivated by talent and values; and have greater sexual drives, physical vigor, and sensitivity. The most common studies of creativity are directed to the creative process itself. The definitions in this chapter represent examples drawn from these process approaches.

One of the first attempts to understand the creative process was made by Graham Wallas in *The Art of Thought* (1920). Based largely upon the writings of creative persons, Wallas delineated four stages of creativity: *preparation, incubation, illumination,* and *verification*. The process of creativity is a continuous one, composed of stages that progress "in and through each other." Preparation entails the conscious investigation of a problem in all directions. Then, during incubation, the problem is not dealt with consciously but simmers, so to speak, on the back burner. Step three, illumination, announces the arrival of a solution or an idea in the person's psyche. This idea is then tested in the final phase of verification. These steps, though apparently simple, provide a powerful and useful explanation of the process. Wallas' model is consistent with more contemporary models of the creative process and has often been used as a basis for these paradigms.

Many theorists have been intrigued by the state of incubation. A problem, already investigated in the preparation stage, enters the unconscious at a time when the individual is engaged in a restful or relaxing activity. Within the unconscious, disorder and chaos prevail; ideas collide with one another to produce combinations that would never have been arrived at through logic or conscious analytical thought. Einstein called this a "play" of the mind's elements. An interesting device to stimulate this stage of innovation and bring it to a more conscious level has been developed by A. F. Osborne.

In *Your Creative Power,* Osborne describes the technique known as *brainstorming*. This technique relates to synectics, as it provides ways to generate spontaneous ideas. The fundamental premise of brainstorming is the need for uncritical acceptance of ideas until they can be tested. Although Osborne was a businessman who invented this procedure as a means to solve problems in commerce, his technique has been used widely to spur creative action in many areas.

Another approach, studies of creative products, attempts to work backward; these studies examine the outcome of innovation in an effort to understand the process. Literary studies of the works of authors are one form of this approach to study creativity. Wherein lies the power of a piece of literature? How and why does a poem move the reader? How does a painting or a concerto convey meaning? These are the questions for which investigators of creative products are seeking answers.

Still further studies of creativity examine environments to identify which stimulate the creative process and which inhibit it. Carl Rogers maintains that the creative environment must be a "nurturing" one that fosters the growth of "psychological safety and freedom." *Psychological safety* is attained by three related processes: (1) accepting the individual as being of unconditional worth; (2) providing a climate that is free of external evaluation; and (3) providing empathetic understanding. *Psychological freedom* is permission to think, feel, and express—with responsibility only to the self. This develops an inner locus of evaluation and encourages actions that are the results of creative, internal processing.

E. Paul Torrance, who has written much about school settings, maintains that these settings must be open, permissive places where teachers relinquish their censorship role to create a nonpunitive atmosphere for students. Environments that facilitate creative behavior must tolerate complexity and even disorder. A creative place encourages innovation; to do this, the teacher must display an accepting, respecting attitude toward pupils. In such an atmosphere, the learner receives permission to give him- or herself over completely to a task.

William J. J. Gordon once described the kind of setting that was necessary for his process of synectics to work. The setting ought not to be plush or comfortable, but rather should provide an uncritical atmosphere where ideas could be freely offered and explored. Gordon's synectics sound much like the school setting described by Torrance or the environment needed for Osborne's brainstorming; all of these are open-ended procedures.

CREATIVE WAYS OF KNOWING: ENDOCEPTS AND JANUSIAN THINKING

The mental processes involved in creativity have long been a perplexing issue for theorists. Some of these processes may be called intuitive, although intuition is often used as a catch-all for any thought process that is not readily explicable. More in-depth conceptualizations of the mental operations that are integral to innovation are offered by Silvano Arieti and Albert Rothenberg.

In *Creativity: The Magic Synthesis* Arieti explores the idea of *endocept*. An endocept is a cognition without representation. This means that it occurs without form; it may be otherwise understood as internal, nonverbal, unconscious, or preconscious thought. It is an emotional construct, a "primitive organization of past experiences, perceptions, memory traces and images of things and movements," which struggles to reach the stage of conscious expression.

Persons experience endoceptual phenomena in dreams and in highly emotional experiences. Endocepts are active during what Wallas calls the period of incubation, as they fight for embodiment in words, actions, and ideas. "Endoceptual processes accrue," writes Arieti. "They are self-enlarging and self-enriching; they add new dimensions even when higher levels of mentation are present."

Arieti's formulation leads to additional understanding and further definition of the creative process. It can be the movement in a person's mind from the holding of an endocept, to its translation or transformation into a concrete image, thought, or expression. Facilitating creative behavior means aiding the movement in a person's cognition from endocept to concept.

Techniques requiring uncritical environments (such as brainstorming and synectics) and ones that lead to bringing together apparently unrelated elements (such as synectics and bisociation) are ways of reaching into the unconscious to give form and substance to what begins as endocepts.

Another type of mental processing that involves the relating of unrelated entities has been formulated by psychiatrist Albert Rothenberg, who identifies *Janusian thinking* as being based on the simultaneous conception of two opposing elements. This principle—metaphorically represented by the two-faced god, Janus, who could see in opposite directions at the same time—is prevalent in works of science and art and is also embodied in metaphor, paradox, ambiguity, and tension. As it does with open-ended thinking, a creative environment can stimulate Janusian thinking.

Rothenberg maintains that Janusian thinking occurs early in the creative process, during the periods Wallas calls preparation and incubation. Even though Rothenberg insists that Janusian thinking is a conscious, content-oriented process, neither its presence nor its effects may be obvious until the action is completed.

This is reminiscent of both Gordon and Arieti. Gordon's mind-stretching through the use of analogy and metaphor (see the discussion of Gordon in Chapter 4) actually demands the integration or relation of opposites or near-opposites. Like Arieti's endoconceptual cognition, Janusian thinking is a way of knowing without realizing that you know until the creative act is complete.

SOME QUESTIONS

This section uses a question-and-answer format to discuss several issues relating to creativity.

1. *Is creativity a process that brings novelty to the world, or can a creative act occur if it provides something new for a single person?* Although this chapter has defined creativity in several ways, theorists remain divided on the issue of novelty. If innovation must bring something new to the universe, then creativity is a process available only to a limited number of people. If, however, innovation must bring something that is new only to the innovator, then the possibility of creative behavior exists for a much larger number.

2. *Is creativity found in all persons or only in those designated as gifted and talented?* Innovation can be facilitated and improved in everyone, regardless of one's mental capacity. All persons—a kindergarten student figuring out a way to keep her crayons sharp as well as the sophisticated computer scientist designing systems for spacecraft—can become more creative. Teachers need to learn to be facilitators of creativity for typical students, as well as for the very able.

3. *Can creativity be taught?* Creativity cannot be taught directly in the manner in which mathematics or history is taught, but it can be facilitated in a number of ways. William J. J. Gordon's process of synectics allows students to use metaphor as a means of developing their own creativity. Psychodrama-trained therapists use a variety of group-process techniques to improve spontaneity and, consequently, creativity. The process of gaming is synergistic with creativity: participating in games can make persons more innovative even as creative persons are better game players. These devices, and others, can be used to improve creative production.

4. *Is creativity synonymous with spontaneity?* Creativity and spontaneity are not the same. Persons who learn to act more spontaneously often increase their creative behavior. Indeed, spontaneity seems to be a prerequisite for innovation. A pleasant circle emerges: as individuals become more spontaneous, their spontaneity increases creativity, and increased creativity stimulates spontaneity, which allows still more creative energy to emerge.

5. *Is creativity in art the same as creativity in science?* Theorists had often been divided on this question in the past, but now most scholars agree that the underlying processes in creative art and creative science are virtually identical. Innovative expression operates in different modes (words, paint, test tubes) producing different outcomes. Yet, the process through which something is created—a medicine, a poem, a painting, a song—seems to be the same.

6. *Can persons working in groups become more creative individuals?* Many scholars, including Torrance and Gordon, have examined this issue. Since creativity requires an individual act, can groups develop it? This issue has implications for the organization of creative education. Most writers agree that group process can facilitate creativity. Many techniques can be used to raise cohesion; this leads to more spontaneous behavior among group members. Spontaneity in turn leads to an increase in creative behavior. Sharing of ideas in a group can increase the production of new perspectives; for example, the process of brainstorming requires group work. Group members also support each other. This makes risk taking less threatening, and this increased security also facilitates creativity.

7. *Is creativity a mysterious process, or can it be studied and understood?* Many persons approach the creative process with a sense of awe, believing that it is not for them and feeling that it involves unknowable qualities. Despite its complexity, innovation can be studied, understood, and facilitated. In his work, Gordon discovered that awareness of the process was in itself an aid to improving it. Others also support this point of view.

COMPONENTS OF CREATIVITY

The work of J. P. Guilford and E. Paul Torrance have led to the identification of many components of creative behavior. For them creativity includes the following parts:

1. sensitivity to problems
2. fluency
3. flexibility
4. originality
5. elaboration
6. redefinition
7. penetration

The first and key component, sensitivity to problems, requires awareness that the odd, the unusual, and the inconsistent may be present in a given situation. Without this sensitivity, the student will find few problems to solve and little opportunity for creative expression. Recognition of the unusual in an assignment demands subjective involvement with a problem. Such involvement is essential for creative problem solving.

Fluency requires multiple responses to the same given information in a limited time. It is the ability to generate multiple solutions to a problem or answers to a question. (For example, how many words can you think of which rhyme with the word *bell?*)

Flexibility calls for the individual to shift trains of thought to avoid becoming locked into one track. The flexible individual is less threatened by a new situation. S/he finds it easier to bisociate matrices or to bring unrelated aspects of experience together. Flexibility facilitates creativity by helping pupils increase their ability to make the familiar strange.

Originality is the quality most commonly associated with creativity. It can be defined in many ways but generally means the ability to see what most people do not. It can be viewed as the acceptance of bisociation.

Elaboration is the ability to expand one's view of a thing or process. A person can take a common object (perhaps a chair) and increase its uses from something to sit on to dozens of other possibilities. (The chair can be transformed into a stationary horse, for example.)

Redefinition refers to the ability to reorganize what is known to make it useful in solving a problem. It too can be related to Koestler's process of bisociation and the Janusian principle discussed previously. It provides new meanings for old words and involves new ways of knowing.

Penetration suggests that the creative person can see more things than what appears on the surface in any given situation. Creative persons are particularly adept at penetration, often going beyond the information given.

CONSCIOUS AND UNCONSCIOUS ASPECTS OF THE PROCESS OF CREATIVITY

In attempting to understand the process of creativity, a distinction can be made between those theorists who pursue an approach based on the study of consciousness and those who approach an understanding of creativity through examining the unconscious. The detailed work of these theorists is discussed in the next chapter but some attention is given in this chapter to the two perspectives and how they affect creative education.

The conscious orientation to creativity involves a perspective based on awareness, cognition, and reflection. It is an approach that requires attention to the world. By and large, the conscious approach to creativity is the basis for intelligence theory described in the preceding chapter. Authors such as Guilford and Torrance have this orientation, which approaches the creative process through a direct means. The reading of Torrance's steps for the creative process indicates a very structured method. Torrance says that, "creative thinking is a natural process by which a person becomes aware of a problem, difficulty or gap in information for which he has no learned response; searches for possible solutions; evaluates these possible solutions and tests them; modifies them and retests them; and communicates the results to others."

This approach becomes a problem-solving one that attempts to use direct means to facilitate creative behavior. In effect, it seeks to achieve divergent production by a convergent pattern. Although it offers much insight into creativity, the conscious approach for gifted and talented students is limited. This approach may set constraints on creative behavior in an authoritarian manner (particularly in the hands of a less than able teacher who converts Torrance's system into a lockstep procedure). The conscious approach to facilitating creative behavior, although successful with many students, can often be stifling for gifted and talented ones.

The unconscious approach holds that creativity rises from within. It stems from Freudian precepts and holds that creativity relates to the role of freely rising fantasies.

For Freud, creativity begins with an internal conflict for which unconscious forces seek solutions. Creative behavior allows for the discharge of pent-up emotions stemming from the struggle that leads to an acceptable level of frustration. Freud maintained that creative thought derives from daydreaming and childhood play. He argued that innovative persons could accept these fantasies *into adulthood* whereas the noncreative people repressed them. In effect, creative behavior can be seen as a continuation and substitution of childhood play.

As noted, the role of the child is seen as important by many creativity theorists. Transactional analysis defines creativity as the nurturing adult ego-state giving the child permission to exist. John Dewey once suggested that grown-ups can learn the spontaneity necessary for creative expression from children.

As consciousness-oriented theorists such as Torrance present problem-solving techniques for the development of creativity (e.g., Torrance provides systematic ways for children to learn fluency, elaboration, and the like) those who view creativity as being highly unconscious have also derived means for facilitating creative behavior. Specific exercises are suggested in Chapter 5, but the general approach can be briefly described here.

The fundamental means for facilitating creative behavior for theorists of the unconscious lies in the role of metaphor. Webster defines metaphor as "a figure of speech in which a word or phrase literally denoting one kind of object or idea is used in place of another by way of suggesting likeness or analogy between them" (*New Collegiate Dictionary*). The importance of metaphor is that it can free the unconscious by making connections that might otherwise elude the censorlike mechanism found in all people. This censor tends to force people toward convergent rather than divergent thought.

Thomas Edison, Albert Einstein, and Will Rogers were creative students who perceived metaphoric, fantasy-oriented connections between things, and this led them to have trouble in school. Persons need convergent thought in order to function in the complex, modern world, but they also need to be divergent thinkers. Metaphor serves as the primary focus of unconscious creativity theory just as problem solving serves as the primary focus for the conscious theorists. In the next chapter, Gordon's metaphoric system for facilitating creative behavior is examined in detail.

FACILITATING CREATIVE BEHAVIOR

Specific strategies and procedures for increasing creative behavior are discussed in Chapter 5, but some general points can be made here about facilitating creative behavior. Creative behavior is increased by those activities that result in deep involvement. From Dewey it is known that these activities must be meaningful. In order to achieve this significance it is important for teachers to become aware of the interests, needs, and perspectives of their students. The opposite of involvement is ennui and the bored student can be a most difficult one with whom to work.

In order to facilitate the process, the teacher should avoid the role of censor. Students flourish in open environments where their minds are free to explore. Within the normal limits of schooling and safety, teachers must allow the free reign of thought and activity that lead to stimulation and excitement. In order to do this, the role of censor must be inhibited.

Creative behavior is facilitated by creating a nonpunitive atmosphere in the classroom. Children can often propose divergent solutions to problems which can be rejected by teachers who may fail to be sensitive to a creative solution to a problem. In extreme cases, teachers may even punish students for divergent production.

Creative behavior can be enhanced by providing challenges and by offering difficult tasks. If students find the typical classroom too easy, this can lead to boredom, potential discipline problems, and a stifling of creativity. Much thought and planning must be given to preparing for teaching. The presence of appropriate amounts of challenge is critical.

Creative behavior is facilitated by the stimulation of curiosity. This can be achieved by what Torrance describes as incompleteness. Rather than providing all of the answers all of the time (which is the usual temptation of pedagogy), the teacher must approach some problems in ways that foster incompleteness. The curiosity this creates is motivating and increases creative behavior.

SUMMARY

This chapter provided an overview of theories of creativity and examined innovation in terms of person, product, process, and environment with major emphasis on the creative process.

It also offered several definitions of creativity drawn from many sources, including transactional analysis theory, humanistic psychology, and the work of Arthur Koestler.

Further, the chapter identified questions and answers on some of the key issues in the study of creativity. These questions concerned the nature of novelty and the issue of who can be creative and whether innovation can be taught. This format is also used to examine the nature of creativity in art and science as well as the role of groups in the creative process.

The discussion in this chapter identified some components of creativity, making a distinction between conscious and unconscious aspects of the process of creativity. Ways to facilitate creative behavior (explored in depth in Chapter 5) were introduced.

Whereas this chapter introduced some theoretical considerations, the next chapter focuses primarily on creativity theorists who have defined the creative act.

NOTES

1. Abraham H. Maslow, *Toward a Psychology of Being* (New York: D. Van Nostrand Company, 1968), p. 136.

2. Quoted in P. E. Vernon, *Creativity* New York: Penguin Books, 1970), p. 139.
3. Rollo May, *The Courage to Create* (New York: Bantam Books, 1975).
4. Arthur Koestler, *The Act of Creation* (London: Pan Books, 1975), p. 35.

CHAPTER

4

Theories of Creativity

INTRODUCTION

A distinction can be made between theories of creativity based on the study of consciousness and those theories that are drawn from the study of the unconscious. This chapter explores each of these perspectives—as well as their major proponents—in detail.

The conscious orientation to creativity is based on awareness, cognition, and reflection—it is an approach that requires attention to the world. This perspective on creativity serves as the basis for the theories of intelligence described in Chapter 1. In general, the study of consciousness, which approaches creativity in a direct manner, can be understood as a behaviorist explanation of the process.

From the study of unconsciousness we develop the perspective that creativity rises from within the psyche. As indicated in Chapter 2, this theory derives from Freudian precepts and relates creativity to the role of fantasy and daydream. It can be understood as a Freudian, psychoanalytic explanation of the process.

This chapter is organized around these two ways of understanding creative behavior. As suggested before, studying the unconscious may be more lucrative for facilitating creative behavior.

THEORIES BASED ON THE STUDY OF CONSCIOUSNESS

The Mismeasure of Man by biologist Stephen Jay Gould provides a beginning for the study of consciousness.[1] Gould traces the history of the study of mental capacity, particularly as it was believed to have differed among racial groups. The earliest construct of intelligence derived from the concept of *polygeny*—a belief that human beings are descended from different Adams. This meant that Caucasoid, Negroid, and Mongoloid peoples stemmed from different sources. Gould indicates that polygeny was part of a movement to create a scientific basis for believing that mental ability differed among races.

From this unsophisticated kind of overt racism, the study of the variation of mental capacity proceeded through many stages including craniometry (the study of skulls), the weighing of brains (which led to a belief that women were less intelligent than men because their brains were smaller, and the study of bodies (in an attempt to discover which races were most apelike).

The modern study of intelligence theory began with the work of psychologist Sir Francis Galton (1822–1911)—a cousin of Darwin—who was interested in the way environment and heredity contributed to the development of mental ability. Galton also investigated the relationship between motor skills and intelligence. Both issues remain controversial and unresolved and the questions formulated by Galton continue to intrigue theorists.

Galton was obsessed with measurement; he believed that *everything* was quantifiable. For him, measurement defined the validity of any science. Galton's perspective, along with his interest in the relationship of heredity to intelligence, established a climate for an increased desire to quantify mental capacity.

The next development came with the work of the French psychologist Alfred Binet (1857–1911), who had been hired by the French government to devise a means of identifying children who might have trouble in school. The government wanted to know which children might be incapable of attending school and which of them might need remediation.

Binet began by identifying behaviors that determined school success. He concluded that these were memory, mental imagery, imagination, attentiveness, and verbal comprehension. In developing a means by which to measure these, Binet used a highly empirical and behavioral approach. He determined the level of achievement on these measures that would be concomitant with school success and then devised instruments for testing these behaviors. He created what today would be called "age-referenced norms" by finding the mean score for each behavior for specific age groups. For example, he tested a representative sample of 100 six-year-olds on a mental imagery test and obtained a mean for that group. This allowed him to make predictions about six-year-olds and mental imagery. Binet derived a composite score for his tests and argued that children above the mean of his examination would probably do well in school and those below it would probably do badly. In this way, Binet met his responsibility; he was able to find a way to predict success and failure in school.

Binet, according to Gould, insisted on three cardinal principles for using his tests. They were:

1. The scores are a practical device; they do not buttress any theory of intellect. They do not define anything innate or permanent. We may not designate what they measure as "intelligence" or any other refined entity.
2. The scale is a rough, empirical guide for identifying mildly retarded and learning-disabled children who need special help. It is not a device for ranking normal children.
3. Whatever the cause of difficulty in children identified for help, emphasis should be placed upon improvement through special training. Low scores should not be used to mark children as innately incapable.[2]

All of Binet's caveats came ultimately to be ignored. Because of a Galton-like obsession with measurement, Binet's tests were transformed by the German psychologist W. Stern and by Lewis Terman at Standard University. Stern argued that the mental age described by Binet's tests (the age-referenced norms described) could be divided by chronological age and then multiplied by one hundred. This is the derivation of the *intelligence quotient* (IQ): mental age divided by chronological age times 100.

Terman, who became an early advocate of IQ testing, created a variation of Binet's test which has become a standard means of determining IQ. This instrument—now world famous—is the Stanford-Binet Intelligence Test. Terman's work concluded a process that reduced the nature of mental capacity to a single quantity; it led to a belief that intelligence consisted of a single, indivisible entity.

This viewpoint fails to differentiate among the many different talents that can be found among human beings. People can reason abstractly and they can draw. They can compose music and they can create categories. They can conceptualize and they can evaluate. The mental abilities of human beings—typical ones and gifted ones—are many and varied.

Binet set out innocently to assess school behaviors and to identify those children who might not succeed in school without receiving special help. His work was reduced into a single measurable quality whose existence is questionable.

Many psychologists reacted against the narrow definition of mental capacity represented by IQ. They sought ways to assess and conceptualize mental capacity in less restrictive ways. This led to the development of the concept of primary mental abilities (PMAs)—a term that indicates that the types of mental capacity are many and varied. Perhaps the most famous advocate of this viewpoint—and the person most influential in the development of a "conscious" theory of creativity—was J. P. Guilford.

Guilford, who earned a doctorate in psychology at Cornell in 1928, spent much of his professional career as a teacher and researcher at the University of Southern California. He became a psychometrician—a person who applies statistical methods to the study of human behavior.

Guilford was one of the many psychologists who objected to the notion that mental capacity could be reduced to the simple construct of intelligence quotient. Furthermore, he was concerned with the lack of attention being given to the study of creativity and with the related assumption that creative persons could simply be equated with those obtaining high scores on an IQ test.

In many ways, Guilford opened the era of research on creativity with his 1950 presidential address to the American Psychological Association. Prior to 1950, there had been little serious study of the process of creativity from a psychological perspective. In his address, Guilford called for renewed interest in the topic and he himself became involved with in-depth research on creativity.

Guilford asked two questions in his 1950 speech: 1 How can we discover creative promise in our children and youth?, and 2 How can we promote the development of creative personalities?

Guilford used multiple factor analysis—a statistical process first developed by L. L. Thurstone—to isolate primary mental abilities which he felt could serve as a measure of intelligence. Through this method of analysis, Guilford created his "structure of intellect" model (see Figure 4.1). Using complicated factor analysis to identify primary mental abilities, Guilford isolated 120 separate measurable abilities.

Guilford's model indicates varieties of mental abilities along three planes. The model can be pictured as a cube with three major dimensions—operations, content, and product. *Operations* are those mental activities by which one processes information from the environment. *Content* relates to the forms the information may take—those discrimi-

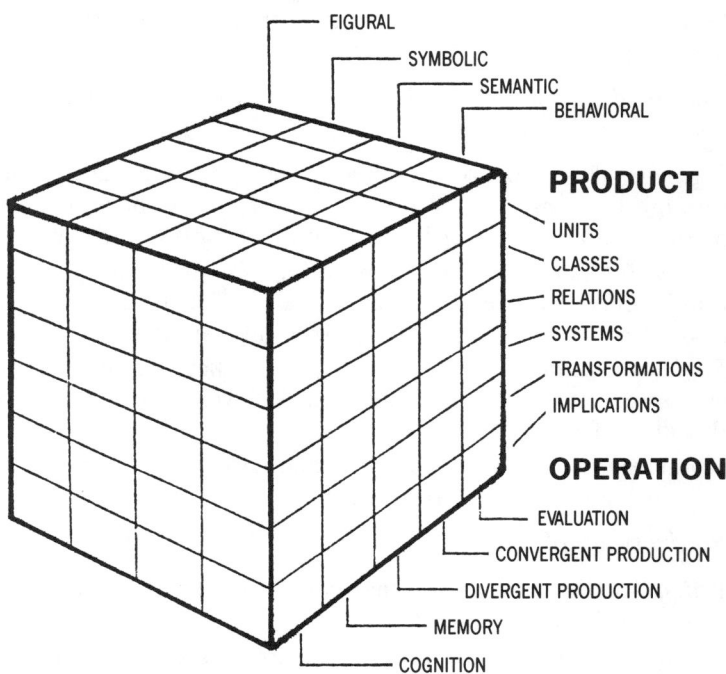

FIGURE 4.1 *Theoretical model for the complete structure-of-intellect.*

nations made by a person about the environment. *Product* refers to the kind of organization that occurs as a result of the processing by an individual.

For each of the major dimensions, Guilford introduced several subcategories. *Operations* contains five types of mental abilities:

1. *Memory:* The ability to recall information to which a person has been previously exposed.
2. *Cognition:* The ability to recognize information that may occur in any form including print, sound, and film.
3. *Evaluation:* The ability to make judgments according to criteria that are either external or internal.
4. *Convergent Production:* The ability to generate information from a stimulus that results in a single and conventional outcome. (This is what Gordon calls making the strange familiar.)

5. *Divergent Production:* The ability to generate a variety of ideas from a stimulus. Furthermore, the ability to see things differently than they are seen by others. (Divergent production relates to Gordon's idea of making the familiar strange.)

The mind, according to Guilford, perceives four different types of *Content:*

1. *Figural:* This type of content consists of information perceived through the senses in the form of sound, shape, or touch. A motion picture is an example of information transmitted through a figure.
2. *Symbolic:* This refers to information obtained through something that is representative of an idea or feeling. The trademark "Coke" on a soda can is an example of symbolic information.
3. *Semantic:* Information obtained from spoken, written, or imagined words represents semantic content. A novel or short story contains this kind of information.
4. *Behavioral:* This type is transmitted through nonverbal action. A wink represents behavioral content.

Products are of six different kinds:

1. *Units:* A unit is something that can stand alone—a single thing. (A Chevrolet is an example of a unit.)
2. *Classes:* When units are grouped together as a result of shared characteristics, they may be thought of as a class. (All different makes of cars belong to the class *automobile*.)
3. *Relations:* The ideas or concepts that allow units to fit into a class are examples of relations. The characteristics of all Chevrolets that allow them to belong to the same class are examples of relations.
4. *Systems:* When two or more units are interconnected, they form a system. The process of producing automobiles may be viewed as an example of a system.
5. *Transformations:* When something is changed, redefined, or modified it represents a transformation. A person who purchases a used school bus and converts it into a mobile home has brought about a transformation.
6. *Implications:* Extrapolation leading to predictions based on information or on previous experience are examples of implications, which often result from what–if statements. ("What if a misunderstanding led to a nuclear war?")

Guilford's work led to an operational definition of creativity as the application of divergent production to any content that results in a transformation.

Guilford's distinction between divergent and convergent thinking has been especially useful in clarifying creativity. Divergent thinking moves away from already known and expected responses, whereas convergent thought moves toward responses that fit what is already known. Traditional measures of intelligence have emphasized convergence—the development of logical thought toward single right answers. Creativity demands new ideas and unconventional behavior that breaks away from expected ways of doing things.

In his 1950 address to the American Psychological Association, Guilford asked for a greater emphasis on research and development in the area of creative behavior. One of the persons who responded to his call was E. Paul Torrance. Torrance, currently a professor of educational psychology at the University of Georgia, studied many aspects of creativity. He was particularly interested in the type of environment that fostered or inhibited innovative behavior. In addition to analyzing conditions favoring creative growth, Torrance also studied the personality of creative persons and the effects of heredity and society on creativity. For Torrance, creative thinking occurred when situations called for nonhabitual behavior in which no learned response existed in an individual.

As a result of his early training as a school guidance counselor, Torrance argued for a particular kind of treatment for those who were perceived as creative. Innovative children need the following kind of support in the school. First, they require a place of refuge; They must be able to pursue their talents in a nonthreatening environment. Second, creative students need the assurance and support of school authorities in ways that legitimize their ability. Third, these pupils must be enabled to accept their own differences so they can become divergent thinkers. Fourth, creative students need the opportunity to communicate their ideas. Fifth, they require recognition. Finally, sixth, they require understanding from their parents and others about their creative ability.

Torrance urged teachers to show respect for innovative ideas. Often students suggest ideas that can surprise and even baffle teachers. Instructors should respond to these notions with respect; when they do, students respond with interest, enthusiasm, and renewed effort. Teachers who react this way help children with their self-images and with their views of their own ideas. Not rewarding or even punishing students for these kinds of differences will clearly have the opposite effect.

Torrance made an important point regarding evaluation. Although judging students' work is always an integral part of schooling, constant evaluation can have a negative effect on children. Torrance indicated that teachers should not judge all of the work of students, who may need large periods of time to engage in unevaluated activity. Torrance argues that this kind of time is helpful to children as they establish the limits of their ability and become familiar with new kinds of materials and situations.

A major contribution of Torrance has been his procedure for testing creative behavior. These tests, which were designed while Torrance was at the University of Minnesota and expanded during his years at Georgia, are known as *The Torrance Tests of Creative Thinking.* Torrance modified Guilford's categories and devised a battery of tests that could assess creative ability. Torrance suggested that the major components of creative behavior included 1) sensitivity to problems, 2) fluency, 3) flexibility, 4) originality, 5) elaboration, and 6) redefinition. Using these constructs and dividing them into verbal and figurative parts, Torrance created a widely used instrument that is generally regarded as a standard for measuring creative behavior.

Torrance argued that in order to develop creative thinking, an individual must be curious. Creative thinkers must want to meet challenges and must develop a tendency to attempt difficult tasks. The person who wishes to develop his or her creative thinking ability must be willing to give him or herself over completely to a task, be honest, and be one who searches for the truth. Torrance argued that persons need to be encouraged in their individuality in order to develop creative behavior.

Whereas Torrance has contributed most to the testing of creative behavior, he also recognized the limits of evaluation. He said in an address to the American Educational Research Association in 1972, "... a fundamental difficulty is that creative thinking can be manifested in an almost infinite number of ways and there is no acceptable way of quantifying all of these different kinds of achievement."

Torrance and Guilford represent the two most significant theorists of the conscious approach to the study of creativity. Before we turn to the work of theorists of the unconscious, we must describe the contribution to the evaluation of creativity of Sidney J. Parnes.

In two major publications on creativity (*Guide to Creative Action,*[3] and *Creative Action Handbook,*[4] the latest editions of which were written with the assistance of Ruth B. Noller and Angelo M. Biondi), Parnes indicated a commitment to two guiding principles: 1) Students, through practice, can increase creative behavior, and 2) whereas education emphasizes facts and information, the deliberate use of imagination is essential for creative production.

In seeking to increase creative problem solving, Parnes suggested several objectives. Students must develop self-confidence in their creative abilities. Through a variety of reinforcements they must learn not to say, "I am not creative." The potential creative student must be highly motivated to use his or her creative power. S/he must learn to feel comfortable with the desire to create. The potential creator must be open to the ideas of others and show increasing curiosity. The potentially innovative person must demonstrate an awareness of the importance of creativity in all facets of life. S/he must evince a sensitivity to problems and a desire to solve them. Finally, creative problem solving should lead to an increase in the production of original and high-quality ideas that solve problems.

Parnes believed that divergent thinking abilities are important because they contribute to a person's ability to solve more quickly and effectively the many difficult problems that life constantly provides. For Parnes, creative problem solving is one of the many strategies people need to learn to adjust to the increasingly complex world of the late twentieth century. Parnes's guidebooks provide teachers with many concrete techniques for the application of the conscious theory of creativity to the classroom. In this way, Parnes—like Torrance—transformed the theory of mental capacity—begun by Galton and brought to fruition by Guilford—into an operational means for effective classroom use.

As indicated in Chapter 2, the conscious theory of creativity (with its deep roots in behavioral psychology) is limited because of the lock-step fashion in which it tends to operate—a manner which attempts to achieve divergence in convergent ways. This does not deny the importance of these theorists to an understanding of creative behavior.

Guilford expanded the definition of mental capacity by his construct called "the structure of intellect." Torrance used Guilford's formulation to provide useful applications for the classroom. A major contribution of Torrance is his description of the creative environment. Furthermore, *The Torrance Tests of Creative Thinking* made an important and useful contribution to those studying and attempting to facilitate creative behavior. Parnes' problem-solving course based on creativity also provides methods for teachers who wish to facilitate creative behavior. All of these are valuable contributions to the study of creativity by the theorists of consciousness who began their work by trying to understand mental capacity.

THEORIES BASED ON THE STUDY OF THE UNCONSCIOUS

Creativity theories drawn from the unconscious begin with the work of Freud, who was the first to conceptualize the unconscious. Freud remains a controversial figure in psychology, and his perspectives have divided the discipline into his supporters and his opponents. Freud's most significant contribution to psychology was probably the understanding that people act for reasons that are different from the reasons they give for their behavior. This is a simple but useful way to state the nature of the unconscious.

Freud studied creativity because of his role as a psychologist and because of his interest in culture. In Freud's view, creativity, like neurosis, originates from conflicts that result from basic biological drives. People who experience internal conflict can deal with it in many ways; one positive type of accommodation of this conflict results in creativity.

Freud asked why writers and poets produce imaginative work, and answered in part by saying:

> We ought to look in the child for the first traces of imaginative activity. The child's best loved and most absorbing occupation is play. Perhaps we may say that every child at play behaves like an imaginative writer, in that he creates a world of his own, more truly, he rearranges the things of his world and orders it in a new way that pleases him better.
>
> Now the writer does the same thing as the child at play; he creates a world of phantasy which he takes very seriously; that is, he invests it with a great deal of affect, while separating it sharply from reality.[5]

Children take their imaginary world very seriously. They treat play earnestly as they borrow events and characters from the real world. As people mature they give up play and its pleasures. However, Freud argued, the pent-up emotion that results from internal conflict demands an outlet. For persons who can no longer engage in the play of childhood, this means the creation of daydreams and fantasy. Freud said:

> So when the human being grows up and ceases to play he only gives up the connection with real objects; instead of playing he then begins to create phantasy. He builds castles in the air and creates what are called day-dreams.[6]

These daydreams and fantasies are, in many ways, the continuation and substitution of childhood play. The person who becomes creative accepts the freely rising fantasies and daydreams; the noncreative person suppresses them.

Freud concluded that the poet or writer presents his or her work as a kind of disguised form of daydream. The creative product brings about a release of the tension built up from the internal conflict and signals that are released by the pent-up emotions resulting from the struggle. For Freud, an unresolved conflict can result in either creativity or neurosis, so that a properly focused program that facilitates creative behavior may also improve mental health.

In a fascinating book, *Freud and Man's Soul,* Bruno Bettelheim argues that Freud studied neurotic adults in order to determine what had gone wrong in their childhood.[7] Bettelheim claims that Freud can best be understood as a person interested in the reform of childrearing practice. Freud's perspective on the creative process can be seen as a way of urging that childhood forces be allowed to reestablish themselves in a way that leads to creative behavior.

Lawrence Kubie, another psychoanalyst who is interested in creative behavior derived from the unconscious, published *Neurotic Distortion of the Creative Process* in 1958, which was reprinted in 1979.[8] Kubie maintains, as did Freud, that all persons have the capacity for creative as well as neurotic behavior, and that both traits manifest themselves in infancy and childhood as a result of early life experiences.

Kubie sees creative activity as containing two essential parts: "cognito" and "intelligo." Kubie borrows a Freudian construct—the preconscious (a sort of filing clerk that mediates between the conscious and unconscious). Cognition, for Kubie, is the work of the preconscious. It uses free association without conscious deliberation to freely gather or "shake together" many ideas that seem unrelated. The shaking together, Kubie believes, is done through the use of analogy. The preconscious then puts these unrelated constructs together into new combinations. Intelligence, which is a conscious process, then chooses among the free associations for new combinations that seem significant. For Kubie, creative activity takes place when both processes work simultaneously: the preconscious shaking together and the conscious selecting from the product of preconscious activity.

This shaking together to form new combinations can be related to Koestler's notion of bisociation described in the previous chapter. Both Koestler and Kubie are trying to account for the appearance of something new into consciousness and both use the existence of the Freudian unconscious and preconscious to do so.

Kubie was highly critical of formal education with regard to creativity. Kubie saw schools as being neurotically rigid. This rigidity has become so entrenched that it is perceived as normal while attempts to bring about change are seen as abnormal. Schools, Kubie argues, tend to favor the certainty of facts and they rely excessively on drill and memorization. These are all aspects of the conscious state that tend to inhibit or even destroy the preconscious process of creativity by not allowing the free association and shaking down to occur.

George Prince, an early associate of William J. J. Gordon, also contributed to the explanation of the role of the unconscious in the creative process in *The Practice of Creativity*.[9]

Prince argues that the human mind consists of three parts—the subconscious, the conscious, and the preconscious. The many experiences which a person has had are stored in the subconscious. The conscious mind, Prince says, is constantly confronted with problems of various kinds that require solutions. The preconscious acts as a "file clerk," receiving data from the consciousness and searching the subconscious for appropriate material for response. A difficulty arises for people because their experiences have been numerous and diverse and require organization. The mechanism that has evolved to provide organization between the conscious and the preconscious, Prince labels "the censor." It tends to reinforce what Guilford described as convergent thinking and it seeks to avoid divergent thought. Put another way, it is the purpose of the censor to resist the kinds of bisociation described by Koestler as necessary for the creative process.

This mechanism exists because convergent thought is an important part of human behavior. Divergent, creative thinking is not superior to convergent thought that provides necessary solutions to the most frequently occurring of life's problems. The censor keeps the mind on track and provides efficient solutions to standard problems (e.g., One must know which key on one's ring will open the car door and which will start the engine. No creative behavior is desired here. Attempting to place the house key into the ignition will ruin the switch.) A difficulty arises, however, because in most people the censor is overdeveloped and it becomes a mechanism for preventing creative behavior.

Traditional educational practice has been very good at building the censor. The mechanism is stronger among typical children that it is in gifted children. Both typical and gifted children, however, need to learn how to weaken the censor so that creative ideas can flow more readily.

Prince and William J. J. Gordon together began Synectics, Incorporated, a company for teaching persons to use the creative process. They applied Gordon's process of synectics—a system designed to weaken the censor and to let the creative processes emerge.

In *The New Art of the Possible* (1987), Gordon described how he first conceptualized the process:

> The first time I witnessed hidden elements of creativity surfacing was during the North African campaign in World War II. I was part of a group that was formed to clear Tripoli Harbor of the wrecks that the departing Germans had sunk across the entrance. Since the use of Tripoli as a support port was necessary for the Italian invasion, our task was crucial. The problem was explained to us by the naval officer in my group.
>
> "The ship we can't seem to budge is right smack in the middle of the channel," he said. "She's sitting bolt upright in the sand with twenty-four holes in her hull. And before Jerry blew the holes he dropped great sheets of three-quarter inch iron inside every compartment so that our divers can't get in to do the patching. If we could

just plug the holes from the inside we could pump enough air into her to float her up a couple of feet and tow her out of the way. But the air blows right by the outside patches we are forced to use."

While the navel officer was talking, a colonel seated next to me had shut his eyes tightly. He began to sway a little and nod his head as thought listening to some voice inside himself. When he finally spoke, he made no immediate sense at all. His eyes remained shut as if he were afraid of losing touch with the inner voice.

"What a bloody paradox," he said softly. "Here is a ship specially built to travel great distances, yet we can't move it a few feet. A most ingenious paradox." He paused and drew in a long breath. "Mother is a wizard paradox fixer," he whispered. "She can grow anything in that tiny walled-in garden of hers in the middle of London. Likes everything tidy, though. When she rakes out her garden, she always ends up with a few high mounds of dirt. They torment her. She must get rid of them. She can't heave the dirt over her garden wall into the street. But no place to hide it inside. So she goes right at those dirt piles with a brisk rake. She rakes away at a pile till the dirt gets spread around and just disappears." The colonel carefully opened his eyes and looked around. He seemed surprised to find himself among us, so far away had his concentration transported him.

"By George, your mother's right. We could do just that," the naval officer said slowly and thoughtfully. "We can blast the whole ship to pieces with small cordite charges. Then we'll all go down and rake the bloody mess till it's level. Might have to drag over it with small boats a few times. We'll level it just as his sainted mother did."

I am happy to tell you that the idea worked. That was the first time I had seen a person deliberately produce an inventive concept. It seemed more than accidental, but exactly how had the colonel done it? I saw him from time to time after that and witnessed more examples of his talent for solving problems that required creative solutions. Every time he needed an innovative idea he went into a kind of trance.

When I asked the colonel how he did it, all he could say was: "I shut my eyes and let my mind wander." Hardly a step-by-step explanation, but the colonel's behavior did offer a clue to the mental process that might reliably produce creative ideas.

The colonel let his mind wander, but on purpose. This aspect of purposefulness was in direct contradiction to what I always had been led to believe about creativity. I was fascinated. What was the actual thinking process that produced solutions that seemed to come out of the blue? I had to find out what went on inside the colonel to what I had always believed about creativity. I was fascinated. What was the actual thinking process that produces analogies that seemed to come out of the blue? I had to find out what went on inside the colonel's mind when he let his mind wander.

The only element I could pin down in the colonel's process was the way his connection between his mother's gardening activity and the problem produced a new viewpoint about removing the sunken ship. Though this insight of mine was fragmented and incomplete, I began to dream about being able to understand the steps in the creative process.[10]

Gordon coined the term *synectics* to describe his approach to creativity. The term, which comes from the Greek, means the joining together of different and apparently unrelated elements.

Gordon assumed that the creative process was not mysterious. It could be studied and understood. He also assumed that creativity in the arts is characterized by the same fundamental processes as it is in science. (Koestler made the same assumption when he indicated that different kinds of bisociations result in different kinds of creative work.) Furthermore, Gordon thought that by bringing creative processes to consciousness, the creative capacity of individuals could be increased. Finally, he assumed that in the creative process, the emotional component is more important than the intellectual, the irrational more important than the rational.

Through his own research, and the empirical work of others, Gordon verified the correctness of his assumptions. Particularly important for facilitating creative behavior is Gordon's third assumption, which means that children can be taught directly about the process of creativity as a way of increasing their innovative capacity. Learning about creativity can increase innovative behavior.

Gordon attempted to determine the psychological processes associated with the creative act. He decided to study persons who were in some form of therapy and also involved in a problem-solving situation. Gordon reasoned that such persons had considerable self-insight and would make good candidates for helping him discover the psychological processes that were associated with the creative act. He asked his subjects to speak aloud into a tape recorder while struggling with their problems. Gordon gathered a large collection of tapes from these problem solvers. As a result of studying them (as well as on the basis of other research he conducted), Gordon concluded that the psychological processes associated with the creative act included the following:

1. **Involvement—detachment:** These are two ends of an emotional-intellectual continuum; involvement means putting oneself (almost lit-

erally) into the place of the object; detachment means remaining objective and analytical about the problem. Creative problem solving requires both states.
2. **Deferment:** This refers to the necessity of not seeking too quick a solution to a problem before all the possibilities are examined and considered. If the person involved in a problem-solving situation fails to deter, then he or she will reinvent the same old, unsatisfactory answer to the problem.
3. **Speculation:** The ability to generate many possible solutions to a problem results from speculation. It requires open-mindedness and a tolerance of ambiguity.
4. **Autonomy of Object:** This occurs when the problem appears to take on a life of its own. As a result, a new viewpoint can be developed.
5. **Hedonic Response:** This is a feeling that the solution is right before its correctness has been established.

In addition to these states, Gordon came to believe that empathy, playfulness, and the use of irrelevance were also important for individuals to develop in order to weaken the censor and facilitate creative behavior.

Gordon then turned to the task of making these psychological states operational. He concluded that they could not be taught directly, and he then remembered the insight he had achieved during the North Africa campaign. Gordon reached a conclusion that has also been discovered by other creativity theorists. He came to understand that metaphor could help persons facilitate creative behavior.

Synectics relies upon analogy to solve problems. Over the years, Gordon developed a variety of metaphorical techniques for facilitating creative behavior. The process often involves groups of persons with different backgrounds (e.g., there may be an engineer, a poet, and a medical doctor in a group) who work together to find a solution to a problem. Gordon avoided overreliance on specialists whom he felt might tend to repeat old unproductive answers. Synectics groups use a method similar to the process of brainstorming described earlier in this volume.

In his earliest work, Gordon advocated three kinds of metaphors. First, he employed the *direct analogy*. This is the standard literary analogy that is a simple comparison of two things. For example: A crab walks sideways like a sneaky burglar.

A second metaphor is the *personal analogy*. This describes how it feels to identify with a person, concept, plant, animal, or nonliving thing. It is more than simple role-play because the person attempts to *feel* what it would be like to become the thing.

Finally, Gordon created a new kind of metaphor that he called *compressed conflict*. This is a poetic, two-word description on a high level of generality where the two words don't seem to fit and sometimes seem even to contradict each other. Gordon indicates that Pasteur used the compressed conflict "safe attack" to discover the concept of antitoxin.

As mentioned previously, in 1987 Gordon published *The New Art of the Possible* which contains his latest refinement of the synectics technique. The book teaches readers to use the process in their own settings, and introduces procedures that come from Gordon's many years of studying methods for facilitating creativity.

The New Art of the Possible introduces a creative problem-solving procedure that consists of six parts. First, the problem must be described. This comes before the actual synectics excursion. It requires a clear statement of the nature of the problem. Once the problem description is completed, the problem solving can begin.

Step one of creative problem solving is called *Paradox*. Gordon believes that all problems have an inherent paradox within them. As an example, Gordon discusses the need to conserve energy while maintaining a warm environment in cold weather. The paradox is that houses should be warm and pleasant at the same time that saving energy requires a cold, businesslike attitude. In a second example, Gordon analyzes Pasteur's attempt to understand the nature of infection. In this case the paradox is the fact that doctors believed that infection came from within persons; however, no soldier became ill until after he was wounded. Step one of the procedure is reminiscent of Gordon's earlier idea of compressed conflict.

Gordon labels step two as *Analogue*. An analogue is a metaphor that describes something that is like something else. It is used to provide a problem solver with a new context for viewing the problem and it can be a direct or personal analogy. In the energy problem, Gordon identifies the analogue as a thermostat. It keeps the house warm but maintains temperature in a businesslike way. Fermentation of grapes is the analogue used by Pasteur to understand infection because the ferment was erroneously thought to come from within the grape.

Step three is called *Unique Activity*. It is a description of the unique way in which a thing works or acts. The unique aspect of a thermostat is that it provides feedback to the furnace, allowing it to regulate temperature in the house. In Pasteur's problem, the unique activity of fermentation is that the grapes must be crushed before the ferment enters from the outside.

Step four involves a new way of seeing the problem that Gordon identifies as the *Equivalent*. This is the application of the metaphor to the original problem. The equivalent can be similar to the description of the unique activity because its purpose is to consider the original problem in the light of the unique activity. The equivalent to Pasteur's notion that grapes must be crushed is the recognition that human skin must be cut to allow infection to enter from the environment.

The culmination of the synectics process is the creation of a new idea. Gordon argues that energy could be conserved if each household had an energy meter installed to indicate how much fuel it was using. This would provide the user with constant feedback and consumption could be monitored. Pasteur's new idea was that infection was spread through the air, and the use of bandages could thus reduce the possibility of people becoming infected.

Gordon believes that using these steps will lead to finding solutions to problems. He argues that the conscious use of this procedure slows the creativity process down and allows the person to obtain control of it. However, once the skill of creative problem solving has been learned, it is not necessary to continue to follow the lock-step procedure each time a new problem is encountered. Gordon writes:

> Your uses of . . . synectics should be an extension of your inner self. You are not exactly like anyone else and your process will reflect your personality and experience.[11]

After a successful number of experiences in using synectics in industry (where his groups invented the space saver Kleenex box and the Pringle potato chip), Gordon turned to education. In 1966, he founded Synectics Education Systems (SES). Under his direction, SES has published a number of publications for facilitating creative behavior. Some of his educational techniques are described in Chapter 5.

Theorists of the unconscious—such as Freud, Kubie, and Gordon—have much to offer those interested in teaching and in creating programs for facilitating creative behavior. These thinkers provide a legitimization for fantasy and daydreaming. The unconscious theorists suggest that such behavior is useful and can lead to increased creativity. From these theorists comes support for play and the free association aspects of the unconscious and preconscious that precede creative products. They encourage the acceptance of unconventional behavior from students. Studying these theorists underlines the importance of metaphorical life.

SUMMARY

This chapter examined theories of creativity, and analyzed theories based on both the study of consciousness and the unconscious. Theorists of conscious approaches to creativity include J. P. Guilford, E. Paul Torrance, and Sidney Parnes. A major perspective achieved by these writers is the distinction between convergent and divergent thought.

Theories based on the study of the unconscious derive from the work of Sigmund Freud and include perspectives developed by Arthur Koestler, Lawrence Kubie, George Prince, and William J. J. Gordon. A major contribution of this group is the identification of the use of metaphor as a way of facilitating creative behavior.

NOTES

1. Stephen Jay Gould, *The Mismeasure of Man* (New York: W. W. Norton and Company, 1981).
2. Ibid., p. 155.
3. Sidney J. Parnes et al., *Guide to Creative Action* (New York: Charles Scribner's Sons, 1976).
4. Sidney J. Parnes et al., *Creative Action Handbook* (New York: Charles Scribner's Sons, 1977).
5. Sigmund Freud, *On Creativity and the Unconscious* (New York: Harper & Row, 1958), pp. 44–45.
6. Ibid., p. 45.
7. Bruno Bettelheim, *Freud and Man's Soul* (New York: Alfred A. Knopf, 1983).
8. Lawrence Kubie, *Neurotic Distortion of the Creative Process* (New York: Farrar, Straus, & Giroux, 1979).
9. George Prince, *The Practice of Creativity* (New York: Macmillan, 1970).
10. William J. J. Gordon, *The New Art of the Possible* (Cambridge, MA: Porpoise Books, 1987).
11. Ibid., p. 164.

CHAPTER

5

Techniques for Facilitating Creative Behavior

INTRODUCTION: JOHN DEWEY AND THE USE OF ACTIVITY IN EDUCATION

Students can become more innovative by participating in carefully chosen activities that are designed to facilitate creative behavior. Effective education requires that class time be used wisely and that activities be selected thoughtfully. In today's schools, pupils have a low tolerance for boredom and they need stimulation.

John Dewey argued that before understanding can take place, the learner must participate in the formation of purposes that direct his or her activities. In order for learning to occur, the goals must seem real to the learner. To accomplish this, Dewey suggested that pupils be involved in the choosing of goals.

Dewey believed that students come to the classroom with much previous experience. In order to produce effective outcomes, these experiences must be taken into account. These experiences must relate to learning in a way that allows new experience to be understood in the context of relevant previous events in the student's life.

This connection between learning, previous experience, and current experience is reminiscent of George Prince's formulation regarding the role of the censor (see Chapter 4), Arthur Koestler's view of bisociation (discussed in Chapter 3), and William J. J. Gordon's construct of making the strange familiar.

For Dewey, experience leads to knowledge and then to growth. If growth fails to occur, the activity has little use for the learner. Dewey denied the distinction between work and play. Work without meaning is onerous toil; play that is purposeful becomes useful work. Learning occurs when play is given purpose and when previous experiences give meaning to current ones. Thus, for Dewey, meaningful labor becomes a kind of enjoyment done for personal growth. The person who experiences toil as fun recognizes meaning in it.

Understanding Dewey's view of the role and nature of experience is important for teachers. Students need to participate in the formulation of goals. They enter the classroom with a rich array of experiences, which can be used to facilitate learning.

PLANNING: A PSYCHODRAMA MODEL

The psychotherapy process called psychodrama applies to teaching in many ways. Its relationship to spontaneity has been discussed and in Chapter 6 its relationship to theories of simulation/gaming is explained. Psychodrama can also provide a model for planning instruction.

A psychodrama is an enactment of a personal problem in front of a therapy group. Several roles exist in psychodrama. First is the director—the trained therapist in the situation who serves in three capacities. As analyst, s/he must use his or her knowledge of human behavior to try to help the person obtain catharsis and insight. The director serves also as stage manager, arranging the components of the drama in an effective manner. Finally, s/he must direct the play. The director uses the stage and his or her knowledge of psychological processes to create an effective session.

The major role in the production is that of protagonist—the person whose drama is enacted. The director helps to raise the protagonist's struggle to heroic proportions as a result of the performance.

A psychodrama also employs auxiliaries, several of whom exist in any enactment. They represent the supporting cast, playing the roles of important others for the protagonist. The selection of these persons is usually left to the star of the production and s/he chooses on the basis of feelings s/he has for particular people in the group.

The final role is that of the audience—persons viewing the play who are also participants in the process. Most often the audience consists of people who are in training or in therapy themselves. From this group comes the protagonist as well as the auxiliaries.

The relationship of psychodrama to simulation/gaming—one of its most important applications to the education—is more fully explained in

Chapter 6. One aspect of psychodrama, however, can be described here. The structure of psychodrama can be viewed as a way to organize teaching. It can serve as a supplement to usual lesson planning (which consists of the need to list objectives, content, activity, and evaluation) or as an alternative approach for planning.

A psychodrama consists of four parts. It begins with a **warm-up**. During this period, the psychodrama director prepares the audience by using group process techniques. The warm-up ends with the selection of a protagonist who will then be led by the director into the next stage—**the action**. In this part the therapist helps the protagonist enact the problem using appropriate auxiliaries. Once this phase concludes and the protagonist has achieved catharsis—relief from the pain that s/he has been experiencing, the director guides the group through a period of **sharing** in which the audience responds to the drama by relating it to their lives in ways that help the protagonist. In a psychodrama training session, where the audience also tries to learn how to use the process, the director concludes the session with a **debriefing** that helps the participants understand what has occurred. The sharing is usually emotional while the debriefing is analytical.

These four components—warm-up, action, sharing, and debriefing—can serve as a means for planning lessons. Every lesson begins with a warm-up in which students are helped to focus on the problem to be examined or the task to be completed. This is followed by the action—participation in the activity itself. Students then share the experience by reacting to the activity as it affected them on an emotional plane. Finally, the instructor should engage in a debriefing period that provides analytical closure to the experience.

This way of viewing a lesson can supplement or supplant traditional lesson planning. It can also lead to better lessons for students and better preparation from teachers.

ACTIVITIES

The remainder of this chapter describes activities for facilitating creative behavior. The activities are listed alphabetically.

The Analogy Game

This activity allows students to develop skill in the use of metaphor. Students play *Analogy* in the following manner: One member of the group thinks of a famous person—living or dead—but does not tell whom s/he has selected. The players then try to discover whom has been chosen by asking the selector to answer questions in the form of analogies. (e.g., "If the person you are thinking of were an automobile, what make automobile would s/he be?" "If the person were a book, what kind of book would s/he be?") The person supplying the answers begins by indicating the sex of the chosen figure and tells whether it is a living or dead person. Then s/he supplies answers to the analogies with appropriate metaphors. These analogies should relate to the essential character of the person chosen rather than to his or her physical attributes. The players are allowed a limited number of guesses (usually three or four). If no one discovers the identity, the person who was "it" wins. S/he continues in that role until replaced by a person in the group who guesses correctly. The person who gets the correct answer then has the opportunity to try and stump the group.

Brainstorming

Alex Osborne's technique for problem solving remains a simple but important procedure. In many ways, W. J. J. Gordon's approach to problem solving, which he calls synectics, is a refinement and extension of Osborne's technique. Brainstorming requires a group to identify as many solutions to a problem as possible (no matter how apparently silly or foolish the answers may seem) in the hopes that some of the ideas might turn out to be productive.

In conducting a brainstorming session, the teacher must be absolutely uncritical in the acceptance of the ideas. Creative problem solving will not work if the teacher reinforces or even becomes the replacement for the censor that the technique attempts to elude.

Some problems that brainstorming might be applied to include the following:

1. How can a person make studying for a dull or boring class more interesting?
2. In what ways can communication between persons of different cultures be made more effective?
3. If you could talk to the leaders of the United States and the Union of Soviet Socialist Republics, how would you help them abolish nuclear weapons?
4. Suggest ways that elections for the President can be improved.

If a local problem is being used, the class can send some the suggestions to leaders as a follow-up activity. These officials will often respond

to ideas from students and may even attempt to implement a proposed solution.
As a variation, students can engage in nonverbal brainstorming. Students can use crayons or magic markers and sheets of paper to brainstorm ideas using drawings rather than words. This technique can be done individually with each student working on his or her own. It can also be done by passing a sheet of paper around and having each pupil add his or her own nonverbal portion to it. At the conclusion of the activity, students can give their drawings titles that reflect the ideas that have emerged. To be most effective, this kind of brainstorming should be done silently with no discussion until the very end of the procedure.

Cartooning

Cartoons have fascinated people for much of history. The varieties, which range from simple Saturday morning violence to the sophistication of Pulitzer prize-winning editorial cartoons, provide many options for expression. Students can develop their own ongoing comic strip. They can draw editorial cartoons on local, national, or international issues or ones that relate to the school. Cartooning can be used in conjunction with the production of a newspaper which can lead to many other creative endeavors.

Still another application involves the use of cartoons in which the captions have been removed. Students write their own captions, which can be shared among the class where many persons may have written a different caption for the same cartoon.

Desert Island

This relatively intense exercise provides students with the opportunity to be creative at the same time that it builds group cohesion.

Students pretend that they have been shipwrecked on a desert island. They create the story of where they were going on their ship, what happened to it, how many people were lost at sea, and how they arrived at the island. Students then physically build the setting in the classrooms (using tables, chairs, and the like). Spontaneously the students enact what needs to be done for survival.

As the action flows, the teacher interrupts and advises the group that a storm is coming. The teacher might have some students create the storm with appropriate sounds. The students are asked to congregate in an appropriate shelter. The story continues to be enacted.

The instructor should interrupt the action again and ask the students what important people in their lives they left behind when they went on the ship. The instructor should ask the students who in the group could take the place of these people. At this point, the students can share their feelings about being stranded on a desert island.

One way to end the exercise is to have the students plan and execute an escape from the island that results in their reaching home safely. Teachers can use additional improvisation students to extend the activity. The need for closure—both emotional and analytical—with this activity should be borne in mind.

Diary and Journal Keeping

Although this technique fits under the general category of writing, it can be listed separately since it generally occurs outside of the regular classroom.

Students should be urged to keep a diary or a journal (the latter being less formal than the former). Teachers can provide many formats for this work and can reinforce it by periodically reviewing what students have written (allowing students the option of keeping parts of the material confidential if they wish to do so). No grade should ever be awarded but instead teachers should offer comments of support and encouragement.

Creative behavior can be facilitated by keeping a diary or journal because it leads to more fluency and because it helps students examine many feelings that may be emerging from unconscious sources. This technique can enable students capture the freely rising fantasies described by Freud.

Discovering the Apple

Students do this exercise by reading the following and working with the apple as described.

> Isaac Asimov writes about the development of artificial satellites for human habitation in several of his books. He advocates the creation of huge space stations that could hold up to 100,000 persons. These "mini worlds" could be orbited in many places in the solar system— around the earth, the moon, and various planets. People might be born, live their lives, and die inside these satellites without ever experiencing any other place. Asimov sees life in space as a more reason-

able solution to population expansion than the settlement of other planets in the solar system or elsewhere in the galaxy.

The advantage of Asimov's solution is that it can solve the growing population problem faced by humankind with technology that already exists. The disadvantage is that people who live in these worlds may be forced to live their lives in artificial environments.

Of course, much that persons experience in the present is synthetic. Consider: The settings where people live and work are carefully regulated—heated in winter and cooled in summer. Persons travel from home to work in air-conditioned cars while playing stereo radios that drown out the sound of the real world.

Much of the food that people eat is artificially colored and flavored; some nutrients have been removed and others added.

Persons tint their hair to hide the gray and some people change the color of their eyes with contact lenses. An individual may have a rebuilt nose or a heart that is aided by a pacemaker. In time, mechanical organs of all kinds may lead to the creation of persons who are part human and part machine.

The contemporary world grows increasingly artificial. Cybernetic intelligence will play an ever increasing role in the future when computers requiring minimal input from human beings communicate with other computers.

In this growing imitation environment human sense mechanisms may atrophy, making it impossible to smell or taste anything real. The process of eliminating genuine smell has already begun. Look on the shelves of any supermarket and you will find:

1. room fresheners to mask the presence of human living
2. deodorants to mask the smell of people
3. perfumes (for men and women) to replace human odors with artificial ones that have names like "Poison" and "Opium"
4. furniture polish designed to make rooms smell like lemons

Look on the box of any common food in the grocery store. See how many artificial additives and chemical preservatives are contained in the product. Manufacturers of diet foods can now produce a low-calorie "ice cream" which is almost 100% synthetic. Despite recent emphasis on "natural" ingredients, the trend toward artificial substances continues.

This exercise is designed to help you rediscover your senses. Pick up the apple that has been provided for you—a genuine fresh, red fruit. Begin with your sense of touch. Feel the surface of the apple. Close your eyes and find every bump. Allow your fingers to take over.

Smell the fruit. Inhale it deeply. Run it against your face. Smell it again. Enjoy the wonderful aroma of a real, fresh apple.

Now cut the apple in half. Feel the juices run out of it. Core and cut one half of the apple into slices. Slowly eat each slice, savoring the cool taste of each piece.

Look at the remaining part of the apple. Be aware of its colors. How many shades of color can you see? Before you cut the core, note the appearance and feel of it. Now bite into the second half and close your eyes as you do so. What do you hear? How does the texture of the apple feel on your tongue? What sensations do you experience? Chew slowly, enjoying each bite as it fills your mouth with pleasure.

Now it is time to write. Do not take too much time to think. Translate your experiences into words as quickly as you can. Describe as many sensations as possible. Continue to write for as long as you need to describe your feelings.

After you and your classmates have completed your discovery of the apple, share your writings in small groups with the others who have had this opportunity to discover the apple.

Fairy Tale Enactment

This activity contains much creative possibility. The teacher begins by conducting a discussion about favorite fairy tales of the group. After a reasonable amount of time, students choose to enact one. The teacher casts persons to play the various roles in the story. As the tale reaches its conclusion, the students can improvise other endings making the story become a kind of "fractured" fairy tale. The activity can also take a more profound turn. Students, for example, can enact Cinderella's life after she goes off with the prince. What happens in their life together? Did they really live happily ever after or did they have to face the realities of everyday family life including children, bills, and so on? This procedure provides many possibilities for facilitating creative behavior.

Guided Fantasy

This technique facilitates innovative behavior resulting from an unconscious approach to creativity and it has much to offer students. The process helps persons experience alternative perspectives and allows them to explore many types of feelings in depth. The following provides direction for conducting a guided fantasy. It focuses on a trip to outer space.

In order to conduct a successful experience, the facilitator begins by helping the participants to relax. To achieve this, students are asked to find a comfortable place in the room. They can lie on the floor or sit restfully in chairs or desks. Persons in the group close their eyes and the lights are dimmed. The students are told that inhaling serves as a source of energy and exhaling as a release of tension. They take strength into their toes and they release the tautness, attempting to be aware of each toe even as they are able to separately perceive each finger in the hand. The subjects continue to breathe energy into all parts of their bodies—legs, thighs, stomachs, arms, shoulders, and head.

At this point the participants imagine the arrival of a letter informing them that they have been selected to go on a trip to outer space. They must decide whom to take along and what things they wish to bring with them. They imagine their arrival at the take-off site and fantasize about how it feels and looks. They contemplate the blast-off and feel their immersion into weightlessness. They think about the landing on a planet in another galaxy with normal air and with gravity so minimal that they are able to fly.

In his or her imagination, each subject creates the physical surroundings of the place and enjoys it with a friend. When it's time to return, the person must come back while his or her friend may choose to remain. Participants imagine the flight back and the landing of the spaceship on Earth. Who is there to greet them? How does it feel to be back? Slowly they return to reality.

The exercise concludes with a crucial step: participants voluntarily share their sense of the experience. The greatest amount of education for creativity takes place as persons have the opportunity to listen and respond to the feelings of others.

Guided fantasy can be used with upper level elementary students and with all secondary students. It is an excellent procedure that allows persons to stretch their creative imaginations. Many kinds of guided fantasies can be conducted including future projections that are discussed in Chapter 9.

Lifeline

Lifeline, originally developed for Jerome Bruner's *Man: A Course of Study,* provides students with much opportunity for self-expression. It also allows for the effective development of the group process.

To begin the activity, pupils are asked to make a list of the seven most important events in their lives. They should have ample time to reflect on these happenings. Once the lists have been completed, the students are given magazines that contain many illustrations, and they are told to find pictures that represent the events on their lists.

Class members are given scissors, heavy twine, paper clips, and masking tape. They cut seven pictures out of the magazines and attach them to the twine using the paper clips. The line of the seven pictures is then placed on a wall in the room using the masking tape.

Students then share the lifelines with each other in pairs. Participants keep changing partners until they have shared all of the lifelines in the group.

To conclude the activity, each student selects one of the seven pictures that s/he feels is the most significant. The students sit in a circle and discuss what the single picture represents and why it is important.

When all students have described their pictures, a debriefing is conducted by asking the students what they have learned from the activity about themselves and about the others. They can be helped to see that people are both similar and different as they go through life's experiences. Students can share whatever feelings about themselves and the others that emerged. The instructor must be sure that everyone has had a chance to express his or her feelings when the session has been concluded.

Logic Puzzles

Logic puzzles, which are excellent techniques to stimulate creative problem solving, meet virtually every criterion for quality activity. They require both convergent and divergent thinking skills—the former because ultimately the puzzle contains only one solution, the latter because intuitive leaps are sometimes necessary in order to arrive at a solution. Logic puzzles develop many skills because they require much thinking in order to obtain a solution.

The following are all good examples of logic puzzles:

LUNCH AT THE BANK

The employees of a certain small neighborhood bank usually bring sandwiches for lunch, but in four recent days, Lee and four other employees who are particularly friendly decided to pool their resources. Four of them prepared for the group what they considered to be their culinary specialties; the fifth claimed an inability to cook and instead paid for the group's beverages, which were delivered by a nearby coffee shop. From the following clues, you should be able to identify the job title that each participant and his or her contribution to the group's lunches.

1. Neither Sandy nor the secretary brought spaghetti or lasagna.
2. Pat eats at the same time as one of the others; the head teller and the secretary eat together at a later time.
3. The manager is a bachelor.
4. The teller eats alone.
5. Chris and the one who brought spaghetti eat together earlier than Kit.
6. Pat did not bring chili.
7. The guard learned his specialty from his wife.
8. The spaghetti, lasagna, and salad were prepared by women.

WHO OWNS THE ZEBRA?

1. There are five houses, each of a different color, and each inhabited by men of different nationalities with different pets, drinks, and cigarettes.
2. The Englishman lives in the red house.
3. The Spaniard owns the dog.
4. Coffee is drunk in the green house.
5. The Ukrainian drinks tea.
6. The green house is immediately to the right of the ivory house.
7. The Old Gold smoker owns the snails.
8. Kools are smoked in the yellow house.
9. Milk is drunk in the middle house.
10. The Norwegian lives in the first house on the left.
11. The man who smokes Chesterfields lives in the house next to the man with the fox.
12. Kools are smoked in the house next to the house where the horse is kept.
13. The Lucky Strike smoker drinks orange juice.
14. The Japanese smokes Parliaments.
15. The Norwegian lives next to the blue house.

Now, who drinks the water? And who owns the zebra?

HONORED GRADUATES

State U's class of '86 elected five of its graduates—all over fifty—to speak at commencement. Can you determine each speaker's full name,

home town, order on the program, degree course, and the long-time occupation he or she will be giving up now?
1. Mrs. Gould was born in Gallup, New Mexico.
2. The man from Rochester, New York, is a gardener.
3. George is a native of Anchorage, Alaska.
4. The first speaker was born in Des Moines, Iowa.
5. The man from Savannah, Georgia, has earned his degree in geology.
6. Richardson will speak after Adams.
7. The real estate agent's degree is in Romance languages.
8. The man getting his degree in accounting and the actress have adjacent spots on the program.
9. Ms. Davis earned her degree in dentistry.
10. Ruth will speak third.
11. The native of Des Moines and Smith will speak one after the other.
12. Al's degree is in sociology.
13. Richardson's first name is Don.
14. The dog trainer and the-soon-to-be dentist will speak in adjacent spots on the program.
15. Sarah is not a secretary.

Lost on the Moon

This activity emphasizes the advantages of the group in creative problem solving. The following handout is given to each person in a class:

> You are a member of a spaceship crew that has landed on the moon. Because of a malfunction of the craft, the landing destroyed most of your equipment except the following list of items. You are on the light side of the moon's surface but you know that you landed 200 miles short of a pre-determined rendezvous point. Before you start out on the journey to meet the mother ship at the rendezvous point, decide what you would take and which is *most important!* Various conditions make it necessary to leave certain items behind. (Label the most important #1, next most important #2, etc.) (15 total)
>
> _____ box of matches
> _____ food concentrate
> _____ 50 feet of nylon rope

_____ parachute silk
_____ portable heating unit
_____ two .45 caliber pistols
_____ one case of dehydrated Pet milk
_____ two 100 pound tanks of oxygen
_____ stellar map of the moon's constellations
_____ life raft
_____ magnetic compass
_____ five gallons of water
_____ signal flares
_____ first-aid kit containing injection needles
_____ solar powered FM receiver-transmitter

After each person completes the exercise, the teacher collects it. The teacher then divides the class into groups and each group completes the form again. When the groups have completed the exercise, both versions are scored using the following key:

box of matches = 15
food concentrate = 4
50 feet of nylon rope = 6
parachute silk = 8
portable heating unit = 13
two .45 caliber pistols = 11
one case of dehydrated Pet milk = 12
two 100 pound tanks of oxygen = 1
stellar map of the moon's constellations = 3
life raft = 9
magnetic compass = 4
five gallons of water = 2
signal flares = 10
first aid kit containing injection needles = 7
solar powered FM receiver transmitter = 5

Scoring consists of subtracting the actual number given for each item from the number chosen by the individual or the group. Always subtract the smaller number from the larger; a zero would therefore represent the best possible score.

Students will discover that the score of each group was better than the *mean* of the members working separately. This can lead to an understanding of the value of group process in problem solving.

Magic Shop

This activity began as a psychodrama warm-up technique. Torrance and other creativity theorists have used it widely in facilitating creative behavior. The teacher (or a student in the class) opens a "magic shop." This store contains an unlimited supply of whatever a customer might want—usually intangibles like self-confidence, security, happiness, or love. The shopper must pay for his or her purchases with something of equal value. The store clerk is wise and will not accept useless qualities (fear, anxiety, or insecurity) for the valuable items in the shop. The customer must trade an item that the shopkeeper can resell to someone else. Thus a person may come to the shop to obtain skills in obtaining a job and may have to part with some traits that can impede finding employment (over-aggressiveness or assertiveness). These traits, however, might be valuable to someone else in a different setting. An example of another exchange might involve trading some independence in order to obtain friendship.

The magic shop technique operates on many levels as it consciously helps persons understand value conflict and unconsciously helps bring other internal conflicts to the surface in ways that can result in creative synthesis. The magic shop can be used at various levels of intensity with students in most age groups.

Model

A model is a metaphoric representation of an object or process—a kind of simulation. Models are extremely important because they help to conceptualize and explain. Students who have been sensitized to metaphor as a way of facilitating creative behavior will be receptive to the development of models.

Models can be physical (e.g., a three-dimensional representation of the solar system) or paper-and-pencil drawings (e.g., a diagram of how a bill becomes a law). Students can construct miniatures of important inventions (e.g., a replica of the first steam engine). There can be many varieties and kinds of models. The use of the technique with its many connections to the creative process can facilitate creative behavior as students learn to make metaphoric representations of real world things and processes. The many kinds of potential models can also be matched to the different kinds of talent found among a group of children.

Mystery Puzzle

This activity comes from *Turn-Ons!* by Stephen K. Smuin. It is another kind of puzzle activity that works to build group process and allows for creative problem solving. The teacher types the following clues on cards and gives the cards to members of the class. If necessary some students may receive more than one clue.

> When he was discovered dead, Mr. Kelley had a bullet hole in his thigh and a knife wound in his back.
> Mr. Jones shot an intruder in his apartment building at 12 midnight.
> The elevator operator reported to police that he had seen Mr. Kelley at 12:15 A.M.
> The bullet taken from Mr. Kelley's thigh matched those used in the gun owned by Mr. Jones.
> Only one bullet had been fired from Mr. Jones's gun.
> When the elevator man saw Mr. Kelley, Mr. Kelley was bleeding slightly, but he did not seem too badly hurt.
> A knife with Mr. Kelley's blood on it was found in Miss Smith's yard.
> The knife found in Miss Smith's yard had Mr. Scott's fingerprints on it.
> Mr. Kelley had destroyed Mr. Jones's business by stealing his customers.
> The elevator man saw Mr. Kelley's wife go to Mr. Scott's apartment at 11:30 P.M.
> The elevator operator said that Mr. Kelley's wife frequently left the building with Scott.
> Mr. Kelley's body was found in the park.
> Mr. Kelley's body was found at 1:30 A.M.
> Mr Kelley had been dead for one hour when his body was found, according to a medical report.
> The elevator man saw Mr. Kelley go to Mr. Scott's room at 12:25 A.M.
> It was obvious from the condition of Mr Kelley's body that it had been dragged a long distance.
> Miss Smith saw Mr. Kelley go to Mr. Jones's apartment at 11:55 P.M.

Mr. Kelley's wife disappeared after the murder.
Police were unable to locate Mr. Scott after the murder. When police tried to locate Mr. Jones after the murder, they discovered that he had disappeared.
The elevator man said that Miss Smith was in the lobby of the apartment building when he went off duty.
Miss Smith often followed Mr. Kelley.
Mr Jones had told Mr. Kelley that he was going to kill him.
Mr. Kelley's bloodstains were found in Mr. Scott's car.
Mr. Kelley's bloodstains were found on the carpet in the hall outside Mr. Jones's apartment.
Miss Smith said that nobody left the apartment building between 12:25 A.M. and 12:45 A.M.

Some class members may end up with more than one clue.
Tell the students they have all the information necessary for them to solve the crime. Tell them that they have thirty-five minutes to tell you who got murdered, who the murderer was, and the time, place, motive, and weapon used to commit the murder. Do not tell them whether they are correct until they have all given their conclusions. Do not indicate which guesses are wrong and which are correct; just indicate that their answers are wrong—this eliminates mere guessing on each item.
Answer: After receiving a superficial gunshot wound from Mr. Jones, Mr. Kelley went to Mr. Scott's apartment where he was killed by Mr. Scott with a knife at 12:30 A.M., because Mr. Scott was in love with Mr. Kelley's wife.

Personal Identification

An interesting approach to facilitating creative behavior helps students focus upon themselves. Many kinds of techniques have been devised to achieve this. Three are described here.

(1) Home Floor Plan

Each student receives crayons and paper. Then s/he draws the floor plan of his or her home. When all the pupils have completed this task, they share these sketches with one another. In addition to helping each student see the homes of other people, this activity helps build group cohesion.

(2) Coat of Arms

Each student uses crayons and paper to produce a coat of arms which he or she believes can represent them and their lives. Once again the activity is concluded by sharing.

(3) Self-Portrait

In this activity students are asked to construct a self-portrait in a representational fashion. Instead of trying to create an exact portrait, pupils draw pictures that indicate how they feel about themselves. The results can be symbols, geometric figures, colors, or any combination of these. When students conclude the drawings, they can share them with other students. The debriefing of this activity should be done carefully.

Puppetry

Puppetry facilitates creative behavior in enjoyable ways. Students respond to the drama that results from making and using puppets. They can be constructed from many materials (including paper maché or potatoes), and they can be used to enact many kinds of stories. Students can use the puppets to present improvisational drama or they can write and enact scripts. This simple technique results in many kinds of creative activity.

Reading

This fundamental human activity should not be overlooked in planning for the development of creative behavior. In today's world of growing illiteracy and overdependence on television for entertainment and information, techniques to encourage reading are important for all students.

Reading can facilitate creative behavior in many ways. Most authors indicate the necessity for writers to be voracious readers. Reading leads to many outcomes. It provides examples of many kinds of writing styles; it builds vocabulary and adds to fluency. Perhaps, most importantly, reading offers vicarious experience that can broaden one's perspective and increase the number of matrices from which Koestler's bisociation can take place.

Any classroom that uses the strategy of facilitating creative behavior should contain a reading program. Students must be encouraged to read widely and to make reading a part of their leisure time. This is not always as easy or as self-evident as it may seem when reading must compete with a large variety of both worthwhile and time-wasting activities.

Students should read biography and nonfiction as well as many kinds of fiction. Biographies provide children with role models; good works of fiction offer a window on the child's world; novels can broaden perspective; mysteries can provide students with still another kind of logic puzzle to be solved, and science fiction increases the opportunity to learn to speculate. All of these forms should be part of a reading program.

Sociodrama

Sociodramatic activity fits best as part of the simulation and gaming activities described in Chapter 8. However, some kinds of sociodrama are relevant to facilitating creative behavior.

Sociodrama relates directly to psychodrama. The technique contains many aspects of psychodrama but lacks a protagonist. Hence it is a nontherapeutic application of the psychodrama process.

The intensity of a sociodrama can vary. It can be based on a general and abstract problem in which few feelings are involved or it can examine a situation closer to the lives of students and therefore having a greater impact on them. An example of the former is an enactment in heaven of a meeting of historic figures (former presidents with the current one, Clarence Darrow with William Jennings Bryan, to cite two examples).

At a more personal level, a sociodrama can examine issues like interfaith or interracial dating—important issues among many teenagers. Still another sociodrama asks students to portray a model family and describe their goals, needs, and perceptions in a way that uses improvisational drama to understand the nature of families.

A sociodrama related to the teaching of English can be one in which students enact scenes from short stories or novels. The teacher can help the students go beyond what is given about the characters and provide them with deeper insight.

Sociodrama can be used at most age levels and can be particularly effective at the secondary level. It allows students, both consciously and unconsciously, to come to better terms with themselves.

Spontaneity Exercises

These exercises facilitate creativity by helping students get in touch with their spontaneous selves. Two different examples are given here. Many others can be devised once the idea of a spontaneity exercise is understood.

1. This exercise occurs in an imaginary small airport terminal with only one telephone. It is five minutes before the player's plane is scheduled to leave. The person has left his or her stove turned on at home and s/he must call a neighbor to have it turned off. The only telephone is in use by a person who has an hour layover and is making an important business deal. The task of the player is to solve the problem spontaneously. The phone user is reluctant to hang up.
2. The place is a market in Budapest in the middle of the afternoon. A variety of persons are present selling various objects in the market. The player must go to the bathroom but s/he cannot speak Hungarian and none of the Hungarians can speak English. The person must make him- or herself understood.

Synectics

These activities come from the procedure devised by W. J. J. Gordon described in earlier chapters. They seek to apply the synectics problem-solving technique to the classroom. Two activities are presented here. The first—*Kamala—Wolf or Child*—is reprinted from Gordon's book of activities called *Strange and Familiar*. The second is an original activity developed by the author.

KAMALA – WOLF OR CHILD?

People are always talking about who invented the telephone or the steamboat or the safety pin. However, people don't only invent things that make life easier. In this Unit you'll be reading about someone who invented a way of life to make existence possible.

Kamala's bare young skin shone white against the fur of the young wolves in the den. Kamala's voice was a low growl, just like the young wolves. She ate with mouth and teeth alone. She sniffed the air, animal-fashion. What was she doing in a wolf den and why did she act like a wolf?

When Kamala was a six-month-old infant her mother left her near some bushes so that she could wash some clothes in the river. While Kamala was asleep in the shade a mother wolf sneaked up, lifted her by her baby clothes, and carried her away. That's how she came to be brought up in a wolf den. In the next eight years Kamala learned to be a wolf. She ran on all fours. She lapped up water with her tongue. While on the prowl at night she howled at regular times to let the 'other' wolves know where she was. She had no fur, but except for that, she was wolfish.

One day she was discovered by a hunter, captured and sent to live with other children. For a long time she continued to act like a wolf—lapping water, growling and snapping at the other children, prowling and howling at night, and curled up sleeping by day.

It was years before she walked about on her feet instead of all fours. Finally she spoke a few words and used her hands to eat. Seven years after she was taken away from the wolf den she began to act like a human being except with the intelligence of a three-year-old.

Now you'll be comparing Kamala to a physical thing. You will need a plastic spoon and a book of matches. Light a match and heat the plastic spoon with just enough heat to bend it slightly out of shape. Let the spoon cool and harden. Now light another match and reheat the spoon, but this time try to get it back to its original shape. You may want to have a partner help you with this.

Even though you are twisted out of shape, at least you have become an individual. Before you were heated and bent you were exactly like all the other pieces of plastic. Now you are different and nobody could possibly mistake you for somebody else. Would you rather look exactly like all the other pieces of plastic or look completely different? _____

Why?

Someone has taken you from your friends. You are stiff and twisted out of shape. You can't straighten up no matter how hard you try. Another match has been lit and your body is being heated again. You can't push back your body to look exactly the way it did before you were heated for the first time. How does this failure affect you?

When Kamala first was discovered and put in with other children she kept on acting like a wolf even though she was living among humans. She was unable to make friends with the other children. She had to walk on all fours and she had not yet learned to speak. Who do you think was better off, the piece of plastic that was twisted out of shape or Kamala?

Why do you think so?

Which do you think was more difficult, making the plastic look exactly as it did before it was heated or teaching Kamala how to live with human beings?

Why?

What do you think worked out better, straightening out the plastic spoon when the second match was lit, or Kamala slowly getting used to life with other children?

Why would you say this is true?

A person in trouble often invents ways to survive, as Kamala did. That kind of invention is very personal. Kamala's invention worked only for her. On the other hand, scientific inventions like the telephone and the computer work for everyone. That's the difference between personal and scientific inventions.

ECONOMIC PRESSURE SUIT

You've seen astronauts and test pilots in pressurized suits. These garments enable the wearer to survive space or space equivalent conditions. How do they work? Let's use some comparisons to begin to understand what makes a pressurized suit work.

The suit may be worn during periods of extremely hot or cold weather because of a temperature control mechanism. What creature in the animal world can survive hot or cold weather because of some kind of temperature control mechanism?

Explain your connection.

Oxygen must be provided for respiration, and the exhaled gases must be disposed of. This requires the inclusion of at least one oxygen cylinder in the suit. What thing in the animal world carries its own oxygen supply in an environment in which it ordinarily could not survive?

Explain your answer.

The complete survival system centers around the suit. The garment must be made of a protective material that is not easily damaged. How is this protective material like the earth's crust over an oil deposit?

How would a tear in a pressure suit be like striking oil?

The actions of the Federal Reserve System to regulate the nation's money supply and availability of credit can be thought of in terms of a pressurized suit. The Fed may pump money and credit into the economy to stimulate business. Too much can lead to inflation while not enough leads to deflation or recession.

Sometimes the Fed must take some money out of circulation and cut down the availability of credit. How is decreasing the money supply and availability of credit like the carbon dioxide and excess water removers of a pressurized suit?

Other times, the Fed must increase the supply of money and credit. How is increasing the money and credit supply like the oxygen and temperature control units of a pressurized suit?

If the space suit had no pressure valve, what would happen?

If no one regulated the nation's money supply, what might happen?

To conclude this exercise, make a diagram that shows how the Federal Reserve system can be compared to the operations of the pressure suit. Perhaps you can begin by picturing an astronaut in a suit that can also represent the nation's money supply.

Totem

Indians built totem poles to inscribe meaningful events in pictorial form. This activity asks students to create their own personal totems to creatively describe themselves to others. A totem can be any kind of physical object constructed to be a representation of one's life. Examples include a collection of photographs, drawings made with crayon or water colors, a variety of musical selections spliced together, or even an abstract portrait made from fruit.

Totems can take a variety of forms, each of which allows the student to say something important about him or herself using a wide variety of media. Totems help students use metaphor to bisociate planes in a way that can facilitate creativity while leading to a meaningful and satisfying outcome that also improves group cohesion when the totems are shared.

Videotape Productions

Videotape equipment represents a creative outlet that is available to children in the context of modern technology. The use of videotapes results in a wide variety of creative products. Students can produce a television movie that includes writing a script, casting the actors, and learning lines. The equipment can also be used to record role-play and sociodramas. When a creative product results from activity, the motivation to continue to engage in the activity increases. The use of video equipment can thus increase interest and involvement as it results in tangible outcomes.

Writing

This activity takes many forms, all of which represent excellent ways to facilitate creative behavior.

Free writing serves to improve skills and can lead to higher-quality products. In the use of this technique, pupils record whatever comes to their minds in a given time period. The results of free writing should be accepted uncritically by the teacher in order to avoid inhibiting the students.

Poetry is another kind of writing that appeals to many students. The teacher should recognize the many legitimate forms of poetry and that all of these are acceptable. The teacher who presses too strongly for structure may destroy creativity.

The writing of fiction should also be encouraged. An instructor who possesses the appropriate writing skills can help make fiction writing interesting and effective. Booklets of student work can be produced and given to other students and to parents.

Many forms of writing nonfiction can also serve to facilitate students' creativity. Writing an essay can provide an exciting outlet for many kinds of innovative energy. The development of articles based on research is also a meaningful application of writing, as is writing letters to the editor, which has the additional virtue of allowing students to see their work appear in print.

Many synectics activities lead to creative writing. In fact, writing of some sort can result from most of the activities described in this chapter.

SUMMARY

The introduction to this chapter offered a perspective on how to approach activity in teaching based on the work of John Dewey and how to plan for this activity based on psychodrama.

The activities described in this chapter are designed to facilitate creative behavior. Only a small sample of the many varieties of techniques has been provided. Other chapters provide additional examples in the areas of simulation/gaming and future studies.

CHAPTER

6

The Process of Simulation/Gaming

INTRODUCTION

Simulation/gaming is a powerful teaching device. Its use can achieve a great variety of results and its potential has only lately been understood. The use of this process can achieve the usual outcomes of teaching: content, concepts, skills, and attitudes. As indicated in this chapter and in the following one, simulation/gaming can achieve much more. It can aid in socialization, improve mental health, facilitate creativity, and help persons prepare for life in the future.

Some of the value of gaming as an instructional technique arises from its ability to motivate and involve students. Traditional views of learning perceive education as an expository process. The instructor presents the students with correct information—this is the *lecture mode.* Sometimes recitation is added: the teacher asks and answers questions about the given material. Another modification permits discussion that more fully involves the learners. However, this procedure focuses largely on the instructor who controls it.

Simulation/gaming represents a form that is neither lecture nor discussion. A *facilitator* arranges activity for the participants. At the conclusion of the experience, the students analyze and learn from what has occurred. This represents the *participative mode,* which leads to greater involvement, motivation, and learning because it is an *autotelic* activity.

The term *autotelic* describes processes such as simulation and gaming. It means that the activity is self-motivating—people take part in it for intrinsic rather than for extrinsic reasons. Ideally, all instruction should be of this nature, but, of course, it is not. Mihalyi Csikszentmihalyi in *Beyond Boredom and Anxiety* studied many types of autotelic behavior including chess, rock climbing, dancing, and surgery.[1] From empirical data, Csikszentmihalyi developed the concept of "flow," which occurs when the challenge of the task is equal to the ability of the person. If too much is demanded of the person anxiety results, whereas too little challenge leads to boredom. Most good games are autotelic activities in which participants are intrinsically motivated; they are balanced between too little and too much challenge.

The simulation process motivates students for other reasons as well. Games are often heuristic rather than didactic and, therefore, less authoritarian, making people feel more comfortable; they can attempt new activities without fear of censure. (This relates to the process of creativity and is explored more fully in a later section of this chapter.) The technique of gaming facilitates learning because although it is serious, it is also playful. Most persons require such an outlet but lack access to one. Simulation/gaming can fill this void. Finally, games motivate because they are concrete, real experiences—demonstrating a relationship between cause and effect. They occur in the here and now and they provide closure. Players receive rapid feedback. Learning requires all these prerequisites but most modes of teaching fail to include them. Their presence in the simulation process accounts, in part, for its appeal to students.

DEFINITIONS

The concepts of theory, model, and simulation all relate to each other. A *theory* is an hypothesis or generalization about the real world that describes, predicts, and has high credibility. A *model* is a subclass of a theory; it represents a real-world phenomenon that can be physical, an abstraction of a process, or both. Models are analogies and as such are powerful tools that can be used to explain and create. The value and importance of simulation/gaming comes in part from its relationship to modeling and to analogy. As model is a subclass of theory, so *simulation* is a subclass of model. A simulation is an attempt to mirror reality in a simplified manner that remains dynamic and compresses time. The purpose of a simulation is, in part, to eliminate the potential danger and the cost that might be present if the activity took place in a real rather than in a simulated setting. A *simulation* is a representation of a real-world event in a reduced and compressed form resulting in a dynamic process that is safe and efficient.

A *game* is a contest between two or more players that proceeds by a set of rules. The basic structure of a game is that it is a zero-sum event; this means that player A can win the game only if player B loses it. there are many variations of this construct, from contests in which everyone can win to those in which everyone must lose, but the basis of all of them is the zero-sum relationship.

A hybrid form of the two exists that combines the elements of a simulation (which can also be a research or evaluation device as well as a teaching tool) with the elements of a game (which can be pure entertainment) into a product called a *simulation/game*. Those elements that are primarily employed for teaching purposes are called *educational* or *instructional simulation/games*. Rather than attempt to make unnecessary distinctions, this chapter follows the practice of using simulation, game, and simulation/game interchangeably.

A simulation/game can be a role play in which players assume specific roles in order to solve a problem or make a decision. It can also be a board game in which players attempt to reach a goal by moving a game piece around a board (similar to the kind of activity that takes place in the commercial game, *Monopoly*). Many games that are used for educational purposes are combinations of role play and board activity.

THE NATURE OF THE PROCESS

Human beings are game-playing animals. The playing of games is serious business which can lead to improved opportunity for socialization. The appeal of simulation/gaming as a teaching technique may be found in the proposition that a useful way to understand human social behavior and interaction is to view it from the perspective that life is a game.

The role of games as socializing techniques has best been explained by Omar Khayham Moore and Alan R. Anderson in their description of the concept of the autotelic folk model.[2] Moore and Anderson argue that people in society must learn to deal with the problems caused by the natural environment. They must learn as well to deal with problems that involve human interaction and with those that are affective. They suggest that people learn to solve these problems in ways that are intrinsically motivating and hence autotelic. To learn how to participate in activity A (where failure may result in serious consequences) societies invent activity A' (which is a simulation). Activity A' lacks serious consequences but is similar enough to activity A to provide for genuine practice. Moore and Anderson call these activities *autotelic folk models,* which are autotelic because they are self-motivating and they are "folk" because they are found in all cultures.

Moore and Anderson claim that there are four classes of these folk models. First, there are those of serious noninteractional problems; these are called *puzzles*. Societies create a variety of puzzles for people to solve, all of which involve little risk. These include crossword puzzles and those that involve the manipulation of small pieces of plastic on a board. The whodunit, developed by Agatha Christie and many others, is also an example of puzzle activity which is nonthreatening. Second, there are games of chance (e.g., card games). Third, there are games of interaction; these are games of strategy such as chess and tic tac toe. Science fiction novels can also be viewed as strategy games in which the reader, through the eyes of the protagonist, must devise and test a strategy for dealing with a very difficult problem and thereby save the universe. Finally, Moore and Anderson describe folk models of the affective aspects of life; these are aesthetic objects treated autotelically. Examples of aesthetic folk models can be found in the variety of kits available which satisfy aesthetic needs (e.g., paint by number, sculpture kits, and the like).

Folk models have the effect of helping to socialize the young, and they help everyone better understand the natural and social environment. These activities are serious and they can accomplish the purpose of preparing people to interact in the natural and social world.

Simulation/games are useful teaching techniques because life may be analyzed from a games perspective. In games (and in life) players have goals that they attempt to achieve. In games (and in life) the action of players is regulated by a set of rules; violation of these rules may result in serious consequences. Eric Berne, developer of transactional analysis (whose perspective on creativity is described in an earlier chapter), wrote a best-selling book entitled, *Games People Play*. Although Berne was interested in gaming behavior among neurotic people, his analysis was applicable to a much larger group, and the continuing popularity of the book supports the hypothesis that there is a connection between games and life.

Simulation/gaming demonstrates the idea of cause and effect more effectively than most other alternatives because it conveys gestalt. Understanding cause and effect is necessary in order to participate in social life and to understand the world. Yet teachers rarely provide students with the opportunity to see the results of their own activities. In the debriefing period, which usually comes after the completion of a game, students learn how their behavior led to the result that occurred. Many simulation/games allow for replay and so in another round the student can try another strategy and obtain a different effect. Simulation/games collapse time and this provides many opportunities for testing the relationship between cause and effect in a relatively short period.

Simulation/gaming is also an activity that provides closure. The student is made aware of a problem; a simulation is played. There is some kind of resolution to the problem and there is a debriefing. This concludes the experience (although what was learned can be applied to another problem in the future). Compare this to the usual situation in which a student reads a chapter, hears a lecture, takes a test, and returns to the beginning. Because there is closure, the process of undertaking the cause-and-effect relationship is facilitated.

Simulation/gaming offers the teacher a new role in relating to students. The model that many teachers follow is a didactic one in which the teacher serves as judge, selects the winners, and often punishes the losers by giving them low grades. In a classroom in which the strategy of simulation/gaming is used, the model is more likely to be an heuristic one in which the teacher is no longer the judge; winning and losing become a function of the activity, allowing the teacher to go on to the more pleasant role of being the facilitator of learning. The process can fail if an attempt is made to recast the experience into a more traditional didactic one. (The teacher, for example, observes a group planning strategy and in his or her wisdom suggests a more effective strategy for winning.)

Some critics of the process have maintained that simulation/gaming, because it is a simplified abstraction of reality, creates distortions and, therefore, is not meaningful. Distortions are created, *but this is true of any other presentation of reality that the student ever receives.* Every lecture ever given and every textbook description ever written is also a distortion. The use of simulation/gaming can serve to supplement and extend the student's perception of reality more directly than any textbook or lecture.

THE HISTORY OF SIMULATION/GAMING

The process of simulation/gaming has an interesting history. It began as part of the need to develop more effective military strategy. It was applied later as a technique for training management in business and industry and was then used as an educational tool. John Raser, whose perspective is examined shortly, views gaming as derived from decision theory, systems theory, and small group experimentation.

All people who study the history of gaming are convinced that the game of chess has its origins as a war game. Although the evidence for this is not clear, the nature of the game tends to support this explanation of its origin. The obvious relationship between the society simulated on the chess board and medieval society, as well as the aggressive nature of the rules, seem to be examples of the use of a simulation/game to attempt to create alternatives that can be pursued in medieval battle.

The development of war gaming began at the turn of the nineteenth century. It was first used by the Prussians, and by the end of the century it had spread to other countries including Great Britain. The phenomenon probably reached its zenith in the Pentagon in the 1960s when computers were used to test alternative approaches to the war in Vietnam. The early war games were called *kriegspiel* and took two forms, rigid *kriegspiel,* in which the rules were carefully specified and followed, and free *kriegspiel,* a form which allowed for improvisation.

The next development of gaming was application in business and industry. In 1956 the American Management Association developed a simulation/game, *Top Management Decisions,* whose purpose was to give potential executives the opportunity to try alternative strategies in order to obtain practice for making real decisions later. Eventually management simulation/games were used with computers in order to refine them and make them more complex. Shortly after its development in business and industry, simulation/gaming was also applied to the problems of land use in urban planning.

The application to war, business, and planning are examples of the process described by Moore and Anderson who maintain that society develops socialization techniques so that persons may learn appropriate behavior in settings that are safe. Only an insane general would risk the lives of his troops unnecessarily simply to gain information about strategy; business executives would obviously prefer to train new managers as inexpensively as possible.

After the development of its applications in war and in business, simulation/gaming was applied to formal education, where it began as a device to train administrators (as a natural development from its use in training business executives). Simulation/gaming was used in the early 1960s in the preservice education of teachers. This use was reinforced when it became an intrinsic part of many of the materials of the federally funded curriculum projects of that era. The best example of this was in the High School Geography Project; this was perhaps the most successful of the curriculum projects and it created many simulation/games for use in secondary school classrooms. Once it was applied to educational settings, simulation/gaming grew rapidly in popularity. Many good classroom simulation/games are now available for use at all educational levels.

John Raser in *Simulation and Society,* argues that in addition to these historical developments, three other intellectual developments are also part of the theoretical basis for the development of simulation/gaming.[3] These are decision theory, systems theory, and small group experimentation theory.

Decision theory, which is used in training public administrators as well as in the study of political behavior, attempts to understand the process of decision making. Simulation/games are used to give trainees practice in making decisions. Raser argues that it would have been necessary to invent the process had it not already developed in the manner previously described.

The same argument, according to Raser, can be made with regard to the development of systems theory. In order to reduce complex systems to a size in which they could be studied and understood, it became necessary to create simulations of systems as a means of making them manageable. Hence the process would have been created in order to devise small, manageable, and safe systems for the purpose of analyzing them.

Finally, the development of small group experimentation, according to Raser, is still another antecedent. Sociologists interested in social interaction concluded that simulations of social interaction in small groups was a way of studying the process in a controlled environment. This too necessitates the development of simulation/gaming.

Simulation/gaming developed from rich antecedents and for many purposes. It is this rich background that accounts for its growth and strength. Many educators viewed the development of instructional simulation/gaming as still another gimmick or fad that periodically occurs in education. Nearly thirty years later the technique is still being applied in educational settings and its use continues to grow and develop.

The introduction of computers into education has further increased interest in, and use of, simulation/gaming in education. It was a natural development to adapt games for the computer and to use them in the classroom. The attraction of arcade games to all kinds of students is evidence of this trend.

FACILITATING LEARNING

Simulation/gaming helps people learn how to learn. Moreover, it is an activity that provides gestalt (it allows players to see problems in their totality better than most other techniques). Persons can understand a process better when they can see it as a whole and when it has closure. At the same time, learning is facilitated because learners who take part in the gaming process do so as active participants rather than as passive recipients of knowledge.

One of the unique aspects of the method is that it allows for individualization of instruction and takes place in a group. This is because a single simulation/game can be played simultaneously at different levels of abstraction by different players. For one type of thinker, concrete experiences are provided; that is, the simulation/game occurs in the here and now. Other students may be involved because it is a concrete experience *and* because they are able to examine some aspects (perhaps cause-effect relationships) in greater depth. Still other students, perhaps the most gifted, may be examining the most sophisticated strategies and alternatives available. All of these learners are playing the same simulation/game at the same time. Because of the element of chance involved in most games, one cannot predict which type of learning style will be most successful in winning the game.

Simulation/games allow students to experience content directly. Players participate in an event rather than experiencing it vicariously by reading about it. Through this participation, players have a concrete experience which can help them to understand an abstract event through an analogy. This ties gaming to creativity.

A widely accepted learning principle—and one that has been documented—is that learning is facilitated when the learner receives immediate knowledge of results or feedback. Unlike most traditional forms of instruction, a simulation/game provides prompt feedback. A decision to make one move or to use one strategy usually leads to immediate results. Success or failure (demonstrated by winning or losing) is known by the end of the exercise. The debriefing which takes place immediately aids the player to learn from the experience. This is more direct than the feedback that occurs from the process of reading a text, hearing a lecture, writing a paper, taking a test, and then waiting days or even weeks for results.

Simulation/gaming is effective in the development of attitudes. Alice Kaplan Gordon, writing in *Games for Growth* says:

> One of the most promising hunches about educational games is that they can influence and alter the attitudes of participants. Specifically, this hunch applies to three areas. First, games can evidently be used to change attitudes about the particular issue a game treats. Second, and even more encouraging, experience with educational games can apparently improve the participants' attitudes toward learning and the school system in general. Third, games appear to influence the student's attitude about his own effectiveness in his own environment.[4]

Research done since 1970 has tended to support these hunches about attitudes; it is now generally agreed that simulation/gaming has its greatest *measurable* effect in the area of attitudes.

GAMING AS INTERDISCIPLINARY LEARNING

Well-designed simulation/games will be more necessary than ever in the future. As indicated in the following chapter, gaming can be seen as a "future's language." Furthermore, the process of gaming can convey gestalt and, as a result, alternative futures may be efficiently predicted. Gaming is a technique that is helpful in understanding the future because it is interdisciplinary.

The academic disciplines as they are now perceived are arbitrary divisions of knowledge. They arose, with few exceptions, through a series of historical accidents. That they are arbitrary can be seen by the way in which they overlap (thus there is political sociology, social psychology, and biochemistry), and by the tendency for new interdisciplinary studies to arise to fill vacuums that exist among the disciplines (thus the development of cybernetics and demography). The problems that humankind faces do not lend themselves to easy solutions by the traditional disciplines. The energy problem, for example, will never be solved through the efforts of any one discipline.

Three concepts can serve as exemplars of interdisciplinary ones that are future oriented: decision making, model, and system. Decision making is a process of choosing among alternatives and it is best accomplished where there is a large amount of information from a variety of sources. Model, which is described earlier in this chapter, is a representation of some aspect of the real world which is analogical. Models are widely used in a variety of contexts; the process of modeling is useful in problem solving. A system is an interrelationship of processes such that any aspect of the system affects any other aspect. Systems analysis is an attempt to understand processes so as to be able to solve problems. All simulation/games involve decision making; simulation/gaming is a subclass of modeling; a simulation/game can be perceived as a system.

The connection between simulation/gaming and interdisciplinary approaches to understanding and accumulating knowledge is in and of itself important and critical to survival in the future. Students respond well to the complexity of interdisciplinary concepts. They enjoy working with models and they are interested in systems analysis as well as decision making.

Simulation/gaming relates to divergent thinking and creative behavior that is also an interdisciplinary process. As simulation/gaming facilitates creative behavior, it does so in an interdisciplinary manner. These connections are further developed in other sections of this chapter and this book.

Arthur Koestler, whose constructs about creativity were described earlier, Part I, developed a concept that is interdisciplinary and related to the process of simulation/gaming. This is the idea of *holon* that Koestler discusses in *Janus: A Summing Up.*[5] Everything in existence, Koestler argues, is part of some system—called a *holarchy*. Each segment fits the Janus principle: it is at the same time an independent entity and a part of a whole. A human being is at once an individual who can be self-assertive, and a member of society, whose behavior must be integrated into the totality. A person who is only self-assertive is an anarchist, untouched by social control. A society of completely integrated members becomes totalitarian—a Nazi Germany where all bend their wills to the state and where individualism is lost. The ideal occurs when each person remains proportioned between self-assertion and integration. Such people will be better able to cope with the rapidly changing future. Koestler presents an analogy that links the Janus principle to games. A holon, he suggests, is like a player—constrained by the rules but free to develop independent strategy within them. The future will require interdependent beings who are also autonomous. Simulation/gaming offers practice in achieving this difficult combination. The ability to be interdependent and autonomous simultaneously is an outcome that needs development in children.

GAMING AND CREATIVITY

Creativity—whether artistic creation, scientific discovery, technological invention, or personal insight—embodies a process that is essential to life. As indicated earlier, the process enables persons to understand the world and share that comprehension with others through the development of creative product. The process of creativity can be developed, strengthened, and enlarged through the use of the strategy of simulation/gaming.

Creativity is frightening. Ultimately, the creative act must be engaged in alone; the individual must confront the inner core of the self. Innovation demands divergence from the things and thoughts of daily life, from the safely accepting public consensus about reality. It requires a faith in oneself to know and act in ways that may not be fully conscious.

Because of these fears, many persons fail to create; they shy away from their own creativity. Simulation/gaming can allay the fears surrounding creativity and can increase human potential through the development of innovative abilities.

Simulations simplify reality while providing a risk-free environment for exercising options. They allow individuals to function originally and spontaneously within safe parameters. Games increase the power and control an individual can exercise over his or her actions and thoughts,

THE PROCESS OF SIMULATION/GAMING   103

over others, and over the environment. Abilities to cope with and respond to the unknown may be developed through gaming. Games bridge the convergence necessitated by daily living and the divergence demanded by the need to create and the need to improve the human condition.

E. Paul Torrance defines creativity as: "... the process of sensing problems or gaps in information, forming ideas or hypotheses, testing and modifying these hypotheses, and communicating the results."[6]

The popular game, *Mastermind,* illustrates this definition of the creative process. This game consists of two players. The first player uses colored pegs to create a hidden design. The second player, through a series of guesses, must try to determine the unknown pattern. The initial sensitivity to "gaps in information" is given in the game's objective: the code breaker must discover the hidden patterns of colors determined by the code maker. The code breaker formulates hypotheses about the pattern, receives symbolic feedback concerning their viability, and then reformulates hypotheses until the code is broken.

This illustration of Torrance's definition may seem rather simplistic and rigid. Where does the "sensing problems" originate? How are hypotheses formulated? Can persons really facilitate the process associated with creativity through gaming?

William J. J. Gordon, whose development of synectics has been described in Chapter 4, maintains that these abilities—sensitivity to problems, hypothesis formulation, and creative process development—may be facilitated by: 1) getting persons to understand their own psychological processes better, 2) according emotional and nonrational components of these processes the same significance accepted for rational and intellectual components, and 3) engaging emotional and nonrational components along with rational and intellectual components in mind-stretching activities.

The gaming process accomplishes these objectives in a safe and enjoyable manner.

To play a game, players must consciously learn the *objectives* (what is the purpose of the game?), the *rules* (what are the conditions under which the player may operate?), the *roles* (how are players to act? What are their personal goals?), and the *sequences of action and interaction* (how does play proceed?). As s/he participates in a game, however, the player may invent new dimensions to roles and new ways in which to communicate with the other participants. These innovations are not arrived at consciously; they may be the result of emotional or intuitive responses to situations within the game, responses which are as unique as is each individual. Being "allowed" to respond in new ways (it's only a game, after all) fosters an understanding of individual psychological processes, as well as the growth of self-confidence in spontaneous action.

Synectics expands an individual's capacity to use metaphor and analogy; games provide metaphors of reality. Simulations also provide players with the opportunity to connect the pieces of simplified reality in the learning and invention of play. Emotion is just as important as intellect. The motivation to play and to reach goals, the ability to internalize and interpret roles, as well as the ability to empathize with other players are largely nonrational strengths.

Although they demand the intellectual abilities of comprehension, reason, and analysis, games also demand and facilitate other ways of knowing and of acting upon this knowledge.

Endoceptual cognition (a formulation of S. Arieti explained previously) is internal, unconscious, nonverbal thinking without form. This type of processing occurs in dreams and in highly emotional experiences, such as an intense simulation. The gaming process, in that it demands original and spontaneous thought unrestrained by precedent, can require and encourage endoceptual cognition and can foster its development within the individual.

The perceptions and orientations an individual brings to a game, the individual's actions in the game, and the perceptions s/he brings away from the experience are as unique as the person is unique. Players preparing to participate in any negotiation game (e.g., *Culture Contact* described in Chapter 8) all have different ideas of what it means to negotiate, as well as certain predispositions concerning how to interact with others and how to behave toward strangers. The play of the game broadens and alters these ideas and predispositions; players define for themselves how they will act and think within the context of the game.

At the conclusion of an exercise, participants have an enlarged understanding of negotiation processes within and between sociocultural groups. They also understand better their own strengths and weaknesses in these processes. This insight comes from the interaction of the player's role perspective in simulated reality with whatever the person brings to it from his or her real life situation. In other words, the understanding comes from playing the game.

GAME AS CREATIVE ENVIRONMENT

Creative action demands courage. In a world where "average" and "normal" are generally synonymous, where mediocrity is all too often lauded, those who choose to deviate from norms in any way risk social alienation and stigmatization.

Simulation/gaming eliminates the fear associated with divergence. This is perhaps its greatest contribution to creative development. Games offer a safe environment in which the individual may test other ways of knowing, thinking, and behaving. The world of game brings a person closer to tapping the source of his or her own creative pool. Hence, the person comes nearer to a state of self-actualization, and closer to realizing his or her potential to see life as it is and as it might be. The gaming environment fosters the growth of creative vision because it provides safety and freedom.

Carl Rogers wrote that creativity must be permitted to emerge under nurturing conditions of psychological safety and freedom. Psychological safety may be attained by three related processes: (1) accepting the individual as of unconditional worth; (2) providing a climate free of external evaluation; and (3) empathetic understanding.

Psychological freedom helps develop an inner locus of evaluation within the individual. It is permission to think, feel, and express with a primary responsibility to self alone. When individuals account only to themselves for their actions, they increasingly behave in ways that can foster internal creative processing. This kind of behavior—free from being externally prescribed—is necessary to foster and support.

Nurturing conditions for developing creative behavior often arise in the gaming environment. Game facilitators provide unqualified support and acceptance of participants. Players can often become secure enough in their roles to interpret them freely. The ultimate evaluation of a player's actions is not made by the facilitator nor by the other players, but by the gamer him- or herself. In order for a productive and stimuating game to progress, empathy must exist among the players. The higher the degree of total participant involvement demanded by a game, the more nurturing the environment becomes.

Role-play situations contain great creative potential. Although opposing goals and interests of players, as well as rules and basic strategies, may be rather well-defined, the use of strategies and combinations of moves offer room for divergence. Since no preferable strategies exist, this often requires spontaneity and originality from the players, even when they engage in simulation for the second or third time. Players remain free to interpret their roles and devise strategies for several diverse objectives.

The gaming environment facilitates creative thought processing within the individual. It encourages spontaneity and originality, and also provides settings that offer persons the opportunity to expand their world views, and simultaneously, the opportunity to expand the self, to come closer to fulfilling their personal potential.

The use of simulation/gaming contains relatively little danger; it is a place in which the individual may accept challenge to create a product that is original, spontaneous, and comprehensive. Although a player's role may be loosely or elaborately defined, it remains a superficial guide; the role must come to life from within the individual. This potential for role creation appeals to the gifted and talented who add rich dimensions to roles they come to play in simulation/gaming.

Within the context of the game, players are not shackled by the constraints of real-life roles as students, friends, or relatives or other participants. The nature of role-play allows the freest, most spontaneous components of the personality to emerge. In so doing, it increases the person's access to these parts of the personality.

Simulation/gaming contributes to the development of many traits associated with creative behavior. A successful gamer must be sensitive to problems. S/he must be aware of personal goals, strengths, and weaknesses, and must anticipate the objectives of other players. The gamer must be flexible in exploring alternatives, and fluent in conceptualizing new ways to achieve goals. Cooperating with players demands sensitivity and resiliency. Solutions to problematic issues often lie in their redefinition. Successful strategies are frequently original and/or complex.

Simulation/gaming, in facilitating the individual's creative development, also aids in the realization of his or her potential to become more powerful socially. Persons who can made sound decisions and formulate realistic goals, who are sensitive to others as well as to their surroundings, and who can readily adapt themselves to rapidly changing situations are those persons who reach higher states of self-actualization.

SIMULATION/GAMING AND GROUP PROCESS

Kurt Lewin, a Jewish social psychologist who fled Hitler's Germany in 1933, systematically studied group behavior in three different types of settings. In the first, he established an authoritarian climate controlled by a powerful leader. The leader directed persons to engage in various tasks constructing simple crafts. The group functioned efficiently as long as their leader was present in the room. Left on their own, the persons deteriorated as a work force and tremendous confusion resulted.

With the second group, Lewin examined the effect of laissez-faire leadership. The facilitator in this model provided little direction; participants were allowed to set their own rules and goals. This approach was inefficient and resulted in extremely low productivity.

A third group setting was based on democratic group process. This group organized itself and set its own goals and rules. The leader obtained consensus and worked democratically with group members. He sought to improve group cohesion and increase effectiveness. Lewin found this environment to be the most successful.

Many simulation/games build cohesive democratic groups. Participation in the gaming process strengthens group process and leads to functioning groups that can aid the creative process within individuals. Alex Osborne's brainstorming technique relies upon the use of group process to foster innovation. W. J. J. Gordon conducted research to determine whether or not creativity could occur in groups of persons working together. After using his synectics technique with groups to achieve divergent solutions to problems, Gordon concluded that innovation could indeed take place in this way.

The process of creativity can be facilitated when it occurs in a supportive group that is cohesive and in which members work together with a sense of mutual trust. This condition occurs in many simulation/games; playing them strengthens cohesive forces. This helps to explain the synergistic nature of creativity and gaming: innovative persons are better game players, and simulations facilitate spontaneity and increase creativity.

COMPUTER GAMING

The newest application of simulation/gaming for use in educational settings is the computer game. The popularity of computer games among students can be seen in the tremendous proliferation of arcade computer games. These games, which were designed for entertainment, involve players in intense and prolonged concentration. The ability of arcade games to enthrall students represents a strong argument for the use of computer gaming in education.

The advantages found in any simulation/game are also present in computer games. They resemble other simulation/games in basic construction and in format. Some computer games are the equivalent of board games as well as those involving role play. Educational computer games have been developed that teach basic skills (such as reading and mathematics operations) and complex computer games are available that teach students more sophisticated concepts.

Computer gaming has a good deal of appeal and it is attractive to students, in part, because of the excitement it engenders. One should keep in mind, however, that in and of itself the computer does not necessarily represent a superior form of gaming. Whether or not to use a computer game depends on the objectives that the teacher has in mind and the most appropriate means for achieving these outcomes. Computers should not be used simply because they represent an innovation in technology. On the other hand, computers have great appeal for gifted and talented students and the combination of them with simulation/gaming increases the power of this tool. Chapter 8 describes several computer games that are presently available for classroom use.

SUMMARY

Simulation/games bridge the convergence that is necessitated by daily living and divergence demanded by intrinsic needs to grow and to create. Games simplify reality as they provide risk-free environments in which to exercise options. Players act in an innovative and spontaneous manner while participating in gaming. As better players become more creative, so do innovative individuals become better gamers. Simulation/gaming increases the understanding, power, and control an individual can exercise over his or her actions and thoughts, over others, and over the environment.

Simulation/gaming aids the socialization of the young. Players learn how to set goals, as well as how to compete with others and how to cooperate with others in achieving goals. Games provide "practice" environments for many of life's activities.

The role of the group is an important one in the process of gaming as well as in the real world. A supportive cohesive group fosters the development of mutual trust; this strengthens problem-solving ability as well as the spontaneity that is so integral to creative development. Games enhance a person's access to the child ego-state in improving spontaneity. They provide strokes for all players, thus improving their mental well-being.

Good games are sociodramas. Players learn new roles, new responses, and new perspectives for the situations in their lives.

Gaming fosters creativity as creative development fosters gaming abilities. As confidence in creative ability grows, individuals attain broadened conceptions of life processes and systems, and of their personal relations to these in terms of understanding and control. This increases human potential as it draws people toward higher levels of not just being, but becoming.

The process of gaming with its many strengths and advantages as a teaching technique is further enhanced by the development of computer-assisted instruction based on the process of simulation/gaming. The interaction of computer and gaming adds to the value of both as tools for improving education.

Simulation/gaming, like the strategy of facilitating creativity, is based on the work of many theorists. The next chapter examines some of their work in order to add to an understanding of the process.

NOTES

1. Mihalyi Csikszentmihalyi, *Beyond Boredom and Anxiety* (San Francisco: Jossey-Bass, 1977).
2. Omar Khayham Moore and Alan R. Anderson, "Autotelic Folk Models," in *Sociological Quarterly* (1960, Volume I), pp. 206–216.
3. John Raser, *Simulation and Society* (Boston: Allyn and Bacon, 1969).
4. Alice Kaplan, *Games for Growth* (New York: Science Research Associates, 1970).
5. Arthur Koestler, *Janus: A Summing Up* (New York: Random House, 1978).
6. E. Paul Torrance, *Creativity* (Washington, D.C.: National Education Association, 1963), p. 4.

CHAPTER

7

Theories of Simulation and Gaming

INTRODUCTION

This chapter describes theories relating to simulation/gaming. Whereas the previous chapter studied gaming as a process, this chapter offers further analysis by examining the points of view of several persons. Some of these theorists have been directly interested in simulation/gaming whereas others offer perspectives about human behavior and learning that can add to an improved understanding of the gaming process.

Garry Shirts, a pioneer in the development of simulation/gaming as an instructional tool, founded a game development center several years ago which he called Simile II. This organization has produced many excellent games (some of which are described in the next chapter). An early statement by Shirts can serve as an introduction to thinking about simulation/gaming from a theoretical perspective. Shirts called his statement, "An Inventory of Hunches about Simulations as Educational Tools." He wrote:

1. Maybe simulations are "motivators." Their main payoff may be that they generate enthusiasm for or commitment to: (a) learning in general, (b) social studies or some other subject area, (c) a specific discipline like history, (d) a specific course, or (e) a specific teacher.

2. Maybe a simulation experience leads students to more sophisticated and relevant inquiry. That is, perhaps the important thing is what happens after the simulation is over, when students ask about the "model" which determined some of the elements of the simulation, about real world analogues to events and factors in the simulation, about processes like communication, about ways of dealing with stress and tension. Maybe participation leads naturally into a critique and analysis of the simulation by students, and maybe this can lead easily into a model-building experience ... And maybe the greatest learning occurs when students build their own simulations.

3. Maybe simulations give participants a more integrated view of some of the ways of men. Maybe they see the interconnectedness of political, social, interpersonal, cultural, economic, historical, etc., factors. Maybe simulations help people understand the idea of "social system." Maybe the simulation experience helps them integrate ideas and information they already had.

4. Maybe participants in simulations learn skills: decision making, resource allocation, communication, persuasion, influence resisting. Or maybe they learn how important these processes are. Maybe they learn about the rational and emotional components of these skills.

5. Maybe simulations affect attitudes: (a) maybe participants gain empathy for real-life decision-makers; (b) maybe they get a feeling that life is much more complicated than they ever imagined; (c) maybe they get a feeling that they can do something important about affecting their personal life or the nation or the world.

6. Maybe simulations provide participants with explicit, experiential, gut-level referents about ideas, concepts, and words used to describe human behavior. Maybe everyone has a personal psychology or sociology ... maybe a simulation experience brings this personal view closer to reality. Maybe people know many things they don't know, and simulations act as an information retrieval device to help bring this knowledge to consciousness.

7. Maybe participants in simulations learn the form and content of the model which lies behind the simulation. That is, in a corporation management simulation, maybe they learn about the ways in which certain aspects of the marketplace are related; in an internation simulation, maybe they learn the relationship between the relative satisfaction of political influentials and the probability that leaders will retain office.

8. Maybe the main importance of simulations is their effect on

the social setting in which learning takes place. Maybe their physical format alone, which demands a significant departure from the usual setup of a classroom (chair shuffling, grouping, possibly room dividers, etc.), produces a more relaxed, natural exchange between teacher and students later on. Since simulations are student-run exercises, maybe they move "control" of the classroom from the teacher to the structure of the simulation, and thereby allow for better student-teacher relations. Simulations are usually very engaging; maybe one product of such engagement is that students drop their usual interpersonal facades, and maybe this leads to a more open classroom atmosphere in later sessions. Maybe simulations have their main effect on the teacher: perhaps he sees his students as more able than he had thought before, and the result may be that he looks to himself more to explain failures in the classroom. Maybe simulations—like any new technique—cause teachers to look at their normal teaching methods with a more critical eye. Maybe simulations' main payoff is that they create student enthusiasm in one classroom which may spread to informal student channels throughout the school.

9. Maybe simulations lead to personal growth. The high degree of involvement may provide some of the outcomes hoped for from T-groups, sensitivity training, basic encounter groups, etc. ... that is, a better sense of how one appears to others; discovery of personal skills, abilities, fears, weaknesses, that weren't apparent before; opportunities to express affection, anger, and indifference without permanently crippling consequences.

Since the time when Shirts first wrote this material, many of his hunches have been proved correct. Simulation/games are good motivators. They provide gestalt—the integrated view of reality referred to by Shirts. Simulation/games can be used to teach many kinds of skills—including computer competence. Research has demonstrated the effectiveness of games in changing many kinds of attitudes. Persons can gain much from the use of simulations in understanding the process of modeling. Simulations change the nature of educational settings, as Shirts indicates, and this provides students with an arena for more productive learning. Shirts' sense of connection between games and growth has been demonstrated in many ways by the relationships that can be made between simulation/gaming and psychotherapy systems such as Transactional Analysis and Psychodrama.

Shirts' hunches can serve as a bridge between the process issues considered in the previous chapter and the nature of gaming theory discussed in this chapter.

JOHN DEWEY AND SIMULATION/GAMING

Any discussion of important trends in education must begin with John Dewey, whose experimentalist philosophy transformed perspectives on learning for all time. Others have periodically suggested alternative kinds of instruction, and occasional attacks based on his approach—the most recent being the "back to basics" movement. But Dewey's insistence that education be based on experience and the scientific method still remains the most widely accepted principle governing the educational establishment from preschool through high school and beyond, as progressive teaching techniques that go beyond lecture and discussion are now finding their way into higher education.

Dewey produced a vast amount of literature on education and experiential learning. The following six propositions relate most directly to the process of simulation/gaming.

The first, and perhaps most important, concerns the role of experience in education. Learning occurs, Dewey argued, only when the student's background is taken into account in providing understanding. An instructional tape produced by the Carleton Video Tape Project shows a student who tells of his father's admonition to him to learn from experience. The young man's reply indicates his agreement with the proposal. He then reports his father's answer: "Then why can't you learn from my experiences?" Dewey teaches that comprehension takes place only when one's *own* experiences are employed in the process of education.

A second significant proposition from Dewey is sometimes labeled "student involvement," which means that in order for understanding to occur, the learner must participate in the formation of purposes that direct his or her activities. Goals must be real ones; therefore the person must have a hand in selecting goals.

Third, Dewey asserts that the only useful kind of knowledge is that which leads to growth. Without this, the process of education results in stagnation.

Dewey advocated democracy in education. Some, for purposes of their own, have chosen to equate this with anarchy. Democracy as a means of government does not require the abdication of authority, nor is it implied in the teaching. Humans grow more successfully under democratic conditions than under authoritarian ones. Simulation/games, by changing the role of the teacher from giver of directions to facilitator, add to the possibility of accomplishing this fourth proposition from Dewey.

Dewey also argued that society should not be viewed as static but as constantly changing. For this reason process becomes more important than any product.

Finally, Dewey denied the distinction between work and play. Work without meaning is onerous toil. Play that is purposeful becomes useful work. Creativity occurs when play is given purpose and when previous experiences give meaning to current ones.

Dewey studied work, play, and leisure, writing about them in the early part of the twentieth century; this served him as one approach to educational theory. The connection he described between work and play and his contention that labor must contain purpose lest it become onerous toil has tended to be forgotten with the passing of the years. The joyless drudgery of the factory became the model for production as well as for education. Without meaning, work often became debilitating. Dewey argued against the factory as a model for the school. The connection between work and play—the idea that significant employment becomes play—supports the use of simulation/gaming—a process that involves fun (as games are played) leading to meaningful work (as students accomplish important outcomes from the use of the technique).

It is commonly said in a psychodrama that a person who has been the protagonist has "worked." This is a further illustration of the proposition that tasks that have meaning become play; when persons learn from playing, it is often labeled work.

For Dewey, meaningful labor becomes a kind of enjoyment—not free play, but nonetheless activity done for personal growth. The person who experiences toil as fun can see meaning in it. This occurs most often when closure takes place.

In many ways, Dewey anticipated the Third Wave of Alvin Toffler (described in detail in a later chapter). Dewey's writing has remained significant after more than a half century because his ideas extended beyond the limits of his time. Though he might have denied it, Dewey was clearly an early futurist—ahead of his contemporaries, anticipating the needs of tomorrow because of his vision of what life could become. In *Democracy and Education* (1916), Dewey wrote:

> Plato defined a slave as one who accepts from another the purposes which control his conduct. This condition obtains even where there is no slavery in the legal sense. It is found wherever men are engaged in activity which is socially serviceable, but whose service they do not understand and have no personal interest in. Much is said about scientific management of work. It is a narrow view which restricts the science which secures efficiency of operations to movements of the muscles. The chief opportunity for science is the discovery of the relations of a man to his work—including his relations to others who take part—which will enlist his intelligent interest in what he is doing. Efficiency in production often demands division of labor.

But is reduced to a mechanical routine unless workers see the technical, intellectual, and social relationships involved in what they do, and engage in their work because of the motivation furnished by such perceptions. The tendency to reduce such things as efficiency of activity and scientific management to purely technical externals is evidence of the one-sided stimulation of thought given to those in control of industry—those who supply its aims. Because of their lack of all-around and well balanced social interest, there is not sufficient stimulus for attention to the human factors and relationships in industry. Intelligence is narrowed to the factors concerned with technical production and marketing of goods. No doubt, a very acute and intense intelligence in these narrow lines can be developed, but the failure to take into account the significant social factors means none-the-less an absence of mind, and corresponding distortion of emotional life.

This quote from Dewey reflects his belief that work have meaning and be social. The use of simulation/gaming as a teaching technique meets both criteria. Whenever games are played, they are filled with meaning for all the reasons described in the previous chapter, and a major value of the process of gaming arises from its social nature.

Dewey's basic constructs relate directly to the development of experiential education. He argues that instruction must prepare people for work of all kinds. The process of gaming leads to experiential learning—it is a real and not a vicarious experience; players become enmeshed in the process. An actual event (the game itself) occurs at the same time that an abstract process takes place in simulation. Games add meaning to schoolwork as students invent strategies for winning. Instructional gaming derives support from the positions developed by Dewey.

Dewey's writings provide theoretical support for the use of simulation/gaming as an instructional strategy. Dewey insisted upon hands-on teaching; he demanded that schools be part of life rather than about it. The student must use previous experience in the acquisition of knowledge and s/he must learn by doing. Labor that has purpose takes on meaning and becomes a creative experience.

ABRAHAM MASLOW AND SELF-ACTUALIZATION

As Dewey is a key figure in modern education, so Abraham Maslow is central for the human potential movement. Maslow is a "third force" psychologist—placing himself between the behaviorism of Skinner and the subconsciousness of Freud. For Maslow, human beings grow toward self-actualization—the point at which they use all of their potential. Few people ever succeed completely in reaching this state, but it is an outcome worth striving for.

Maslow expounds a positive psychology. Behaviorists condition and Freudians psychoanalyze, but Maslow helps people grow into full human beings. Maslow argues for the extension of psychotherapy from ill people to healthy ones. Neurotics in therapy may become healed; healthy people in therapy can begin to achieve their potential.

Maslow's best-known idea remains his hierarchy of needs. Higher-level desires cannot be satisfied until lower ones have been accommodated. The physiological requirements for air, water, food, shelter, sleep, and sex come first. Second come the needs for safety and security, and third comes the necessity for love and belonging. The desire for self-esteem and esteem by others appears in fourth place on the ladder. Finally, there is the drive toward growth, which includes meaningfulness, self-sufficiency, playfulness, order, justice, perfection, individuality, aliveness, beauty, goodness, and truth.

Another key concept (one very important for simulation/gaming) is that of "peak experience." One lives through a moment of feeling self-actualized, which is a brief period in an individual's life when he or she functions completely, and feels self-confident, strong, and self-assured. At times this borders on the mystical, but most people have taken part in such events occasionally. Every person can recall such times in their own lives. These memories may be seen as examples of Maslow's concept.

Characteristics associated with self-actualization include: 1) the ability to see life as it is rather than as one would like it to be, 2) a deep commitment to one's task—whatever its nature, 3) the ability to be creative—including flexibility, spontaneity, courage, and openness (Maslow compares the creativity of self-actualized persons to that of children), 4) a desire to be with people and an absence of hostility to them, 5) the strength to make unpopular decisions, 6) the ability to develop intense sexual involvements that improve with time, 7) a lack of fear of those things in life that frighten others, 8) the ability to relate to children in a friendly way, and 9) philosophical patience.

Maslow agrees that self-actualized people have problems, but these concerns are important ones—loneliness, guilt, sadness—based on the nature of the human condition. These worries are to be preferred to false ones that lack importance—jealousy, rivalry, and a need for an overabundance of material things. The self-actualized person goes about the existential task of defining his or herself.

Maslow attempts to avoid the atomism of science: the attempt to understand things by breaking them down. He urges instead a holistic perception: comprehension of things in their totality. Maslow discourages perceptions of dichotomies—love-hate, good-bad, happy-sad; he urges instead the integration of opposites. There is love in hate, good in bad, happiness in sadness, and vice versa.

SIMULATION/GAMING AND HUMAN POTENTIAL

Dewey and Maslow are *both* human potential, third force psychologists. Their work can provide understanding of how human potential can be facilitated by simulation/gaming.

Dewey's demand for meaningful experience can be related to gaming. A worthwhile game is a significant event for the players. This helps explain the high level of involvement and motivation. Those who take part in a game have the opportunity to plan strategy and to learn to respond to the moves of others. This represents Dewey's notion of participation in the formation of goals. Students who play games grow as a result of the experience; they obtain feedback that is immediate and helpful. Simulation/games enlarge one's sense of efficacy as participants learn to cooperate and as they occasionally win. In fact, more can win this way than in the contest of taking tests. Because of their nature, cooperative games further the development of democratic processes. Games illustrate Dewey's description of a changing rather than a static society as well as his concept that work and play can occur at the same time.

The higher needs on Maslow's hierarchy can be related to the simulation/gaming process. Those needs that lead to growth can often be simulated in nonthreatening ways. This allows practice for actual living while providing perspective. A student understands concepts such as justice, completion, and order more clearly in a game than in life since the former operates under better control.

Games provide peak experiences (moments when one knows what self-actualization is like). Persons who have played a large number of games have experienced this and have observed it in others as well.

Maslow's desire to understand wholes rather than parts fits the simulation experience. A game supplies gestalt and closure by having a beginning and an end that are visible to players in a reasonable period of time. Such an exercise provides better closure than most other learning devices.

The many problems facing society in the closing years of the twentieth century can be related to gaming as well as to human potential. Games by their very nature provide opportunity for problem solving and they often allow for practice in decision making.

PSYCHOLOGICAL ASPECTS OF GAMING

The synergism of creativity and gaming that is fostered by group process has already been described. This synergism is in many ways a therapeutic one. Games not only encourage creativity as they facilitate group process but they also improve mental health. Transactional Analysis (TA) and Psychodrama, already alluded to in other portions of this book, demonstrate this. We now turn to a more detailed description of these therapies and their relationship to gaming.

Eric Berne, creator of TA, used the concept of games to describe human behavior. Each individual has three ego states: Parent, Adult, and Child. In the Parent ego-state, persons repeat behaviors that they learned from their parents; an example of this would be attitudes toward minority groups or sex-role biases. The Adult is the reality-oriented component of human personality; it is objective and rational. The third ego-state, the Child, is characterized by playfulness and creativity. Although each ego-state has appropriate uses, persons function best when all three ego states are integrated. Simulation/gaming facilitates this integration.

When a participant is given a role to play and a goal to achieve in a simulation/game, s/he must first understand these objectively. The player may listen to Parent "tapes" in interpreting the role. The player may consider the goals to be achieved from the Adult perspective, that is, in a rational manner. It is within the Child, however, that curiosity is aroused and the player is motivated to participate. Also from the child come many divergent suggestions and impulses concerning the attainment of goals and implementation of the role. These may be kept in check by the Adult or by the Parent; for example, screaming or stealing may not be appropriate behaviors.

Another concept of TA found in games is that of *stroking*. Children receive physical strokes which make them feel loved and needed and good about themselves. Adults continue to need these strokes—not just physical ones but those that come in the form of praise and reward. Bad strokes, that is, attention received because of negative behavior, may be better than none at all.

Students who are too old for pats on the head from teachers can only obtain reinforcement in the form of verbal praise. This severely limits the amount of strokes available to a student who may express frustration in a disruptive or antagonistic manner. This fate can affect the gifted and talented student whose achievement often comes to be taken for granted and hence the frequency of praise declines. An achievement of a more typical student will be praised highly, whereas the same achievement by the able one will be undervalued because it was expected. This too can increase frustration and can also be applied to adults. In the workplace or in social settings adults may not receive enough positive stroking from their colleagues and friends, so they may resort to subversive, catty, or otherwise destructive behavior.

Simulation/gaming provides people with strokes in a number of ways. Winning is not the only form of positive attention; players may receive praise from teammates or they may invent successful strategies. The mutual trust and support that develops within a cohesive group can also be a source of stroking. This connection between Transactional Analysis and gaming adds to the importance of TA as a teaching strategy and a life activity.

Psychodrama is a therapy that enables clients to learn new roles. J. L. Moreno, the founder of Psychodrama, used improvisational drama to help persons gain insight into their lives. The process, as indicated earlier, also depends on the competent use of group dynamics.

As indicated in Chapter 5, during a psychodrama session the therapist warms up the audience—the people who have come to participate—using a variety of group process techniques. From this a protagonist emerges. The director (the trained psychotherapist) helps the starring player set a scene to deal with a problematic situation in his or her life. The protagonist chooses auxiliaries from the audience—persons to play significant others in the life of the person whose drama is to be enacted. Psychodramatic techniques used in the production include role reversal, mirroring, and doubling. Following the drama, members of the audience share experiences from their own lives with the protagonist. This helps the person understand that many people have had similar experiences.

Psychodramatic situations occur in the here and now, as do simulation/games. Participants learn how to respond to situations in new and healthier ways. They learn new roles or new dimensions to transform already existing roles. The basic tool that brings about this transformation is spontaneity.

Simulation shares many qualities with Psychodrama. Childlike spontaneity often provides the base for play. Protagonists choose auxiliaries on the basis of *tele*—a mutual exchange of empathy and appreciation. Having empathy for other participants in a simulation/game is requisite to successful play. Frequently, simulations become sociodramas.

Sociodrama, as indicated before, is a form of Psychodrama that has no protagonist. Instead of a personal problem, a group issue is examined. A sociodrama contains role-play and often provides significant insight and emotional impact for participants.

When, for example, teachers play Robert Horn's *Participative Decision Making,* they assume roles of members of a community trying to reduce a school budget. Teachers deal with emotion-packed issues within the safety of the roles they play. The therapeutic value of this is that it leads to insight and often to a redefinition of values and priorities for all participants from several role perspectives.

Because of their sociodramatic nature, games can increase mental well-being. Transactional Analysis offers evidence that the healthy personality is one in which the ego-states of Parent, Adult, and Child are integrated; simulations facilitate this integration. Games, sociodrama, and Psychodrama share several qualities that foster improved mental health. They construct a reality in the here and now in which participants may feel safe and free. Within this context, persons can develop empathy for one another. A common problem is explored as participants learn to respond to it and understand it in new ways. Gaming, sociodrama, and Psychodrama lead to insight and provide emotional well-being through a cathartic experience. Good simulation/games elicit strong emotions and are capable of changing attitudes. Quality simulation/games, which use role-play, lead to creative role-creation. Games demand spontaneity and empathy (and thus facilitate the development of tele).

The simulation called *Culture Shock* is an example of a game that becomes an important and meaningful sociodrama. It simulates the bringing together of a group of sailors to confront a nation of islanders. Both have needs the other can meet but differences arise based on varying cultural perceptions. The two cultures must create an accommodation in order to achieve their goals but the structure of the game makes it difficult. Therefore, the negotiation between the two sides becomes an intense sociodrama. All elements of a simulated Psychodrama are present in *Culture Contact* and it often affects the players in a powerful manner.

Simulation/games in the classroom accomplish much; their relationship to Transactional Analysis and Psychodrama is still another reason for their use.

SIMULATION/GAMING AS FUTURE'S LANGUAGE

In *Gaming: The Future's Language* Richard Duke describes languages of the future.[1] These modes of communication allow persons to anticipate the time to come (socially as well as technologically) in ways that can lessen the impact of the increasing rate of change—Toffler's concept of future shock.

For Duke, many future's languages exist including cartography, flow charts, and the simulation/gaming process. They contain the following characteristics:

1. A future's language conveys *gestalt,* presenting a holistic view of a situation. Simulation/games describe complete experiences as players are able to perceive a totality in a relatively short time.
2. *Universality*—another feature of this mode—requires that the communication address a general problem. Games usually examine specific issues but they lead to solutions that can be generalized, therefore meeting this criterion. Simulations have "frames"—the specific problem can be changed within the same structure.
3. Future's languages require *spontaneity.* Quality simulations must contain this feature, which allows participants to invent strategies and interpret roles.
4. *Mutability*—the ability of a process to change while in use—exists in future's languages and in gaming. A game often proceeds in a direction charted by the players and not necessarily in the direction of the designer. The facilitator too can affect the nature of the game to make one point instead of another.
5. Future's languages offer a *future's orientation,* occurring in epochs other than the current one. A game takes on this characteristic, creating its own time frame, past, present, or future.
6. Future's languages provide for the *"explication of linkages."* Duke says:

> Future's languages have the ability to display, make explicit, or permit the recording of linkages between major segments of the holistic imagery; they create an awareness of feedback. As a formulated inquiry is pulsed through the Future's Language, the participants obtain, through both direct and serendipitous means, an awareness of the complexity being explored. Games are particularly valuable for making the linkages between the major components of a system being represented explicit. These linkages are discovered during the play of the game, and they should be emphasized during the critique process.[2]

7. Finally, future's languages provide for *multilogue*—a form of communication in which several groups discuss the same issue simultaneously. Robert Horn's game, *Participative Decision Making,* requires sets of six persons to discuss a school budget. Each panel reaches an independent conclusion and shares its decision. This concurrent examination of a problem serves as an example of multilogue.

As the third section of this book indicates, it is critical that persons learn strategies for coping with the future. The fact that a game is a future's language at the same time that it achieves many other outcomes (e.g., the facilitating of creative behavior, socialization, and the improvement of mental health) adds to its value as a strategy.

SUMMARY

This chapter has explored the use of the strategy of simulation/gaming by relating it to theories that can increase an understanding of the significance of the process. Hunches about gaming written by Garry Shirts were described and this was followed by an analysis of the work of John Dewey as it relates to simulation/gaming. The human potential movement, which includes Dewey as well as Abraham Maslow, also received attention. The chapter focused upon the psychological aspects of gaming including its relationship to Transactional Analysis and Psychodrama. The nature of simulation/gaming as a future's language was described.

This theoretical examination of the process of simulation/gaming can perhaps best be summarized by quoting from Alice Kaplan Gordon's book, *Games for Growth:*

> The term "game" connotes fun. And activities that are fun seem to be incompatible with activities that are serious. Everyone knows that education is a serious business . . . The fundamental deficiency of the school system is its failure to motivate the youth of the country to want to learn. This is probably due as much to the methodology used as it is to the fact that what the schools teach is perceived to have little connection with the real world . . . Of the many educational innovations, games and simulations offer great promise of transforming the classroom from an assembly of passive, if not bored spectators into a laboratory of active participants in the learning process . . . A game is essentially a simplified slice of reality. Its structure reflects a real-world process that the designer wishes to teach or investigate; the game serves as vehicle for testing that process or for learning more about its working. . . . In playing games, students tend to develop feelings of effectiveness and control, because the actions they take in the game produce results . . . There is no way to remake or cultivate attitudes in one grandiose stroke; but teachers can help students to study them by providing opportunities for actually playing out their implications and effects in classroom situations. . . . Nobody suggests that games should be used all the time to teach all things. But if they are as effective in altering attitudes and teaching processes as has been suggested, all other media can be utilized more effectively.[3]

NOTES

1. Richard Duke, *Gaming: The Future's Language* (New York: Halstead Press, 1974).
2. Ibid., p. 54.
3. Alice Kaplan, *Games for Growth* (New York: Science Research Associates), 1970.

CHAPTER

8

Using Simulation/Games

INTRODUCTION

This chapter describes the use of simulation/games in daily classroom practice, and discusses the evaluation and design of these games. Three complete games for classroom use are presented, as well as an annotated list of 26 other games that can be helpful in a wide variety of teaching situations. This annotated list is but a small sample of the thousands of games that are now available to teachers. The best source of these simulated games (a listing of hundreds of games) is *The Guide to Simulation and Gaming for Education and Training,* edited by Robert Horn and Anne Cleaves and published by Sage Publications in 1980. Many school supply companies sells simulation/games (e.g., Social Studies School Services) and many of the games described here can be obtained from these companies. The following are also sources of simulation/games:

Abt Associates, Inc.
55 Wheeler Street
Cambridge, MA 02138

The Games Preserve
R. D. 1355
Fleetwood, PA 19522

Information Resources, Inc.
Box 417
Lexington, MA 02174

Interact
P. O. Box 262
Lakeside, CA 92040

National Game Center and
 Laboratory
University of North Carolina
 at Asheville
One University Heights
Asheville, NC 28804

Simile II
218 Twelfth Street
P. O. Box 910
Del Mar, CA 92014

Urban Gaming/Simulation
  Conference
School of Education
The University of Michigan
Ann Arbor, MI 48109

Social Science Education
  Consortium, Inc.
855 Broadway
Boulder, CO 80302

Wiff 'N Proof Learning Games
  Associates
1490 South Boulevard
Ann Arbor, MI 48104

USING GAMES

The use of simulation/games in daily classroom applications requires an understanding of how to use them, how to evaluate them, and how to design them.

The first step in using a simulation/game is to decide the objectives that one desires to achieve. Although this may seem obvious, this step is often *not* the first step in instruction. However, without a careful consideration of objectives in the use of simulation/games, the possibility of significant accomplishment by their use is diminished.

In the second step one answers the question of whether or not a simulation/game is the most appropriate technique to use to accomplish the objectives. Experience in their use will help one to make this determination. (Part of the decision, of course, will depend on the availability of an appropriate simulation/game.) Some objectives may be better achieved by the use of another technique, and sometimes a simulation/game may not be an appropriate choice for reasons relating to available time, the kind of activities that have come before and which follow the simulation/game, the nature of the class, the nature of the course and its content, and even the cost.

In step three, one selects a simulation/game (or perhaps designs one). In order to do this, it is necessary to become familiar with the variety of available games. The resources listed in the introduction to this chapter can be helpful in this regard. Many school districts have learning resource centers that contain games, and some State Departments of Education also maintain resource libraries that provide simulation/games for those seeking to use them in the classroom.

Becoming familiar with the simulation/game is the fourth step, and playing the game with colleagues or friends remains the most effective way to do this. If this is not possible, then the instructor must carefully read the rules and examine all the component parts. Often it is not possible to really get the feel of a game without first playing it. The facilitator needs two or three experiences with a game before s/he will be able to provide players with the opportunity to derive the maximum benefit from its use.

In step five, the teacher introduces the simulation/game to the students. Most good simulation/games provide detailed instructions on how this should be done. Instructors should not overwhelm students with information or give them data that could ruin the game, and the facilitator should not offer advice on strategy. The rules have to be explained in a way that keeps the students interested.

Playing the game is the sixth step. The role of the facilitator becomes crucial at this point. The instructor ought not to play unless the game contains a specified role for him or her (such as moderator). The facilitator serves in the role of resource person (who also has the responsibility for pacing the exercise) and should have little personal involvement in the game. Those who are new to this technique may have difficulty with the transition from traditional instructor to facilitator of simulation/gaming. They may approach the process in a didactic fashion, lecturing on the rules, describing the outcome beforehand, lecturing on strategy, and urging players to one course of behavior and not another. These actions can destroy the possibility of success and interfere with the learning.

The seventh and final step involves a debriefing session. The debriefing should refer to the objectives which were the reason for using the technique in the first place. The instructor should not begin the debriefing by evaluating the simulation/game itself (although this should be done eventually so s/he can receive feedback about the effectiveness of the experience from the perspective of students). Debriefing should focus on the experience that took place, on an analysis of what happened, on conclusions that can be made from the events, on an examination of the feelings of the players, and on an attempt to discover if the conclusions can be generalized to other experiences. Most good simulation/games provide a debriefing guide that can be adapted to the needs of the instructor.

Teachers need to evaluate simulation/games by measuring student achievement and by obtaining feedback from the perspective of players on whether or not to use the game again. Some people argue that simulation/games are of limited value because it is impossible to test students on what they have learned as a result of the experience. They assume incorrectly that the only good activities are those which can lead to examination questions. They also fail to understand that it is possible to write useful examination questions based on experiences that take place during a simulation/game. The examination can be based on the objectives and on the debriefing which also focused on the desired outcomes.

The second part of evaluation is the question of whether or not the simulation/game was successful. Were students involved and did their motivation increase? Were the results positive? Many good simulation/games are available and an instructor who obtains some experience with them can generally avoid using one that does not work (although sometimes circumstances may lead to failure even with the best game). This kind of evaluation can be done after the debriefing, partly by the instructor who analyzes the experience, and in conjunction with students who can share their feelings about the simulation/game.

Ideally, instructors need to learn to evaluate simulation/games before they determine whether or not to employ them. As one gains experience with simulation/games, one develops the ability to do this. Several factors need to be considered in deciding on whether or not to use a particular game. A game that is too complex may be almost impossible to understand and may require long, boring, and confusing lists of rules. A good simulation/game corresponds to reality in ways which are neither overly simplified nor overly complex. The cost of the game must also be considered. Some games are very expensive but are no more effective than other alternatives which are available at a lower cost.

Other issues must also be considered. A simulation/game may play well but have little value as a learning device. Many commercial games have this problem. Although these games are fun to play, little is accomplished by their use. They often distort the real world so badly that they are capable of doing harm. Some educational products on the market use a simulation/game format but are devices for exercising rote memory; each carefully recited fact allows the player one more move on the game board.

The evaluation process can be summarized with the following questions: Does the simulation/game allow for the accomplishment of objectives? Does it work? Do the students enjoy it? Can it be played in a reasonable amount of time at reasonable cost? Does the simulation/game correspond to reality in an appropriate way? Does it lend itself to meaningful debriefing? Does it leave players desiring to play another simulation/game on another day?

This examination of the use of simulation/games can be concluded with some attention to the process of design—a difficult task at best. Hundreds of poorly designed games exist and nothing is accomplished by adding to their number. One should not attempt to create a game until one has had considerable experience playing games invented by others. Some of the process of design is based on mimicry; thus the first step in learning to design is to become familiar with what already exists. The next step is to determine the objectives one wishes to achieve. Third, the designer must devise a plan which indicates how the simulation/game is arranged, how it proceeds, what kind of equipment is necessary and how it fits together. Only then should the actual construction of the game take place.

Designing a simulation/game also involves the following tasks. One must decide whether it is to be a board game, a role-play game, or some combination of these. A scenario must be created along with the parameters under which it will proceed. People who have experience with the design of games always advise that in setting the parameters it is necessary to focus on what to leave out as well as what to include. Decisions must be made about how the simulation/game will operate with regard to the actions of the players. If they are to play roles, this should be decided and the roles created. The resources available to each player, the basic moves required, and the decisions the players must make should be determined. The way in which players interact with each other and with the setting must be specified. A scoring system (if one is to be used) should be created and a device for ending the game should also be included. Finally, a guide to debriefing is usually necessary.

The design of games is a highly complex task. It often leads to ineffective results when persons who are poorly prepared attempt the process. Four useful principles of design can provide a summary of this aspect of gaming.

1. *Understanding the nature of gaming theory.* The chapters in this book can serve as an introduction. A great body of literature on simulation/gaming exists. Before trying to create a game, the potential designer should have a reasonable acquaintance with this material.

2. *The designer must fully comprehend the problem being simulated.* This requires additional examination of literature. Designers face the problem of reality orientation: the game should be a simplified sample of the real world. If it includes too much, it becomes difficult to manage. If too much is excluded, the game results in distortion. Finding an appropriate balance becomes critical; it comes from an in-depth study of the problem being simulated.

3. *In order to be effective, the designer must participate in a large number of games.* This point is crucial. One must have experienced many games as a player in order to develop the skills necessary to create new ones. Understanding the process comes only with experience. No amount of reading can replace this step.

4. *Once it is designed, a great number of trials are required before the game can be considered complete.* Good designers employ dozens of

trials before they conclude that an exercise is finished. Each trial adds perspective on ways to improve the simulation/game.

THREE GAMES

The following three games are complete. One—Command: The Norm Game—was written by the author. The other two were written by others as indicated. The games are listed in alphabetical order.

Command: The Norm Game

This game, which was originally created to teach the concept of norm, can also teach various aspects of language.

In a class of any size, the group is divided into two equal parts. Three students from each half are chosen by the facilitator to represent the team. The two teams receive the following instructions:

> "I am going to give each of you in turn a command and when you do what I expect you to do, you will receive a point. The team with the most points at the end of the game wins."

The facilitator uses four commands:
WALK
SIT
STAND
WRITE

Whenever a player on Team 1 performs the task indicated by the command, the team receives a point. For Team 2, however, the facilitator changes the meaning of the commands. When s/he says WALK (to any member of team two), the facilitator means WRITE. When s/he says SIT (to any member of team two), s/he means WALK. When Team 2 hears STAND, the facilitator means SIT and WRITE for Team 2 means STAND.

Team 1, since it does not need to break a code to proceed, quickly racks up points. Team 2 cannot get any points until it breaks the code. However, its first task is to understand that the terms have different meanings to the two teams. The facilitator can make this easier by repeating the original directions and suggesting that other members of the team who are not players help the three who represent them.

Eventually, Team 2 will break the code and this concludes the game.

As part of the debriefing, the facilitator begins by asking the players about the fairness of the game. This can ultimately lead to a discussion of what a norm is (an expected pattern of behavior that most people will follow) and how language must be norm-based if it is to be understood. The discussion can be extended in many directions depending on the objectives of the facilitator (e.g., students can learn that a law is a norm that will be enforced by the use of force if necessary). This simple game has many applications in many settings.

Freeway Planning Game
Michael Chester

Rules:
Participants are assigned to one of the following groups:
- City Council
- Taxpayers' Association
- University Archeologists
- Residents' Association
- Merchants' Association
- City Engineers

Participants must select a freeway route which goes from any one of the bottom-most hexagons (see map, Figure 8.1) to any one of the six top-most hexagons.

Participants try to plan their freeway so it will cost the group they represent the fewest points—like a golf score. They receive a penalty for length—5 points for each hexagon used, plus a penalty for going through the hexagons with symbols. Each group is penalized differently according to the chart (Figure 8.2). (Note: Penalty is for each symbol, so a hexagon with 2 hills costs the engineer 19 points—five for the hexagon and 7 for each hill.)

First, select a route as an individual with an assigned role.

Second, select a route with all others of the same role (e.g., all engineers, or all City Council members must be grouped for this task).

Third, select a route in a group made up of one member from each role (e.g., 1 engineer, 1 archeologist, 1 City Council member, and so on).

At the end, compute the difference score (e.g., the points received when all members of a group were engineers minus the points received when the group has members representing different roles). Each person and group uses the same scoring system for all sessions. (For example, when there is one person from each role, the engineer scores 7 points for a hill, the taxpayers' association scores 5 points for the same hill, and all others score the hill as 1 point.)

132 CHAPTER 8

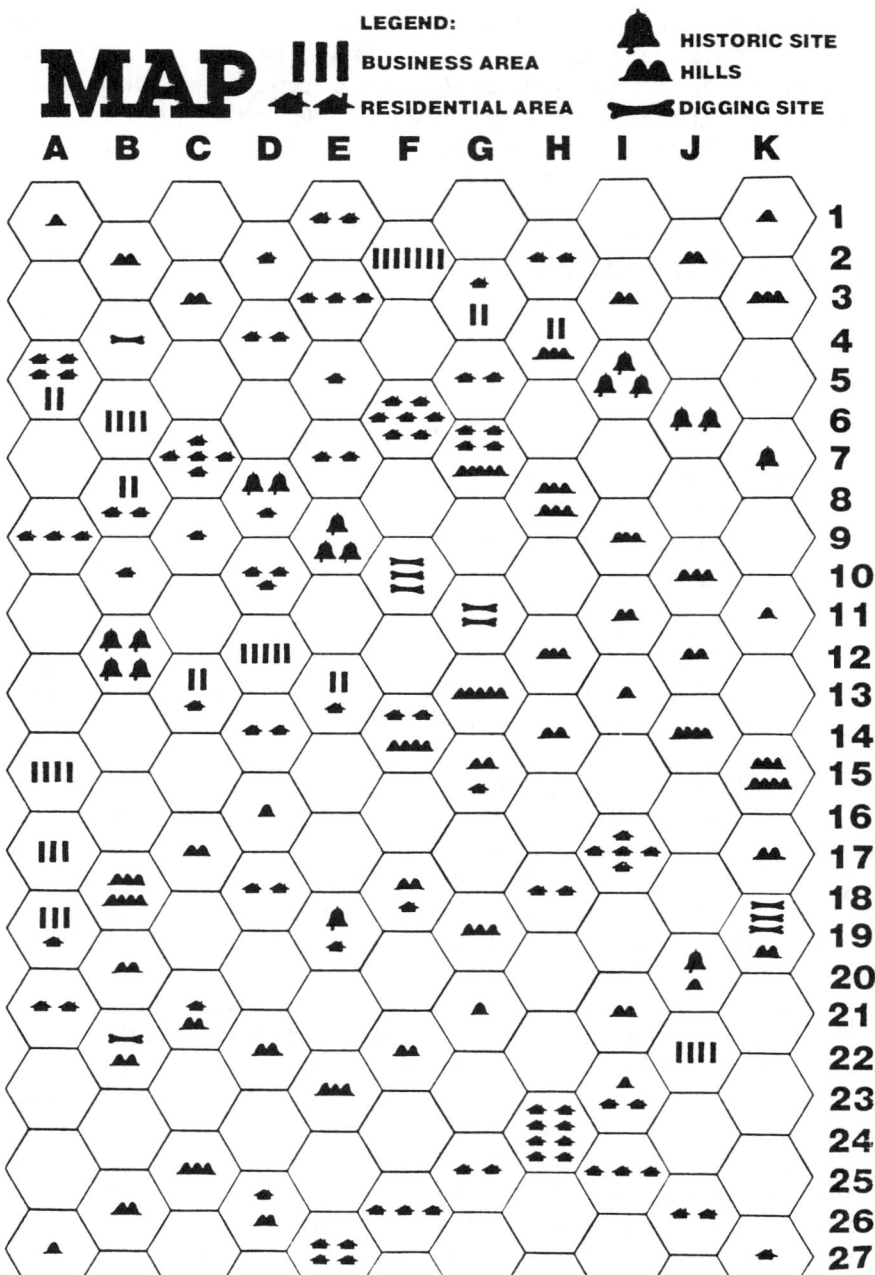

FIGURE 8.1 *Freeway Planning Game (Simile II, P. O. Box 910, Del Mar, CA, 92014).*

		⬆	⬗	▲	🔔	🦴
City Council		5	3	1	1	1
Archeologists		1	1	1	3	5
Taxpayers' Association		1	3	5	1	1
Residents' Association		7	1	1	1	1
Merchants' Association		1	7	1	1	1
City Engineer		1	1	7	1	1

FIGURE 8.2

In the end the group that has the lowest difference score among the six groups (found by adding the second score from each group achieved by members of the original group and dividing by six) wins.

Quick City: A Societal Simulation
P. Douglas McConatha

Quick City is our present condition. The rapidity with which our technological society operates provides us with an ever increasing amount of information about our shrinking world. Yet with the increasing speed of communication and amount of information, there seems to be an inverse response to the credibility of this information. Who is to be believed in our society? We must choose who are to be the "Truth Givers" in our society.

In Quick City as in the larger society, interest groups control our lives and it is necessary to join, voluntarily or involuntarily, such aggregates. In a competitive system like our own capitalistic society, economic powers have a strong lobby for their particular interest. But we also have its counterpart: the social conscious. Social welfare advocates have often found themselves in direct opposition with economic interests in our capitalistic society. There is, however, a supposedly unbiased arbitrator for these conflicts: our political system. (This is true in theory if not in fact.) However, political interest groups also have their interests to protect. Oftentimes, the political segment may play the interests of one group against those of another group and then summon itself as the final arbitrator to benefit the particular administration's goals. This is a practice that is accepted and often condoned.

What of the rest? Apathetic... our silent majority. The apathetic public in Quick City relinquishes its social rights and obligations to any group whose interests are stronger and seemingly more stable than theirs. Occasionally, the apathetic public will bond together and form goals, but usually only after one of two things takes place. One reason may be centered around their increased victimization by other groups, and secondly, there is some degree of infiltration by revolutionaries who have become disenchanted with the structure and objectives of the prominent interest groups.

Any society is vastly more complex than the analogies made in this superficial analysis. But, it is not difficult for one to find a place in this simple society; we are all inhabitants of Quick City. Our personal interests and ideas may be a combination of the various groups in the system, but typically, we align our basic conception of ourselves and of society with one particular group. Broadly speaking, we may fit ourselves into one of the four interest groups which make up Quick City.

This selection of a place in the social structure is the initial requirement for being a citizen of Quick City. The rest is simply a process of determining how one wishes to structure the priorities in the value system of the group and how one goes about accomplishing them.

The purpose of Quick City is to point out realistic community and national conflicts between various interest groups in our society. The game is geared primarily toward our capitalistic economy and democratic form of government; however, the simulation can be employed successfully without these prerequisites.

Some simulations have strict rules governing the number of people who may participate, in addition to crucial time and space allocations that are necessary for conducting the game successfully. Quick City is designed to be extremely flexible in all these areas. Quick City has been conducted with as few as 15 people and with as many as 150. In both extreme cases, as well as the average case (about 40–50 people), the participants became highly involved and the effect was carried off well. In the case of larger numbers, the activity is much more dramatic and audible than with the lesser numbers.

Time allocation is very important in simulations. To gain full impact from most simulations, it is often necessary to continue the game from four to six hours or more, mainly because of the involvement with rules and in order to evoke some ego or self-involvement from the participants. Quick City is designed with a time from one to three hours. The session is usually followed by a group discussion of those elements that are important to the particular orientation of the participants and relative to the interaction that has just transpired.

The number of participants will dictate the size of the room needed for the game. Generally, however, a normal size classroom will suffice;

nevertheless, only one room is required for conducting the simulation. The only requirement is that it be possible for the groups to discuss things without being easily overheard by other groups.

The following directions for administering the game are guidelines based on the experience the author has gained from participating in and running the game. Only five basic rules must be followed and the director of the game must be the final arbitrator in any ambiguous discrepancies that arise. The five basic rules about which the game is conducted are:

I. The four basic interest groups:
   A. Political
   B. Economic
   C. Social Welfare
   D. Apathetic Public
II. Priority system for goals
III. Communication gap
IV. Time sequences
V. Money and power cards

The following instructions for the societal simulation Quick City should be read to the participants prior to beginning the game, and may be repeated throughout the session for clarification purposes.

I. In Quick City, there are four basic interest groups, each with a set of specific goals to achieve. These groups are:
   A. *The Political Group* whose goals are:
      1. to distribute money and power among the other groups as they see fit.
      2. to gain support from all groups (i.e., the other groups must trust your motives. This is assessed by a majority show of hands from the other three groups).
      3. to maintain the power equilibrium in the society (i.e., each group should have one power card).
   B. *The Economic Group* whose goals are:
      1. to obtain 50% of all the power.
      2. to obtain 50% of all the money.
      3. to choose one of the following:
         a. maintain the system.
         b. maintain only the political system.
         c. maintain the political system and Apathetic Public. ("Maintain" means that the group to be supported or maintained must achieve its particular goals during this time

sequence. If the group is not maintained, then the goal has not been accomplished.)
C. *Social Welfare Group* whose goals are:
1. to distribute money and power evenly.
2. to establish communications with all groups (i.e., the groups must trust your motives. Assessed by a majority show of hands from the other three groups).
3. to create goals for the Apathetic Public. (These goals must be in written form and in the possession of the Apathetic Public.)
D. *Apathetic Public* whose goals are:
none. The Apathetic Public must submit to the wishes of any group (e.g., relinquish their money cards) until they, by majority vote, have agreed on at least one specific goal for the group. The goals created by the Social Welfare Group may be used for this purpose. (This group is a catch-all for students who do not wish to participate or who wish only to observe. It is also the focal point for activity as the game progresses.)

After these groups and goals have been expressed to the class, the instructor asks the participants to join the group in which they see their own particular interests aligned. The participants are asked to reseat themselves in the assigned manner.

The choices having been made and the groups separated, each group then receives a blank 4-by-6 index card.

II. Each group must now, by majority opinion, be asked to structure its goals on a priority system. The three goals for the group are numbered in the order in which the group decides to achieve them. Priority 1 is achieved first, priority 2 is achieved second, and so forth. The goals can be structured in any order, but emphasis should be placed on realistically structuring the priorities. The group may want to achieve the most difficult goal first and save the easier ones for last or vice-versa. In any event, the goals are to be approached and solved in the order of priority set up by the particular group.

III. The communication gap in our society is an accepted part of social behavior. The question is: How much of the information we receive daily do we believe as truthful? In general and from discussions with original groups, it was found that only 25 percent of the information that is received is considered trustworthy. In order to include this element of realism in Quick City a communication device is introduced. Each group may select one other group from which it will receive truthful information, as indicated on the reverse side of the priority card. The group so designated will be instructed by the game director to tell the truth to this group again by indicating so on the reverse side of the priority card. Any group may withhold information from another, but if information is given by a designated group, it must be truthful. Truthful information may be provided to other groups at the discretion of the group providing the information. Lies may be told as they are in the real world. After the priorities have been set and the trust group selected, the director temporarily collects the cards and makes the necessary indications for truth giving. The cards are then returned.

IV. In line with the three goals that each group must achieve, the game is divided into three time sequences, each of an arbitrary length, depending on the time allotted for the entire game. (They are usually about 15 to 20 minutes each but are flexible at the discretion of the game director.) The action of the game is concentrated within each of the three time sequences and the game is in progress only while the time sequences are in effect. During the first time sequence, the groups are concerned with achieving their first priority goal only. For example, if the Economic Group has chosen as its first priority to obtain 50 percent of all power, then at the end of the first time sequence it must possess 50 percent of all power in Quick City (i.e., two power cards). Once the goal has been met or the time sequence ended, the group is no longer concerned with that goal.

The consequences for failing to achieve the particular goal during its corresponding time sequence result in a penalty for the group. This penalty is the focal point for action in Quick City. When failure to achieve a certain goal occurs, the penalized group loses one-third of its total population to the Apathetic Public. Failure to achieve any goal results in a one-third depletion of the original population of the group. It can be seen that failure to achieve all three goals would result in a total depletion of that group's population. At the end of each time sequence, then, one-third of each group that has failed to achieve its particular goal must remove itself and sit with the Apathetic Public. The decision as to who is to be removed is left up to the public. This rule does not apply to the Apathetic Public.

V. In Quick City, as in any city, money and power are tools for exchange. They exist as Money and Power cards—which are fashioned out of 4-by-6 index cards. On four cards the director should write the word, "POWER," and on four other cards, s/he should place a $ sign. Possession of at least one Money or Power card is necessary for the survival of a group at the end of the third time sequence. In order for a group to be considered a viable and participating part of the city, it must present *either* one Money *or* one Power card at the end of the game. These Money and Power cards are given to the Political Group at the beginning of the first time sequence to do with as it deems fit.

Debriefing the Game

The debriefing of Quick City should include the following: 1) initial perceptions of the simulation; 2) the model itself; 3) the operating sessions and their progress; 4) the results of the simulation itself; and 5) the learning achievements.

Quick City can be scored by giving each team one point each round for achieving its goal and subtracting one point from each team each round for failing to achieve a goal. If no goal exists for the Apathetic Public for any given time sequence, it receives zero points. Thus for each group, the score can range from -9 to $+9$. Since being ahead or behind after each round is clearly visible to the participants by the number of persons remaining in the group, scoring is optional and can perhaps be most effective if left to the very end after the game has been concluded.

AN ANNOTATED LIST OF SIMULATION/GAMES

Hundreds, perhaps thousands, of quality simulation games are available for use in the classroom. The following, listed in alphabetical order, represent but a small sample. They are drawn from many different areas and they indicate the many types of games that are available. The resources provided at the beginning of this chapter offer additional sources of games—the number of which grows continually. Additional games are discussed in Chapter 10.

Auction **(Creative Learning Systems, Inc.)**

This simulation helps students become aware of how attitudes and values affect their choices. It simulates a real auction in which players have 200 "dillies"—play dollars. All participants receive catalogues which describe items available for purchase at the auction. They also obtain budget and bid sheets to help them plan strategy. They can purchase perfect health, revenge, a homework machine, intelligence, a terrific party, and other such items in a catalogue that contains twenty-four items. The actual auction is conducted by the auctioneer—either the teacher or a competent student. Players must be careful not to spend more than their 200 dillies. The debriefing of this game leads to much helpful value clarification and value analysis.

Bafa Bafa (Simile II)

Bafa Bafa simulates two different cultures—alpha and beta. Each society has its own rules of interaction and behavior. The details of these rules are basically unknown to the other society. The game's purpose is to facilitate the ability to interact with an alien culture. To this end, the game is divided into three stages: 1) Players learn and practice the rules of the culture. 2) They visit the other society in order to figure out as much as they can about the people's rules. 3) Students engage in discussion and debriefing about their experience.

Part of the strength of the simulation comes from the fact that the two cultures have very different sets of values and this makes understanding between the Alphans and the Betans difficult to achieve. Differences in language and behaviors also contribute to the problem.

Bafa Bafa is one of the many Simile II games which are fun to play and profound in their contribution to understanding through the process of simulation and gaming. Courses in sociology, anthropology, and history can benefit from its use.

Beat Detroit (Antler Productions)

This is a board game in which the players learn to deal with problems that arise from automobile ownership. The primary objective of each player is to be able to own, maintain, and drive his or her car without going broke. Participants must examine all of the issues related to ownership (warranties, insurance, repair costs, recalls, used vs. new cars, and status) in a way that provides improved strategies for owning a car. *Beat Detroit* can be used with economics courses, consumer economics courses, and courses related to personal growth.

Computerize (KaySibs Ltd.)

This game bills itself as a cross between a board game and a computer. Actually it is a board game which teaches about the use of computers to beginners in computer studies. The object is to have each player purchase all the components and accessories listed on the shopping list that comes with the game. The first person who becomes fully computerized is the winner. The game is fun to play and provides an excellent introduction to the confusing world of computers. It helps players learn how a computer fits together and how to make good choices about accessories. The package provides a useful glossary which makes playing the game easier and which adds to an understanding of the process.

Culture Contact (ABT Associates)

This exciting simulation examines some of the same issues as *Bafa Bafa* but in a somewhat simpler manner. (Actually, both games could be used in the same course to teach comparative cultures by having students examine the reality orientation of the two games with relation to the particular society they are studying.) *Culture Contact* examines the problems that occur when a group of sailors is forced to land and to negotiate with a group of islanders. The simulation/game can lead to either accommodation between the two groups or destruction of one side by the other. Players often become so deeply involved in the role-playing that in the debriefing session it is easy to demonstrate the occurrence and intensity of conflict between cultures. *Culture Contact* can be used in sociology and anthropology courses as well as in classes that examine conflict.

Dangerous Parallel (Foreign Policy Association)

This game simulates the events of the Korean War. It teaches about a real and significant historical event in an exciting and interesting manner at the same time that it examines the many complexities of foreign policy issues. The simulation presents a situation in which a conflict threatens world peace. Participants are divided into six imaginary nations. Each nation has a chief minister and two to five supporting ministers in his or her cabinet. During each round, students go from one country to another hoping to negotiate a peaceful solution to the crisis. The teacher acts as Control, interpreting the results of each round. Although the game is based on the Korean War, it allows for other outcomes than those that actually occurred. Students learn how nations enter into violent conflicts and how these conflicts might be avoided. The game can be used effectively in history and government courses.

Democracy (Western Publishing Company)

This highly successful simulation/game has players assume the roles of legislators who try to pass bills into laws through a process of negotiation and lobbying. *Democracy* demonstrates the potential conflict that exists between a legislator's own point of view and the needs of his or her constituents. The simulation consists of several versions; this allows the teacher to introduce increasingly complex aspects of the legislative process as succeeding versions are played. The game is useful for government courses as well as any course that studies the complexities of decision making.

Energy X (Ideal School Supply Company)

This simulation thoroughly examines the problem of energy in the United States. *Energy X* contains a multimedia kit that includes a slide tape presentation and other data presented in interesting ways. It is essentially a role-play game in which players take the roles of representatives of different sections of the United States who try to convince a board of control to give a new and limited energy supply to their region. This complex and somewhat lengthy exercise is not difficult to play. It requires several class periods and it offers suggestions to teachers to expand it to a consideration of the many issues surrounding energy. *Energy X* can be used in many types of courses including geography, science, and courses that are interested in future studies.

Expressway (Scholastic TAB Publications, Ltd.)

Expressway demonstrates the competing demands that occur whenever decisions must be made about the environment. The players assume various roles. Some play members of a legislative committee attempting to decide on whether or not an expressway should be completed. Others portray persons who are for or against the project. The roles are very well defined for the players. It can be played in a relatively short time (forty to sixty minutes). *Expressway* teaches much about geography and social issues. It works well with many age levels from middle school to graduate school. It emphasizes the interdisciplinary nature of social problems such as highway construction that cannot be solved or understood from the perspective of any single discipline.

Failsafe (The Minnesota Education Computing Center)

This game is based on the book by Burdick and Wheeler and is played on a computer. *Failsafe* is an exciting experience based on role-play. It examines the process of executive decision-making. Players attempt to arrive at a solution to the problem of runaway bombers aimed at the Soviet Union. In addition to learning about decision making, the game provides a useful way to acquaint students with computers and hence can be used as an introductory activity in the many computer courses now being offered in the schools. *Failsafe* always leads to intense involvement on the part of players who achieve an affective as well as cognitive understanding of the problem of controlling the nuclear arsenal.

Flight (Interact)

This game helps players develop map-reading skills as they practice small-group decision making and incidentally learn about the hazards of flying in lightweight aircraft. *Flight,* primarily for use in geography classes, is excellent in that it can teach the necessary but not always interesting skill of map reading in an exciting way. Students play the game in teams consisting of a pilot, co-pilot, and navigator. As the exercise proceeds, players must change their plans to adjust to weather, geographical hazards, availability of fuel, and rules relating to elevation and mileage. The simulation ends when a team completes a race over an imaginary continent. The winner is determined by the distance flown and the quality of the diary entry kept by the co-pilot. *Flight* has many applications and is an excellent game for teaching skills.

Future Decisions—The IQ Game (The Simulation and Gaming Association)

Future Decisions uses role-play to orient players to future studies. The scenario describes the discovery of a drug that can raise IQ scores. This miraculous material, however, is available only in limited quantities. Players must decide who gets the drug; they become aware of the problems that may exist in the future as a result of such findings. Students also understand the increasing difficulty of attempting to cope with such changes. This simulation contains a systematic debriefing procedure. It offers a vivid experience to students about a problem that comes to feel frighteningly real. Sociology courses and courses dealing with future studies will find this game useful.

The Game of Farming (Macmillan Publishing Company)

Originally produced as part of the High School Geography Project, this game reflects actual events that affected Midwestern farmers during three periods of American history. It remains a highly relevant exercise today as American farmers continue to battle for survival. Players assume the role of farmers and try to anticipate climate and market conditions in order to make a profit. *The Game of Farming* can be used in economics, history, and geography courses. It demonstrates the multitude of difficulties involved in farming in the United States, and also develops empathy for the farmer, a quality often missing among those who live in urban areas.

Inner City Housing

(In *Simulation Games* by Samuel Livingston and Clarice Stasz Stoll, Free Press, 1973)
    This simulation examines problems of inner city housing from the perspective of both tenants and landlords. Players must first take one role and then the other. This role reversal allows them to gain insight into the problem from the point of view of everyone concerned. *Inner City Housing* develops empathy for both landlords (who often have problems not perceived by the general public) and tenants (who often have difficulty getting their needs met). The game provides appropriate balance and is useful in sociology, economics, and geography, as well as in courses that seek to develop sensitivity to the plight of the poor.

Interdepartmental Decision Making

(In *On College Teaching* edited by Ohmer Milton, Jossey Bass, 1978)
    This role-play simulation examines the process of decision making in higher education as it responds to the competing demands of the various constituencies in academic life. The scenario involves the need to dispose of a surplus of funds before the end of the current fiscal year. Six department heads from Metropolitan College meet with the dean to decide what to do with the money. The remaining members of the class play the roles of college trustees who have the ultimate authority to make the decision. If the chairpersons cannot make the decision, the choice is made by the dean. Each department has legitimate needs and achieving agreement seems very difficult. The game demonstrates how needs in an institution usually exceed the resources available. *Interdepartmental Decision Making* can be used in courses studying economics, sociology, government, or decision making.

Kommisar (Selchow and Righter Company)

This board game is commercial rather than educational in origin. It parodies the Soviet system as a kind of "Russian Monopoly game"—presenting Russia as seen by Americans. The goal of the players is to amass enough wealth to be able to escape the Soviet Union. *Kommisar* is fun to play. Its major educational value lies in the satire which is so broad that it can be used as a means of reality testing in conjunction with studies of the Soviet system. It could be played before and after such a study as a way of seeing to what extent students can see the difference between how the Soviet Union really works and the stereotypes by which people in the United States often perceive it.

Lifestyles (World Future Society)

The objective of this interesting board game is to have players live as happily as possible. It enables players to explore their own ideas of happiness while examining their reactions to the kinds of personal experiences and world conditions that may occur in the future. Students work their way around a board that represents years of living. As rounds take place they grow older and experience things that happen in life (marriage, birth, promotion, demotion, death, and the like). The game helps students examine their values as well as their ability to accommodate to the unexpected. It allows players to probe future events in both the world and in their own lives even while helping them experience the present. *Lifestyles* is a useful game for any course examining future studies and value clarification.

Mankala (Brookstone Company)

Mankala, a board game which originated in Africa, requires two players. Each player tries to capture more of the thirty-six stones on the board than the other. The game ends when one side of the board is completely emptied of stones. *Mankala* is a kind of African checkers game. Players must learn good strategies and it thus fosters critical thinking skills. When players become adept at the game, they move the stones rapidly (something Africans can do easily and westerners have trouble accomplishing). *Mankala* is exciting to play and enlightening because it introduces an authentic activity from another culture. This game can be played in any course that examines cross-cultural studies as well as courses in which strategy skills are being taught.

Mastermind (Invicta Plastics)

This is one of the most successful board games ever. Its sales in one year briefly surpassed those of *Monopoly*. The object of the game is for one player—the code breaker—to discover a secret code established by the other player—the code maker. The original version of the game uses codes based on colors (six of them). More recent versions of the game also use words and numbers in place of colors. *Mastermind* is also available at varying levels of difficulty. An outstanding game that includes chance, strategy, puzzle-solving, and an aesthetic dimension, it can be used to teach logic and critical thinking skills. Computer versions are also available under different names and slightly different formats.

Nostalgia (Creative Communications)

Nostalgia is difficult to classify but fun to play. Players draw cards requiring them to enact scenes that are based on events that occurred in the 1920s and 1930s. Following each enactment, the other players rate the performance and the higher the rating, the further the person who has done the acting may proceed on the game board. The first person to reach the end of the board wins. *Nostalgia* is suitable for history, English, and drama courses; it can be used by teachers to prepare students for more spontaneous role-play.

The Propaganda Game (Wiff 'N Proof)

In this game, players compete to be the most effective in identifying a variety of propaganda techniques. The game contains fifty-six techniques and divides them into six categories. One player reads an example of a device and the other participants must determine what type it exemplifies. The player who is most effective in identifying persuasion devices wins the game. *Propaganda* is one of the best games designed especially for teaching critical thinking skills. It is nicely balanced in that it offers some depth with regard to its content but does not overwhelm the players with material to be learned. This game can be used in many courses (e.g., English, social studies, logic) that seek to improve thinking skills.

The Railroad Game (Xerox Education Publications)

The Railroad Game, developed as part of the Harvard Social Studies Project by Donald Oliver, Fred M. Newmann, and James Shaver, simulates the intense competition between American railroads in the 1870s. Players divide into four groups representing four different small railroads. The companies seek to cary iron ore from Oretown to Steeltown. Each round in the game represents one business day. The object of each team is to make a profit while working with fixed and variable costs. This game is useful both as a historical game and one from which students can learn economics. It also provides opportunity for value analysis.

Starpower (Simile II)

This is one of the best-known and most successful of all simulation/games. *Starpower* builds a three-tiered society in which those at the bottom are placed permanently into a caste whereas those at the top make rules and begin to discriminate against those below them. The game has great emotional impact. It teaches the effects of rigid social stratification in an extremely dramatic way. Students playing the game report a remarkable level of frustration and anger since the exercise is only a simulation. *Starpower* has great potential as a device for teaching attitudes and it can be very effective in helping students clarify their own values. It can be used to teach sociology, human relations, and much else.

Values (Friendship Press)

This board game forces players to examine their values. The longer the game is played the more intense it becomes. *Values* can lead to an emotionally meaningful experience, and it is an excellent value-clarification exercise. The object of winning is soon lost in the process of value examination. Players move around a board and draw questions. They can elect to pass, state their own values, or ask other players to expound on their points of view. The many courses that examine values (English, social studies, and so on) will find this game useful. Because of its sensitive nature, the role of the facilitator is crucial.

Voyage of the Mimi (Holt, Rinehart and Winston)

This game is a computer simulation in ecology. The exercise has two parts. In the first, plants and animals are selected for a balanced ecosystem. During this phase, students are required to set up a food web. The players receive cards containing information about the plants and animals. The building of the ecosystem usually generates much discussion among the players. The second phase of the exercise involves an adventure where activities directly affect the populations of plants and animals on the island. The participant goes through a year of survival. Random events can occur that affect planning and final outcomes. *Voyage of the Mimi* can be used in science classes as well as social studies classes. It is an interesting computer simulation that can acquaint students with computers.

What Would You Do? (Minnesota Educational Computing Consortium)

This computer simulation requires decision making and the planning of strategy. The scenario involves a fur trapping expedition in northern Minnesota. The object is to complete the trip in the least amount of days while obtaining the largest amount of furs. At the beginning, each player decides how many supplies to take along and s/he must choose between such items as clothing, gunpowder, food, tobacco, and trading goods. As the trip progresses, the computer provides updates on conditions and morale. The successful player reaches Rainy Lake with large quantities of furs. This interesting game is both fun and enlightening. It can be useful in American history courses and for teaching the concept of culture contact.

SUMMARY

This chapter has described ways to use the process of simulation/gaming. It began with a discussion of how to use, evaluate, and design games. Mastery of this material is critical for one who wishes to become an effective game facilitator in the classroom. The chapter also provided resources for those who wish to pursue the use of games in further depth. It offered readers three complete games which can be used in a variety of classrooms. The use of these games can serve as an introduction to the process of simulation/gaming. The last section of this chapter annotated twenty-six games, drawn from a wide variety of disciplines, in order to help the reader understand the breadth of available resources and in order to help him or her begin the process of learning to select games for use in his or her own setting.

CHAPTER

9

Future Studies

PROLOGUE

Students stretch out on the carpeted floor of the classroom or lounge back in their chairs. Phyllis has kicked off her shoes and now lies comfortably prone with her hands folded upon her stomach, her eyes closed.

"Breathe energy into your body," the soft voice of the instructor is saying, "breathe tension out. Breathe the energy into your body, way down into your toes. Feel the energy in your toes. Be aware of each toe, relaxed and energized. Breathe the tension out." He continues with soothing instructions for the participants to breathe energy into the feet, the knees, the thighs, the hips. "Stomachs," he goes on, "are a source of tension for many people. Breathe the energy into your stomach. Feel each muscle relax in response to the energy. Breathe that tension out . . ."

Phyllis is mildly aware that her body feels cooler, looser; she is more in sync with its rhythms.

"Feel the tension roll off your face as you breathe energy into your cheeks, your nose, your lips, your chin. Feel it slide off your forehead as you breathe energy in."

Students have lost all awareness of one another. Each is a cool, relaxed body floating somewhere between consciousness and sleep.

"You have just received a letter," says the instructor. "Picture yourself opening the letter to find out that you have been selected to go on a trip to outer space. You may choose a friend to go along with you, or you may go alone. What things will you bring with you?

"See yourself arriving at the take-off site. You're impressed with how it looks, with how it feels to be here. You board the ship, buckle your belt, and await the blast-off. 10, 9, 8, 7, 6, 5, 4, 3, 2, 1 . . .

"You feel the gravitational pull drop away and you gradually become weightless as the rocket travels further away from the earth. In a short while, you arrive at your destination. You step off the ship and look out into the world about you. What things do you see? Are there colors? What sounds do you hear? What does this new world smell like?

"You discover you are weightless and you bounce away from the ship into your new environment. Take a few moments to enjoy this world by yourself or with your friend."

The instructor has paused, noting the deep breathing and happy faces of the students. Phyllis and her boyfriend are bounding off into a land of polka dots. They discover that they can play with the dots, bouncing them and throwing them, or they can eat them. What an unusual, delicious flavor! They can take two or more dots and put them together. Phyllis sees herself laughing, feeling light-hearted and very, very happy.

"Okay," says the instructor, "it's time to return to earth." You and your friend say your good-byes to your new planet and board the spaceship once more. You buckle yourself in and begin the flight home.

"After touchdown, you disembark and see who is there at the spaceport to greet you. You begin to tell them about your trip . . .

"Slowly, at your own pace, come back to this room with your experience. Gradually you may open your eyes."

Students begin to stir, slowly stretching their bodies, opening their eyes, and sitting up. Faces wear looks of fresh awareness and rest. When they are all 'back', they form a circle and begin to share their experiences.

The technique of guided fantasy sends people on excursions into their imaginations. It is a creative exercise that is often used as a warm-up for some kinds of therapy.

In the trip just described, persons examine a new planet; they construct pleasant scenes in their minds. In another kind of guided fantasy, participants recall a childhood toy. They return to a day in their lives when they were young, reliving a happy time in the past. Another exercise offers persons the opportunity to project themselves into the future. They travel one year, five years, or perhaps fifty years, into the future.

Then the facilitator slowly brings them back to the here and now.
When people participate in guided fantasy that takes place in the past, they use their minds and memories readily. When they experience a fantasy that requires the construction of alternative imaginary surroundings, positive feelings generally result. They remember their childhood fondly, or they arrive on new planets and enjoy them. But when the facilitator asks them to project themselves into the future, many persons become anxious. They report uncomfortable emotions as they think about the time to come; often they feel frightened. Students who take part in several guided fantasies usually enjoy the ones about the future least of all. They fail to understand the future and they approach it not with excitement and anticipation, but with dread. All persons, however, must enter the future, willingly or not. What is amiss?

Another teaching technique also demonstrates this difficulty. A class is divided into two parts and is given a story to complete. The tale describes a parent who discovers that his or her child is experiencing a problem. The two parts of the class write about the same incident. But unknown to them, one half of the group has received the story written in the past tense, whereas the other half has obtained it in the future tense.

When persons are allowed to write as long as they wish, those receiving the event described in the past tense compose significantly longer endings than those who continue the future scenario. This suggests again that the future, although it demands accommodation, remains formidable for many persons to contemplate, despite the absolutely critical need to do so.

In Chapter 10, a game entitled "Building a Future Community" is presented. This simulation asks students to arrange pictures representing various aspects of society to create a community they desire. The game also contains blank cards on which players must add new institutions that do not exist in the present but could exist in the future. Students find it much easier to arrange the given pictures than to create new institutions for tomorrow. They resist the open-ended part of the exercise, often leaving this task to the end. They need constant support from the facilitator in order to complete it. This, too, is evidence that contemplating the future often fills persons with anxiety.

INTRODUCTION: THE NEED FOR FUTURE STUDIES

The future frightens many people. Yet it demands accommodation. The need to prepare students to anticipate life in the future supports the need for future studies. This strategy helps students go beyond problem solving (an outcome resulting from the strategies of facilitating creative behavior and simulation/gaming) to problem anticipation. In order to survive in the world to come, human beings will need to become aware of problems before they become so difficult as to be insoluble.

Three contemporary thinkers—Isaac Asimov, John Brockman, and John Naisbitt—have written books that demonstrate the need for the study of the future.

Isaac Asimov: *A Choice of Catastrophes*

In this book, Asimov examines many potential catastrophes that could lead to the end of human existence.[1] He describes five classes of catastrophes.

The first type might occur if the universe experiences a change so drastic as to become uninhabitable. Asimov labels this a "Catastrophe of the First Class." He also describes a "Catastrophe of the Second Class," which would take place if something happened to the sun that led to the end of the solar system. A third-class catastrophe is one in which the solar system survives but the planet earth perishes. A fourth-class catastrophe is one in which the universe, the solar system, and the earth all remain intact but human life ends. Finally, Asimov discusses "Catastrophes of the Fifth Class." He defines these as situations in which human life survives but civilization, as it is now constituted, is destroyed, leaving persons to live in a primitive kind of subsistence culture.

Asimov describes the kind of events that can bring about each kind of disaster and indicates the probabilities of their occurrence. First-class catastrophes involve black holes, quasars, and the changing nature of gravity. The most serious of these disasters is based on current scientific theories about the nature of the origin of the universe. These theories hold that the universe originated from the explosion of a "cosmic egg" that expanded and continues to expand to a finite limit. When that limit is reached, the process will reverse itself. The universe will contract and return to the cosmic egg, ceasing to exist in its present form. Scientists believe that this will cause another explosion and the entire process will repeat itself. Current scientific thinking, according to Asimov, is that the end of the universe is inevitable. However, it will take trillions of years for this to occur and therefore it is not a problem that requires much concern.

Catastrophes of the second class are also ones that will occur in the very distant future. The most likely is the inevitable death of the sun. This will take millions of years; it is a problem that humankind will have to face if it still exists during the final stages of the solar system.

Catastrophes leading to the destruction of the earth before the death of the sun are less likely, according to Asimov. The planet faces some danger from bombardment by extraterrestial objects like comets, asteroids, and meteorites. The earth also faces destruction from the removal of magnetism and from glaciation. Some possibility exists that volcanoes, earthquakes, and the changing nature of tides can destroy the earth, but these catastrophes are less likely than the certainty of the sun's death and the ultimate contraction of the universe.

Fourth- and fifth-class catastrophes contain the most imminent danger. Fourth-class catastrophes include the danger of infectious disease, war, and nuclear destruction. Asimov discusses the development of nonhuman intelligence which could compete with human life and ultimately destroy it.

Catastrophes of the fifth class—situations in which human life survives but civilization perishes—are the most likely and the most immediate threats that face humankind. Disasters involving the diminishing energy supply, the end of renewable items (including water, minerals, and certain precious metals), and the danger that population growth will reach a point resulting in mass starvation are ones that threaten life as it now exists.

The potential catastrophes described by Asimov support the need for future studies. Asimov is relatively optimistic about humankind's ability to avert the most immediate catastrophes, and he is even optimistic about the possibility of human life surviving the death of the sun. But in order to survive these potential crises, humankind must prepare for life in the future. And it must do this in the face of evidence that indicates anticipating the time to come is a very difficult task for most people. Therefore, developing a future studies strategy—one that prepares persons to anticipate and define problems in time to find solutions—is imperative.

John Brockman: *Einstein, Gertrude Stein, Wittgenstein & Frankenstein*

In this book, writer John Brockman presents the thesis that reality is not objective but rather invented by human beings as a means of explaining and bringing closure to the world around them.[2] Brockman describes five "invented" universes. These include the cosmological universe of astronomy, the quantum universe of physics, the biological universe, the mathematical universe, and an unorthodox universe that includes religion. Humankind devises these constructs in order to understand the complexity of the phenomena confronting them.

As an example of invention, Brockman describes the search for unification theory in science. He indicates how theories of electricity were connected to theories of magnetism. This paved the way for electric engines, x-rays, and telecommunications. Brockman says that further unification theory (including an ultimate one which explains everything from a single perspective) will bring about even greater technological change than the tying together of magnetism with electricity.

Like Asimov, Brockman is concerned with the question of the development of artificial intelligence. In discussing the work of Norbert Wiener, Brockman says:

> Norbert Wiener once warned that the computer revolution should be greeted as being even more transformative than the Industrial Revolution was. As Wiener pointed out, whereas the Industrial Revolution changed society, the computer revolution will change the nature of change itself. For just as the Industrial Revolution extended our muscle power, computers are extending the powers of our minds, the organs responsible for inventing the technology in the first place. With the advent of computers capable of mimicking human thought, the inventing process will bend back upon itself; what new universes this feedback loop between man and machine will invent is anyone's guess.[3]

Brockman's central thesis is that humankind advances by reinventing the universe regularly—by redefining it in ways that lead to technological and social progress. The ultimate reality need not concern thinkers as long as the invented reality functions. However, as he suggests with regard to the computer revolution, each redefinition creates new issues and problems to be solved. Furthermore, each reinvention opens the possibility for still further redefinition.

The strategy of future studies can provide human beings with the ability to solve these new problems and ultimately to become adept at the reinvention process itself—a necessary procedure if further progress is to be made and if the catastrophes described by Asimov are to be avoided.

John Naisbitt: *Megatrends*

The complex issues demanding the development of future studies described by Asimov and Brockman have been captured in a less abstract and perhaps more easily understandable manner by John Naisbitt in his book on trends.[4]

Naisbitt identifies ten megatrends that require understanding as the United States continues to move toward the twenty-first century.

First, Naisbitt argues, there has been a shift from an industrial society to one that is based on the creation and distribution of information. This relates to the development of computers addressed by both Asimov and Brockman.

Second, Naisbitt indicates that the United States has moved from what he calls "forced technology" (based on the industrial machines) to high tech-high touch—a process in which each high-tech invention requires a particular human response.

A third megatrend identified by Naisbitt is the development of a world economy that has replaced the national economies of the past. The implications of this are enormous. This development requires that persons view the nature of work in a totally different manner.

Naisbitt also sees a shift from short-term rewards to long-term ones. This trend applies primarily to American business where companies, according to Naisbitt, are willing to take a longer-term view of success than they have in the past. This represents a fourth trend.

A movement from centralization to decentralization is still a fifth trend identified by Naisbitt. He offers the growing efficacy of state and local government in the United States as an example of this and he believes that Congress will become an obsolete institution.

There is also a trend, Naisbitt says, from institutional help to self-help. This can clearly be seen in the approach of the Reagan administration toward many social problems and it can also be seen in developments in other western nations as well.

Related to trends five and six is a trend toward participatory democracy to replace representative democracy. Naisbitt sees more and more direct voter participation in decision making (through referenda and through voter-initiated proposals). Consistent with this is the eighth trend in which networking among people replaces hierarchies.

In the United States, Naisbitt sees a trend from the North to South as the southern part of the nation becomes a more crucial part of the national economy.

Naisbitt concludes his discussion with a tenth megatrend—a movement from either/or decisions to decisions based on multiple options. This follows from the other trends since most of the changes Naisbitt sees result in a greater number of choices at all levels of decision making.

The first two paragraphs of Naisbitt's concluding essay (with ideas related to a conceptualization first advanced by Toffler) indicate the ways in which a study of megatrends underscores the need for the development of the strategy of future studies. Naisbitt writes:

> We are living in the *time of the parenthesis,* the time between eras. It is as though we have bracketed off the present from both the past and the future, for we are neither here nor there. We have not

quite left behind the either/or America of the past—centralized, industrialized, and economically self-contained. With one foot in the old world where we lived mostly in the Northeast, relied on institutional help, built hierarchies, and elected representatives, we approached problems with an eye toward the high-tech, short-term solutions.

But we have not embraced the future either. We have done the human thing. We are clinging to the known past in fear of an unknown future. This book outlines one interpretation of that future in order to make it more real, more knowable. Those who are willing to handle the ambiguity of this in-between period and to anticipate the new era will be a quantum leap ahead of those who hold on to the past. The time of the parenthesis is a time of change and questioning.[5]

Undoubtedly time will demonstrate that some of Naisbitt's megatrends are only superficial changes that do not last. Time will also support the accuracy of some of his projections. *Megatrends* adds to the need for future studies because it indicates the broad scope of changes that are occurring in American and world society. The enormity of these changes requires the kind of skills obtained from the formal study of the future.

THE NATURE OF FUTURE STUDIES

A number of generalizations concerning the nature of future studies can be made as a means of defining the process.

Future studies seeks to enlarge and extend social perspectives about the time to come; this remains its primary purpose. It seeks to help students develop better and more sophisticated ways of thinking about the future. Future studies, as a strategy, attempts to reduce the anxiety that many people feel when they try to anticipate what is yet to be. Over the last decade, growing numbers of scholars have used increasingly sophisticated methods to study the future. Beginning as an esoteric rarity, future studies has become a respectable academic pursuit.

A goal of future studies is to predict and make forecasts about the future. As indicated in Chapter 1, attempts to extrapolate the future from the present often fail. Therefore, the strategy of future studies includes not only sophisticated techniques for prediction but also means for enabling students to anticipate problems more effectively. The strategies of facilitating creative behavior and simulation/gaming are synergistic with the process of future studies. Helping persons become more creative makes them better gamers. The technique of simulation/gaming facilitates creative behavior. Creative persons are competent game players and are also more able to anticipate the time to come. The development of effective skills for anticipating the future requires that persons have knowledge, skills, and attitudes that enable them to more effectively cope with change. Future studies also seeks to provide students with a sense of the social responsibilities that are necessary for living in a technological society.

One premise of future studies is that the future cannot be accurately predicted. Rather the time to come must be conceptualized in a variety of ways. The strategy of gaming, for example, has been described by Duke as a "futures language." Varieties of futures languages exist (including systems analysis and cartography). Some of these are presented in the next chapter on techniques for facilitating future studies.

Social life in the future will be increasingly global in nature. A premise that underlies future studies is that it must prepare students to understand the worldwide nature of life in the future. Future studies seeks to make students less provincial, more open to the perspective that human beings consist of a single family of persons who share the planet earth and must deal with its survival together.

Futurists believe in the existence of many possible futures rather than a single determined one. Therefore the technique seeks to identify many possible scenarios and to evaluate the advantages or disadvantages of each. Hence, part of the strategy of future studies involves the study of how to clarify and analyze value choices.

The analysis of the nature of change is one aspect of the study of the future. Futurists recognize that the rate of change has accelerated (causing what Toffler has described as "future shock"). The effect of change on individuals and on societies is part of the process of future studies. Furthermore, the strategy seeks to prepare persons for change and to make it less frightening and less threatening.

Future studies, like gaming and creativity, is a highly interdisciplinary strategy. It represents one of the new subject matters invented in the latter portion of the twentieth century to deal with problems that did not fit into any of the established disciplines. Future studies seeks answers to problems about the time to come by drawing on the many areas of human knowledge and seeking to integrate them.

As a result of its interdisciplinary nature, future studies seeks to understand the nature of many systems and how they interact. Thus the strategy of future studies can be applied to economic systems as well as ecosystems. It can be applied to natural as well as social ones. Futurists are concerned with environmental issues and with issues relating to the quality of social life for individuals. Future studies also seeks to explore the boundaries between the natural world and the social one.

Those who study the future tend to be optimistic. Isaac Asimov, for example, sees a futuristic solution to the enormous problem of overpopulation. In his book, *Extraterrestial Civilizations,* Asimov suggests a solution to the problem of accommodating to the rapidly expanding population.[6] First, he rejects the colonization of other planets as a possible solution; his interpretation of the data leads him to conclude that journeys to other worlds for living space cannot succeed. Those planets that could be reached in reasonable time would not be suitable for human habitation. Appropriate alternatives probably exist in other galaxies. Unfortunately, they could not be reached in a feasible time span. To arrive at them would require travel at speeds faster than light—a physical impossibility.

Asimov suggests the more viable possibility of building colonies in space stations. The construction of huge satellites to hold two hundred thousand or more persons could ease population pressure. Room enough exists for this to happen in near outer space. The development of small space stations in the present foreshadow this development. In order to solve the population problem by colonization in space, a high level of human cooperation is required along with sophisticated technology. Asimov believes that the technology will be found and the cooperation will occur. This optimistic view of the future is one shared by many futurists.

The strategy of future studies offers a valuable payoff in the present. As persons study the time to come and ways to solve problems in the future, they also become more effective in dealing with problems in the present. This is true, in part, because understanding the future requires an awareness of how the present will affect the time to come. It is also partially true because the boundary between the future and the present is not clearly defined. Future problems become present ones at an increasingly accelerated rate.

CONCEPTUALIZING THE FUTURE

Draper Kaufman in *Teaching the Future* suggests four alternative metaphors for conceptualizing the future:

I

The future is a great roller-coaster on a moonless night. It exists twisting ahead of us in the dark, although we can only see each part as we come to it. We can make estimates about where we are headed, and sometimes see around a bend to another section of track, but it doesn't do us any real good because the future is fixed and determined. We are locked in our seats, and nothing we may know or do will change the course that is laid out for us.

II

The future is a mighty river. The great force of history flows inexorably along, carrying us with it. Most of our attempts to change its course are mere pebbles thrown into the river: they can cause a momentary splash and a few ripples, but they make no difference. The river's course can be changed, but only by natural disasters like earthquakes or landslides, or by massive concerted human efforts on a similar scale. On the other hand, we are free as individuals to adapt to the course of history either well or poorly. By looking ahead, we can avoid sandbars and whirlpools and pick the best path through any rapids.

III

The future is a great ocean. There are many possible destinations, and many different paths to each destination. A good navigator takes advantage of the main currents of change, adapts his course to the capricious winds of chance, keeps a sharp lookout posted, and moves carefully in fog or uncharted waters. If he does these things, he will get safely to his destination (barring a typhoon or other disaster which he can neither predict nor avoid).

IV

The future is entirely random, a colossal dice game. Every second, millions of things happen which could have happened another way and produced a different future. A bullet is deflected by a twig and kills one man instead of another. A scientist checks spoiled culture and throws it away, or looks more closely at it and discovers penicillin. A spy at the Watergate removes a piece of tape from a door and gets away safely, or he forgets to remove the tape and changes American political history. Since everything is chance, all we can do is play the game, pray to the gods of fortune, and enjoy what good luck comes our way.

These four views of the future are vastly different. The first assumes that the individual may exert control over predetermined events. The second maintains that the course of the future may be altered only by tremendous effort; the individual has the singular freedom to adapt him-

or herself to life's natural course. The third espouses a somewhat existential view: individuals may, except in extreme circumstances, control their destinies. The fourth asserts that chance is the single most significant element in life.

There can be, of course, no "correct" answer, nor is there a most popular answer. Large numbers of persons choosing among these metaphors distribute their selections rather evenly over the four. This indicates in still another way the problematic nature of understanding and perceiving the future.

The trouble that people have in conceptualizing and anticipating the time to come helps to explain a generalized feeling of malaise that they often feel—a sense of impotence regarding the control of their lives and the institutions around them. Individuals live in a world of sophisticated technology, yet their intellectual and emotional capacities for sensing the world seem limited.

In *The Culture of Narcissism,* sociologist Christopher Lasch writes of a "sense of ending" that he finds pervasive in American culture.[7] The Nazi holocaust, threats of nuclear annihilation, and possibilities of ecological collapse help create a feeling of impending disaster. The effect of this is that people turn away from events of the recent past—political turmoil of the 1960s, Vietnam, Watergate—to look inward at themselves. Lasch writes:

> To live for the moment is the prevailing passion—to live for yourself, not for your predecessors or posterity. We are fast losing the sense of historical continuity, the sense of belonging to a succession of generations originating in the past and stretching into the future.[8]

This "waning sense of historical time," a growing denial of the past, leaves persons stupefied and helpless to face the future.

Psychologist Rollo May describes today's world as "schizoid"; that is, a world that is out of touch, a world in which people avoid close relationships and opportunities to feel.[9] Technological society is so overwhelming that people often protect themselves by stepping back from the things around them and retreating inward. Contemporary life, in effect, "empties" persons of the ability to feel anything but impotence with regard to the future; people grow increasingly apathetic about present events. May articulates the problem: "The present prepares us to embrace the future, even though we cannot anticipate it, even though it always surprises us. . . . Do we freeze or act?"

Alvin Toffler has examined these phenomena in his classic work, *Future Shock,*[10] in a second book called *The Third Wave,*[11] and in a more recent book entitled *Previews and Premises.*[12]

Future Shock conceptualized a phenomenon that many had felt but few had understood. Future shock occurs because the rate of change has increased so dramatically as to make people feel that events of all kinds are out of control. Because of this, the future contaminates the present, causing reaction rather than planning. A better understanding of the time to come, and a better preparation of persons for it, can help overcome this sense of helplessness.

An age of transcience, Toffler argues in *Future Shock,* has replaced an era of relative permanence. The actual rate at which things change—relatively constant throughout human history—has itself accelerated. Because human beings orient themselves so strongly to the past, people are unwilling to confront the reality of this acceleration. Persons accustomed to encountering innovation at a regular pace find it difficult to accommodate themselves to its ever increasing speed. The higher proportion of new situations in daily life (what Toffler calls the "novelty ratio") leads persons to perceive their environments as chaotic. Future shock, a feeling of great stress resulting from too much change in too short a time, leaves persons feeling that events of all kinds are out of control.

In *The Third Wave,* Toffler argues that the current period of time represents a transition between the old world of the Industrial Revolution (the Second Wave), and the post-industrial world to come (the Third Wave)—the First Wave being the time of agricultural civilization. The Second Wave has been relatively short in historical time—approximately 300 years; to people now living, its institutions seem permanent but in fact they are transitory.

Many changing structures already reflect the Third Wave. The nuclear family, for example, existed to meet the needs of industrial society. The factory required workers; therefore large numbers of births occurred. Because children remain dependent for long periods of time, one parent stayed home to provide care while the other went to the factory. Since this usually required heavy labor, and since it was believed that men were physically stronger than women, the female stayed home and raised the children while the male went to work. As evidence of the fact that we live in a transitional period, Toffler cites the statistic that today only 7 percent of all people live in families in which only the male is employed. The increasing divorce rate serves as further evidence that the Second Wave is ending.

Toffler also cites the decline of the efficacy of government, in the United States and elsewhere, for further support of the transition. Governments in most Second Wave societies met the needs of industry. They functioned well in this context without regard for their particular form (democratic or dictatorship, socialist, capitalist, or mixed economy). However, as the Second Wave ends, problems exist in most nations.

Toffler suggests that new forms of government will emerge in the post-industrial world.

Toffler's discussion of the nature of work in the Third Wave is most significant for teachers who are charged with preparing children for life in the future. Toffler anticipates multiple sources of energy well beyond the current dependence on fossil fuels. The factory in its present form will disappear and will no longer serve as a model for other institutions (including the school). Mass production will be replaced by customized products—a phenomenon already visible as persons create their own T-shirts and limited reproductions of phonograph records are available at a reasonable cost.

For Toffler, the workplace will as often be at home as away; people will live in what he calls an "electronic cottage," where they can produce in a humane and pleasant environment. Toffler forecasts the rise of "prosumption"—the reuniting of production and consumption (similar to their role in the First Wave). In this period, manufacturing will be for use rather than for exchange—a process based on do it for yourself rather than do it for the market. In *Previews and Premises,* a third book by Toffler on these issues (written in the form of an interview), Toffler summarizes ideas he introduced in *Future Shock* and in *The Third Wave.*

The key theme of *Future Shock* is presented as the notion that the acceleration of social and technological change has reduced the ability of humankind to cope. Toffler argues further that it is not only change that must be accommodated to, but the acceleration itself. It is the pace as well as the direction of change that make it so difficult for people. The pace continues to grow at an increasing rate between the time of *Future Shock* in 1970 and the publication of *Previews and Premises* in 1983.

In summarizing the thesis of *The Third Wave,* Toffler's third book adds the notion that industrial society has reached a general crisis in which the institutions of the Second Wave simply do not work.

Previews and Premises is an important work in that it allowed Toffler to assess the projections he made in his earlier works. In doing so he finds that for the most part the work he did in 1970 and 1980 was on target. Toffler feels that time has verified his construct of "future shock" (a point of view shared by most futurists); he finds three years later that the transition to the Third Wave is continuing.

Toffler makes an interesting observation about his work in *Previews and Premises.* He writes:

> Futurism is an art, not a form of engineering. So I can sum up my view simply:
> Use science in support of art.

Remember, too, that I come from a tradition which places great respect on first-hand observation and reporting. For many years I was a reporter, a journalist.

Reading books, technical and scholarly papers and journals is essential to me, and I do a lot of it. But unlike many specialists, who have been taught to ignore their own raw experience in favor of the printed page, I also use real-life encounters, personal impressions, travel and face-to-face interviews with relevant people to help me set the statistics and academic studies in perspective.[13]

In a concluding chapter on the roots of change, Toffler restates a perspective on future studies which is an essential one to all who seek to understand the time to come. In discussing his metaphorical description of history as occurring in waves, Toffler makes the point that no future is inevitable. He argues that the Third Wave is no more definite than any other possible future. There is, he argues, an interaction between necessary response to change and chance. When transformation demands a response, the response is partly determined by circumstance and partly determined by pure chance.

Because the interaction of these factors cannot be accurately predicted, the ability to extrapolate the future is limited. Therefore the study of the future must also include the development of persons who can cope with the continual acceleration of change. Toffler's works provide further support for the development of the strategy of future studies.

CREATIVITY THEORISTS AND FUTURE STUDIES

A central thesis of this book is that the strategies considered here—facilitating creative behavior, simulation/gaming, and future studies—are synergistic. Creative persons are better gamers. Learning to be an effective simulation/gamer can make one more creative. And both of these strategies provide persons with problem-solving skills that can make preparation for life in the future more effective. The final section of this chapter turns to an examination of the relationship between creativity theorists (already considered earlier in this volume) and future studies.

Creativity and future studies are inextricably related. The present is a unique time in human history. Because it is an era of rapid change and explosion of knowledge, people encounter difficulties in conceptualizing the future and in attempting to anticipate it. As has been demonstrated in the works of Toffler, among these difficulties is the discomfort and even paralysis of future shock.

As indicated earlier in this book (Chapter 1), there are at least two ways in which persons try to avoid this sense of powerlessness and impotence with regard to the future. One attempt at accommodation is based upon future projections drawn from extrapolations of current trends; this approach has been largely unsuccessful. Another pathway to future adaptation lies in the process of helping people increase their creative potential. In this way people can adapt to whatever the future brings.

Ideas developed by creativity theorists relate directly to future studies. The development of fluency and other primary traits associated with innovative persons is necessary for vocational success and mental stability. Role training is an essential aspect of the journey toward self-actualization. Other ways of thinking and perceiving—those demanding the integration of emotion and reason—are necessary for human adaptation to the time to come. Creative development must be supported by individuals and by societies at large.

> We are called upon to do something new, to confront a no man's land, to push into a forest where there are no well-worn paths and from which no one has returned to guide us. This is what the existentialists call the anxiety of nothingness. To live into the future means to leap into the unknown, and this requires a degree of courage for which there is no immediate precedent and which few people realize.[14]

In this quotation, Rollo May identifies the courage to create. Creativity can aid people to minimize future shock as they develop their personal potential. Several creativity theorists suggest ways to improve the ability to accommodate to life in the future.

J. P. Guilford uses a psychological approach to creativity based upon trait concepts, or ways in which persons consistently differ from each other. Several primary traits relate to the creative process. The development of these is necessary, Guilford maintains, in order to deal with political and personal problems in today's and tomorrow's world.

A generalized sensitivity to problems, or a judgment that things are not all right, is the first primary trait concept. This intuitive ability acts as a key to start productive thinking. Persons who develop this trait and act upon its message are those who will readily adapt to the ever new situations of the future.

The trait concept of fluency involves the fertility of ideas. It signifies skill in spontaneously generating varieties of alternative perspectives. Fluency aids innovation by providing wide alternative possibilities. Types include word fluency, associational fluency, expressional fluency, and ideational fluency. Skill in generating new possibilities of solutions usually means that problem resolution occurs more quickly and more accurately. Creative development entails the growth of this trait and this aids effectiveness in the time to come.

Flexibility is also a necessary behavior for the innovative person, especially when changes in life come rapidly and cannot be anticipated. Originality, elaboration, and redefinition are the other teachable outcomes. All of these trait concepts represent additional tools for coping with tomorrow.

Two nonaptitude examples delineated by Guilford are pertinent to future studies. The ability to work hard for long periods of time, sustaining focus on a single problem or group of related difficulties, is a skill common to innovators (and lacking in many people today). Many activities in society continue to be reduced to smaller and smaller fragments of time; the need to sustain attention receives little support in daily routine. Tolerance for ambiguity, the ability to entertain two or more conflicting meanings at once, represents still another trait. This Janusian talent will be helpful in a future which may require the reconciliation of opposites.

E. Paul Torrance has given much thought to developing a rationale for creativity as a means of future preparation. He sees creativity development as a component of sound mental health. In a future that promises to hold more, not less, stress for individuals, innovative abilities can relieve tension and avoid breakdown.

Creative thinking serves also as a high indicator of vocational success, according to Torrance, even in the most mundane occupations. Torrance insists that the innovative thinker becomes a fully functioning person. Without divergent thought, he writes, "one's capacity for coping with life's problems is indeed minimal." For Torrance, it is imperative that people become more creative. He asserts, "It takes little imagination to recognize that the future of our civilization—our very survival—depends upon the quality of the creative imagination of our next generation."

Role training that leads to increased innovation can achieve the behaviors recommended by Torrance as well as those outlined by Guilford. Eric Berne's psychotherapy of transactional analysis describes three ego-states: parent, adult, and child. These may be viewed as roles. TA theorists suggest that the integration of these states improves mental health, and they indicate that a creative person is one in whom the nurturing parent gives permission to the child to exist. Stronger mental health and improved creative behavior result from TA training—not just for those in need of therapy but also for those who wish to become more effective persons.

The use of psychotherapy with healthy persons is an idea advocated by Abraham Maslow. His hierarchy of human needs begins with the basics of food and shelter and leads to the need for self-actualization. The person who reaches this stage then becomes more creative and adaptive to the demands of an intruding future. Theorists like Moreno and Berne, whose primary focus has been psychotherapy for the improvement of mental health, also provide ideas that aid the development of creativity and improved future orientation.

J. L. Moreno, the psychotherapist who invented Psychodrama, wrote of three concepts which aid innovation and future studies. A central idea of psychodrama is that of *spontaneity*. This trait allows persons to learn new roles and become more adaptive. *Role* is another key notion from Moreno; the learning of new roles leads to the ability to adjust better to a world of transcience that requires constant redefinition. *Tele*—the ability to understand empathetically—is also important for the time to come. As the future requires persons to think and move rapidly in response to new situations, they will rely more upon these intuitive ways of knowing and feeling.

William J. J. Gordon, in his process of synectics, defines creativity as a procedure that makes the familiar strange, or one that enables persons to understand old things in new ways. (Learning, on the other hand, makes strange things familiar or it assimilates new things to those a person already understands.) As time progresses, what is viewed as familiar continually becomes strange and loses meaning; for example, family and sexual mores have undergone radical, dramatic transformation and continue to do so. Creative persons are able to obtain newer, stranger perspectives and therefore become less disoriented when what is known and comfortable becomes unknown and unusual. This, of course, aids accommodation in the future.

For British creativity theorist Edward DeBono, civilization has reached the end of an intellectual era.[15] One result of the accelerated rate of change today is the fact that people live longer than ideas. Survival in the future requires the ability to generate and adapt to new concepts. Traditional thought is a closed, yes/no system—inadequate to meet the needs of tomorrow. Although persons have been taught to make use of fixed ideas and to manipulate them toward logical conclusions, they are not proficient at devising genuinely new perspectives. Traditional thinking helps to verify ideas, but it does not aid in changing them.

DeBono offers the concept of PO as a basic tool of creative thought. PO is the use of feeling, not intellect, in the first stage of thought perception. "This word PO," he writes, "is the name of a system, a concept, an attitude, an indication of the patterning nature of mind, and an invitation to break away from the obvious way of looking at things in order to find new ideas." The process of PO is called lateral thinking, the thought pattern of the future.

Lateral thinking (as opposed to vertical, sequential logic) is DeBono's formulation for creative thought. The lateral thinker can tolerate ambiguity because s/he can reorient a frame of reference, or make what DeBono calls "universe changes." He maintains that persons can be trained to develop these skills, and that they are necessary for living in the time to come.

Silvano Arietti believes that the potential for creativity is much greater than its actual occurrence.[16] He posits that cultures either promote or inhibit creativity. Creativogenic societies, those which enhance innovation, contain many of the following characteristics:

1. Cultural means are available; political leaders promote the growth of cultural media.
2. The people are receptive to and desirous of cultural stimulation.
3. The culture stresses *becoming,* as it fosters growth (opposed to *being,* which fosters stagnation).
4. All citizens have access to cultural media, without discrimination.
5. Freedom, or retention of moderate discrimination, following oppression stimulates creativity among certain groups within a culture.
6. Persons are exposed to different and even contrasting stimuli.
7. The culture encourages a tolerance for and an interest in diverging views.
8. Significant persons interact with one another.
9. Incentives and awards for creative action are given.

Arietti explains that only the first characteristic is absolutely necessary, as the lack of the other eight may be overcome by creative persons individually. If future survival depends on the need for divergence in all people, then societies will have to assume even more of these creativogenic qualities.

For Arthur Koestler, human creativity signifies the only "alternative to despair" with regard to the future. He writes of the "paranoid streak" in humankind that has produced tremendous scientific advances, yet has left humanity utterly powerless to eradicate the social ills of war, poverty, pollution, and misunderstanding. This human paranoia will ultimately lead to extinction, Koestler writes, unless immediate steps are taken to cure it. In one of his last books, *Janus: A Summing Up,* Koestler offers an explanation of this sickness as well as his own solution to this human dilemma.[17]

The source of this paranoid streak, as Koestler sees it, lies in the structure and evolution of the human brain. There are essentially three parts to the brain: the old reptilian brain, which functions together with the later evolved paleo-mammalian brain, and the specifically human neo-cortex, which evolved only lately.

The two old brains act upon instinct and emotion; the new brain is responsible for logical thought. Where the corpus collosum integrates horizontal brain functions, that is, from right to left, there is no such structure to integrate the old and new brains vertically. Hence, persons are physiologically unable to integrate emotion and intellect (or at least they are not able to maintain that integration except temporarily in creative activities).

The "alternative to despair" for the future lies in creative development, in finding a means by which these three brains may be integrated vertically. "The creativity and pathology of man are two faces of the same medal," he writes, "coined in the same evolutionary mint." Koestler asserts that is not beyond the scope of modern biology to develop a substance in the laboratory to make humans mentally stable, to correct our "endemic schizophysiological disposition." He concludes:

> To hope for salvation to be synthesized in the laboratory may seem materialistic, crankish, or naive; it reflects the ancient alchemist's dream to concoct the elixir vitae. What we expect from it, however, is not eternal life, but the transformation of homo maniacus into homo sapiens.[18]

The perspectives of the creativity theorists on the role of future studies are clear. They posit an effective way by which to temper the paralysis of future shock: human creative potential must be realized in ever increasing dimensions.

Fluency traits may be developed to promote vocational success and mental well-being. Persons must learn to unleash spontaneity and develop a tolerance for ambiguity as they learn new role behaviors and new perspectives from which to view the world. Innovations must be designed and tested in laboratories, classrooms, and technological settings.

The ultimate aim of this is the evolution of societies of autonomous, growing people who can think and live for themselves in ever bigger and new ways, who can adapt to swiftly changing structures about them, and who can reach out to each other without avarice or pettiness.

SUMMARY

This chapter has examined future studies as an innovative strategy for use in the classroom. It began by describing a phenomenon that can be labeled "future anxiety." This affects people when they must face the unknown time to come and it is demonstrated by the avoidance and discomfort that occurs when persons must speculate about or anticipate the future.

Writings by Isaac Asimov, John Brockman, and John Naisbitt were used to demonstrate the need for future studies. Asimov's book on catastrophes indicates that human beings must maximize their own potential if they are to stave off catastrophes that can affect human survival. These catastrophes range from the destruction of the universe to the destruction of human civilization. The ability to use future studies strategies can help prevent some disasters and can increase the possibility of survival.

John Brockman examined the way in which human beings continually reinvent the universe—a process that leads to more complexity and more difficulty in coping with life now and in the future. Improved knowledge (e.g., the search for a unification theory in physics) can improve human existence but it can also produce stress by increasing the demand for understanding. One way to cope with the reinvented universe is through the use of future studies.

Megatrends, a book by John Naisbitt, examines the major trends that will significantly alter the nature of life in the future. Naisbitt's book supports the need for future studies by indicating that the world will continue to change; humankind must learn to adapt to these changes in effective ways or face immense suffering both materially and emotionally.

This chapter sought to define the nature of future studies by examining a number of generalizations that can be made about the strategy. It described how futurists function and how they can help to prepare humankind for life tomorrow.

A section of this chapter provided a number of ways for conceptualizing the future. Writings by Rollo May and Christopher Lasch were cited to develop this perspective. Considerable attention was paid to the work of Alvin Toffler who has given scholars the terms "Future Shock" and "Third Wave"—important conceptualizations that have defined futurism and have helped to make an understanding of the time to come easier to achieve.

This chapter concluded by examining the work of a number of previously cited creativity theorists and demonstrating how the development of creative behavior can add to the ability of humankind to overcome future shock and to adapt to life in the time to come.

NOTES

1. Isaac Asimov, *A Choice of Catastrophes* (New York: Simon and Schuster, 1979).

2. John Brockman, *Einstein, Gertrude Stein, Wittenstein & Frankenstein* (New York: Viking Press, 1986).
3. Ibid., p. 203.
4. John Naisbitt, *Megatrends* (New York: Warner Books, 1982).
5. Ibid., p. 279.
6. Isaac Asimov, *Extraterrestrial Civilizations* (New York: Crown Publishers, 1979).
7. Christopher Lasch, *The Culture of Narcissism* (New York: W. W. Norton and Company, 1978).
8. Ibid., p. 5.
9. Rollo May, *The Courage to Create* (New York: W. W. Norton and Company, 1975), p. 2.
10. Alvin Toffler, *Future Shock* (New York: Random House, 1970).
11. Alvin Toffler, *The Third Wave* (New York: William Morrow and Company, 1980).
12. Alvin Toffler, *Previews and Premises* (New York: William Morrow and Company, 1983).
13. Ibid., p. 187.
14. Op. Cit., May, p. 2.
15. Edward DeBono, *Po: Beyond Yes and Know* (New York: Simon and Schuster, 1972).
16. Silvano Arietti, *Creativity: The Magic Synthesis* (New York: Simon and Schuster, 1972).
17. Arthur Koestler, *Janus: A Summing Up* (New York: Random House, 1978).
18. Ibid., p. 106.

CHAPTER

10

Techniques for Studying the Future

INTRODUCTION

This chapter offers ideas for the teaching of future studies in the classroom. Facilitating creative behavior and the technique of simulation/gaming—strategies already described in this volume—also help prepare persons for life in the future. All innovative strategies that enable people to live more effectively and solve problems more easily can prepare them for life tomorrow.

This chapter focuses on some specific ways to study the future in the schools. It begins by examining curricular concerns: What topics make up the future studies curriculum? What will be the nature of a Third Wave curriculum? How can it be implemented? Following this, the chapter describes the World Future Society, an organization concerned with preparing people for life in the future. Several sample activities for use by teachers in the classroom are presented. Two simulation games are described along with information on where to obtain them. Two complete simulation games are also included.

CURRICULAR CONSIDERATIONS

A future studies curriculum should include at least six different kinds of objectives. These outcomes can be accomplished by specific courses in future studies (which are found in some school districts), or by adding future studies components to other classes in the curriculum. Teachers of all disciplines can and should be responsible for teaching students about the future. Effective study of the future requires both separate courses about the nature of the future and the integration of future studies in most other subjects in the curriculum.

The six different kinds of objectives include: 1) information-gathering competence, 2) critical thinking skills, 3) the ability to communicate effectively, 4) knowledge about the environment, 5) knowledge about human institutions, and 6) personal effectiveness.

(1) Information-Gathering Competence

One of Naisbitt's megatrends (discussed in the preceding chapter) is the move from an industrial society to an information one. This is clearly happening already. Students who are able to cope with the future will need to know how to gather information. This outcome must be a primary concern for all areas of the curriculum. The single, most important information-gathering skill is the ability to read. As fundamental as reading is, deterioration in this ability has occurred in the United States over the last few decades. Effective reading is a necessary component of a future studies program.

Information-gathering competence also requires the ability to use libraries and reference tools. The use of computers for information retrieval is critical. More and more data will only be available on computers and a person who cannot use one to locate information will lack a major skill necessary for survival in the future. Persons who cannot gather information effectively will be at the mercy of those who can.

Gathering information competently includes the ability to organize information in ways that prevent overload. Students must also learn to judge the reliability of information. Effective listening and viewing skills are also part of this outcome.

(2) Critical Thinking Skills

Survival in the world to come requires the ability to think critically. Persons must know how to gather information and manage it; they must also be able to evaluate it. As a result, critical thinking is an essential part of future studies. The ability to distinguish fact from opinion, the ability to detect bias in writing and to be aware of propaganda techniques are all skills necessary for accommodation to the future.

In the future pupils will be required to understand and use the scientific method as well as deductive logic. A rudimentary understanding of modern mathematics is also necessary. This includes comprehension of statistics and probability theory as well as the ability necessary to create simple computer programs. Thinking critically requires an understanding of systems theory and its applications to problem solving. Finally, critical thinking requires comprehension of the strengths and limitations of forecasting and prediction.

(3) The Ability to Communicate Effectively

As information gathering depends on reading, so effective communication depends on writing. But like reading, the ability of students to write clearly is becoming less common at a time when it is most needed. The two problems are related: a significant way to improve writing is to read voraciously. Writing is an outcome that must be fostered in all courses in the school curriculum, and must be reinforced by parents who recognize the need to balance television viewing with reading.

After writing, the next most important communication skill needed for a future studies program is the ability to express ideas orally. This skill too must be strengthened in the curriculum.

Nonverbal communication must also be developed. Drawing, sketching, photography, and film making are all communication modes that can contribute to survival in the future.

At a simple level, students need to learn to outline. At a more complex level, pupils need to learn graphing and flow-charting—these, along with systems analysis, are the languages of the future. All students who need to communicate effectively in the future should learn typing as an introduction to computer literacy.

(4) Knowledge About the Environment

Understanding the environment requires solid scientific study. Students must learn physics, chemistry, and biology as first steps toward coping with the future. They must also learn genetics, applied mechanics, and the fundamentals of modern technology if they are to have the skills necessary for life in the future. In addition to understanding the environment, students must also respect it and be committed to its care.

(5) Knowledge About Human Institutions

An understanding of human institutions begins with an in-depth understanding of the social sciences. Students must learn history and they must learn the geographic context in which the story of humankind has occurred. The wide variety of cultures existing on the Earth must be studied through anthropology. Sociology provides knowledge about the limits of racism, ethnocentrism, and xenophobia. Psychology teaches about human behavior and political science offers perspective on the changing nature of governance. The role of change, a central issue in future studies, can best be understood through the study of human institutions and their continuing evolution.

(6) Personal Effectiveness

Knowledge of self provides one kind of personal effectiveness. The person who approaches the future with confidence is one who knows his or her own strengths and limitations. Before one can address the global issues of futurism, one must be able to understand the micro issues existing in one's self.

Personal effectiveness also includes the development of personal living skills. The effective person is an intelligent consumer who is not swayed by the irrational appeals of advertising. S/he is one who comprehends nutrition and hygiene in ways that maximize personal health. An effective person is one who stays in good physical shape and respects his or her body.

Personal effectiveness includes creative behavior. The effective person can make the familiar strange for him or herself in satisfying and meaningful ways. S/he can also obtain enjoyment from the creative products of others by learning to appreciate a wide variety of the fine arts.

An effective person—one prepared for life in the future—is someone who has a sense of political efficacy and is able to participate in public life with a sense of control over an increasingly complex political world.

CURRICULUM AND THIRD WAVE SOCIETY

In 1981, William C. Miller, a Michigan school administrator, published a short book entitled, *The Third Wave and Education's Future*. In it he describes an imaginary scenario for a Third Wave school. Since this scenario offers a view of a school of the future, it is reproduced here.

A SCENARIO FOR A THIRD WAVE SCHOOL

The only thing certain one can say about the typical day in a school during the Third Wave is that there will be no typical day. Participation, personalization, and flexibility will characterize the program of the Third Wave school. Gaining practical skills and education for personal growth and employment will be part of the lifelong learning in a Third Wave society. Let's look at a student and the program, but let's recognize that we will see how only one school provides experiences for one student.

The School: Community High School is three years old. It is a former factory completely converted for education purposes when large numbers of families moved back into the city. The mass migration was precipitated by the greater efficiencies of enery and transportation and because of access to the wealth of cultural resources that have come as part of the rebirth of the urban areas.

The Organization: The school is organized to serve as the students' home base where scheduling, contracting, counseling, and guidance take place. The Development/Resource Center provides necessary support and information to students and faculty. A school-within-a-school organization is used to foster communication and a sense of belonging. There is no set time to enter Community High. Students come and go at all times of the year to pursue interests or work on learning contracts. There is no specified duration for a student's association with Community High, nor is there any age limit.

The Staff: A student's mentor/guide maintains contact with the student throughout his or her association with Community High. Depending upon the learning contract, a student will have an occupation and/or community adviser. Both are volunteers and provide help and support during a student's work or community service contracts. Diagnostic/prescription staff, the student, and the mentor/guide identify needs and plan appropriate learning experiences. The Development/Resource Center staff cooperate in providing needed drill, practice, and skill development. Instructors are available in major content areas, and psychological and other support personnel are on call. As needed, representatives from each of these areas are called together by the mentor/guide to meet with the student and parents to block out an individual learning plan.

The Program: The curriculum is heavily based in the community. As much as half of a student's time is spent in either civic or social projects and/or on-site work experiences. Another 25 percent of the student's time involves counseling about these assignments and learning the skills necessary to be successful in the roles. For more mature, experienced students, national or international assignments are provided. The ultimate aim is to identify, in cooperation with the student, a major learning quest that will challenge the student and use the knowledge and skills gained to date. The remainder of the student's program which has no predetermined starting or stopping time, focuses on personal enrichment and is likely to involve the arts or sports.

The Student: Kelly is seventeen years old and has been at Community High for three years. Planning and building a cabin in the school's recreation/conservation park is a major off-site activity. The current civic service involves helping with registration for the election primaries. Volunteer work with handicapped elementary students is another challenging contract. Because Kelly is considering a career as a forest ranger, a work contract has been arranged with the State Conservation Department with Ranger Doson serving as an occupational adviser. These more responsible assignments were selected and designed in cooperation with Kelly's mentor/guide with the support and suggestions of the members of the individual learning plan team. New skills in math and architecture are required to successfully carry out the cabin building assignment. Biology and science courses are also part of the formal school program because they are required for conservation work. Glee club, swimming, and basketball are also serious interests. With the mentor/guide's urging, both painting and theater are being explored to assure a well-rounded series of experiences.

A Typical Day: Kelly is up early today in order to have access to the main computer and its mechanical drawing capability, so there is a need to be on time. The final computations and the machine-generated architectural drawings should be ready unless the input was goofed up. The staff at the Development/Resource Center were of great help with the project, and the math instructor used the cabin design work as the basis of most of the skills work Kelly needed. Kelly hoped the design would be accepted. Applying academic skills to specific field projects made sense to Kelly, because it allowed for exploration of several potential career areas. Kelly felt completely comfortable with knowledge gained from the project, with the practical nature of the assignment, and with the working conditions. After three hours at the Development/Resource Center, the drawings were ready to be delivered to Ranger Doson. Doson, together with Kelly and the Supervisor, will review the plans. If approved, Kelly will appear before the next student assembly to describe the project and request volunteers to work with Ranger Doson to construct the cabin under Kelly's direction.

Kelly went home for lunch and decided to take some time at the home terminal to check on the status of voter registration and to complete and enter a math assignment on the computer so it would be available for the math instructor to retrieve and check in the afternoon. Kelly looked at the clock and realized it was play practice time. The play is based on an original script that Kelly had a hand in writing.

Even though Kelly enjoyed the autonomy possible with the individualized contracts, the group activities were also a source of pleasure. Student government, glee club, and sports all provided interaction with others. In addition, since Community High was available to anyone in the community, it offered an opportunity to learn from older adults and to work with younger students. It was particularly gratifying to be able to tutor older persons and at the same time gain from them the insights of their vast experiences.

Play practice went well, which was reassuring with the performance only a week away. On the bus ride home Kelly thought through the remaining tasks to complete the learning contracts. Obviously more time on the home terminal would be needed this evening.

With the assignments up to date, Kelly decided to take the next morning off and with a few phone calls arranged a swimming party with friends for the next morning. Kelly snapped off the light and studied the patterns of light on the ceiling above the bed. Kelly was content; much had been accomplished. While not all decisions about the future had been made, the firsthand work and community service projects provided a secure foundation on which to plan next steps. With the backup and support of the mentor/guide and the other advisers, Kelly was certain that the years ahead would be satisfying, enjoyable, and productive.

Kelly's "typical day" has been condensed to provide information about the variety of experiences that might be possible in a Third Wave school. No student's program would be so hectic every day. Note the emphasis placed on guidance and counseling and how the teacher's role is not one of dispensing information. Socialization is not ignored. Third Wave students are comfortable with the use of technology. Observe too the extensive use of community resources, and how education has become a multiagency responsibility. From the scenario it is impossible to discern whether Kelly is a male or female student. Freedom from sex stereotypes is another characteristic of a Third Wave school.

No brief scenario can provide a comprehensive view of education in the future, but by exercising the imagination one can conceive the vast possibilities.

The preceding curricular considerations and the Third Wave school scenario should be read with a note of caution. A problem inherent in future studies is that the future that actually arrives is often different from the one that was projected. This occurs, in part, because of the interaction of change with pure chance. The difficulty of accurate forecasting adds to the sense of future shock. This section of this chapter has offered a perspective on a possible curriculum for the future but it must be recognized that it is only a suggested one; rapidly changing circumstances may make it less than accurate.

THE WORLD FUTURE SOCIETY

An important source of many kinds of resources available for those who wish to teach future studies is The World Future Society. It is the largest and most important of the futurist associations, formed in Washington, D.C., in 1966 as a nonprofit, nonpartisan scientific and educational association. It now has members in more than eighty countries around the world. The society takes no stands on what the future should be like. Instead, its purpose is to promote the study of the future as well as the development of futuristic methodologies. It seeks also to serve as a clearinghouse for ideas about the future as well as to educate the public about possible future developments. The World Future Society is open to anyone who is interested in the future and its membership includes academics, authors, political leaders, teachers, and students. Annual dues in 1987 were $25 per year. The society publishes a journal, *The Futurist,* and also conducts international conferences. In addition, the society produces a weekly program for public radio.

Those who join *The World Future Society* receive *The Futurist,* a bi-monthly journal which is a valuable teaching resource. A recent issue of *The Futurist* (November–December, 1986) contained articles on developments in architecture (raising the question of whether bigger is better), foreign trade, the nature of the twenty-first century corporation, and an analysis of science fiction movies. Each issue contains a section called "World Trends and Forecasts." In the November–December 1986 issue, the journal examined transportation, business, and the development of large dams, the application of technology to commerce, environment, and health.

The Futurist also contains a number of regular "departments" including "Anticipations," "Tomorrow in Brief," "Future Scope," "The Futurist Bookshelf," and "Outlook." The nature of the material published in the journal can be seen from the following quotation taken from the "Outlook" department:

Technology

Technology will continue to be the driving force for change in the future. Each category listed in Outlook—as well as virtually all other areas of life—will feel the impact of the ever-increasing pace of technological development.

Society is moving rapidly toward universal technological competence. Today, even small children can operate computers and other complicated equipment; in fact, the younger you are, the more likely you are to possess basic technical skills. As today's children age, computer competence in the United States will approach 100%.

Unanswered are questions about the implications of this technological growth. Will future generations expect there to be a technological answer for everything? How will the overwhelming presence of technology affect such areas as intuition or faith? And could machines eventually challenge humans as the predominant force on earth?[1]

The World Future Society regularly issues a catalogue called *The Futurist Bookstore.* It lists books, tapes, and other products that are available in a bookstore in Bethesda, Maryland. Members receive a 10 percent discount on all items found in *The Futurist Bookstore.*

The Winter, 1987, catalogue contained listings for books on alternative futures, business, communications, environmental resources, futuristics, habitats, human values, life-styles, science and technology, as well as space and work. This continually updated catalogue contains a wide range of materials that teachers can use in the classroom.

The address of the organization is:

World Future Society
4916 St. Elmo Avenue
Bethesda, Maryland 20814

ACTIVITIES FOR TEACHING FUTURE STUDIES

Reading

An important way to approach the study of the future is through reading. *The Futurist Bookstore,* described previously, represents one important source of reading material. Many of the items are inexpensive and they can be used as supplemental material in courses studying the future.

Another important source of reading for facilitating future studies is science fiction. Authors such as Isaac Asimov, Arthur C. Clarke, Robert Heinlein and a host of others have provided a huge body of literature which can help students anticipate the time to come in exciting and interesting ways.

In Chapter 6, on simulation/gaming theory, the idea of autotelic folk models—a construct developed by O. K. Moore and Alan R. Anderson—was introduced. Autotelic folk models are found in all cultures; they are self-motivating activities used by societies to socialize persons for solving puzzles, developing strategies, coping with chance, and learning aesthetic behaviors. Chapter 6 suggested that part of the popularity of mystery stories can be related to their being autotelic folk models that are puzzle-games. Science fiction stories can also be viewed as autotelic folk models but they are primarily strategy games rather than puzzles. Like mysteries, science fiction stories appeal to readers on more than one level. This increases their value as material for the classroom. Science fiction has always appealed to younger readers and hence the transition from material for entertainment to material for studying the future will be an easy one.

A wide variety of reading material for future studies has been produced. Senior high school students can read books on the future written by people like Asimov, Toffler, and Naisbitt. Materials also exist for less able readers and for those who are younger. An interesting junior high school series has been written by Harriette S. Abels and published by Crestwood House in Mankato, Minnesota, in 1980. The series is called *Our Future World* and contains nine easy-to-read short volumes. Each book is well illustrated and contains about fifty pages. Each addresses one aspect of the future. Topics in the series include business, communication, food, family, government, medicine, science, space, and travel. This series is illustrative of the kinds of materials being developed for the study of the future for younger and perhaps less able readers.

Film

The use of film has been discussed earlier in this volume. It is also an important vehicle for studying the future. With the development of videocassette recorders, the availability of excellent films for the classroom in a relatively inexpensive format (since tapes can be rented for only a few dollars) has increased. Science fiction movies are the most significant for studying the future for the same reasons that science fiction novels make excellent books for reading about the future. A large number of quality films are available. Series such as *Star Wars* and *Star*

Trek are very popular with students and can be used to discuss perspectives on life in the time to come. Many less popular and less well-known films (e.g., *Soylent Green* or *Starman*) are also worthwhile. Film catalogues list science fiction movies and describe their content and quality. Using these as guides to find science fiction films can result in adding valuable resources to the future studies classroom.

The World Future Society collects and sells videotapes for classroom viewing. Many contain interviews with people such as Toffler and Asimov. These tapes, too, can be used to investigate the future.

Future Planning Games

Future Planning Games, a series of activities for studying the future, has been developed by Greenhaven Press of St. Paul, Minnesota. These exercises contain classroom activities that help students focus on important problems. Two examples of *Future Planning Games* are *Determining America's Role in the World* and *Determining Family and Sexual Roles.*

Determining America's Role in the World consists of four activities. The first is called "Constructing and International Philosophy." It presents two different philosophical perspectives about foreign policy. The first is labeled "Cooperation" and the second, "Competition." The class divides into groups of four to six students. Each group examines the two perspectives. They must decide which point of view will best meet the needs of the United States in the future. Pupils must also determine which philosophy can help lead to the solution of crucial world problems including war, poverty, pollution, overpopulation, and racial conflict. Each group must reach a consensus and report it to the entire class. A general discussion with all classroom members participating concludes the activity.

A second part of the game, called "World Order and American Policy," acquaints players with several alternative models for world organization. Pupils study the implications of peaceful coexistence among the superpowers, a continued cold war, a world based on a revitalized United Nations, and the enforcement of world law. The exercise also asks students to examine the consequences of protracted world conflict.

Once again students work in small groups; they rank and evaluate each of the models and seek to achieve agreement about a model for world order. The findings of each group provide the basis for a classroom discussion.

The third activity in this *Future Planning Game* asks groups of four to six students to determine the future of U.S. foreign policy. They discuss U.S. relations with China, Russia, Europe, South Africa, the Middle

East, and Asia. Pupils also examine the future of foreign aid and nuclear policy. In their groups, students devise a statement on foreign policy that responds to the many issues confronting the United States.

The culminating activity of this game requires the students to use what they have learned about foreign policy to analyze an issue that they have not yet examined. It helps students apply what they have learned to a new situation.

Determining Family and Sexual Roles is a second example of a *Future Planning Game* developed by Greenhaven Press. This simulation consists of five related activities. It too uses small groups and again the findings culminate in general class discussion.

The first activity asks students to examine alternative family patterns. These structures range from traditional monogamous families to those consisting of partners of the same sex. Students also discuss single parenthood and life in communes.

Another activity in this game asks students to write a marriage contract. In order to do so, they receive information about many of the issues that confront married couples. The exercise helps students examine a future which is very near in most of their lives.

The game also asks students to examine the rights of homosexuals. It concludes with an activity to help students develop an appropriate premarital sexual philosophy for themselves.

A major strength of the *Future Planning Games* is that they strive to provide a balanced viewpoint without advocating any particular position about the issue. The games allow teachers to help students anticipate future problems—personal and societal—while at the same time providing for meaningful value clarification.

Greenhaven Press is currently revising its *Future Planning Games*. Further information can be obtained by writing:

Greenhaven Press
577 Shoreview Park Road
St. Paul, Minnesota 55126

Futurism and Population

Turn-Ons, a book on strategies by Stephen K. Smuin, has a section on activities for teaching future studies. The following is reprinted from that section:

> Propose to students that conceiving the world's entire population is a problem which can be solved by "compressing" the earth's population to a representative 1,000. Have students develop a profile of the

make-up of the 1,000 using whatever resources they can think of. Then compare their profile to the following accurate composite:

Of the 1,000, 305 people are white, 695 are nonwhite; 60 are American, 64 are Russians, 225 are Chinese Communists. The 60 Americans have nearly half the total income, with the other 940 sharing the other half. The 60 Americans have a life expectancy of 70 years while all the others can expect to live less than 40 years. The Americans have up to now had 10 times as much to eat per person as all the rest of the people. The Americans produce 16 percent of the world's total food supply, eat all but 1/2 percent, and keep part of that for future use. More than 400 people cannot read or write. Of the 1,000, 330 people are Christian, while 670 either belong to other faiths—Jewish, Hindu, Buddhist, and so on—or have no formal religious beliefs. Of the 1,000, 320 people live on land controlled by communists. More than half the group have never heard of Christ, while more than half have heard of Marx.

After you have discussed this composite profile, tell the students that beings with greatly advanced intelligence from another planet have decided to take this 1,000-member group (represented by the class) to another planet to live. The group must decide unanimously whether they wish to (1) begin all over again to build a civilization, in which case the beings from the other planet will erase their *total memory,* including language, or (2) remember all that they are and all that has been accomplished on Earth and build from that.

Debrief. Would it be preferable to enter the new world with no memory of war, racism, sexism, population problems, and so on, or would Earth experiences prove helpful in resolving these problems should they arise?

Scenarios

The use of imaginative scenarios can be an important future studies technique. They enable students to view the future in a personal way that helps make possible futures more meaningful. These activities have potential emotional impact; the teacher who uses them should do so carefully.

(1) Survivors

In this scenario, students are told that a nuclear holocaust has struck the Earth and that they are part of a small group of survivors. Have the students enact their perception of life on Earth after a nuclear disaster.

Encourage them to describe what they see. Ask them to consider what decisions they must make to protect themselves from further calamity. The teacher begins this activity by vividly describing the situation using his or her imagination to create the scene. At the conclusion, the teacher must allow the players to describe their feelings during the activity so that emotional debriefing can take place.

(2) Life on a Rejuvenated Earth

This scenario represents a time in the future when human beings have solved most of their environmental and social problems; they have arrived at a time of abundance. The teacher begins this activity by describing the scene and letting the student enact it in a spontaneous fashion. The students should be asked to make decisions about life in this happy future. At the conclusion, the teacher should ask the students to examine their feelings about living with plenty.

(*Note:* Maximum benefit for future studies can be obtained by having groups of students participate in both of the preceding scenarios. The teacher can ask pupils to compare their experiences either orally or in writing.)

(3) A Picture of the Future

The teacher brings in an empty picture frame. A simple one can be constructed from cardboard. Students then fill the frame by describing scenes from life in the future. The teacher can suggest a variety of settings. S/he might have the students experience a future supermarket, a future hospital, or perhaps a future school. One approach to this scenario asks several groups of students to simultaneously fill the same picture frame and then compare the different views of the future that have been generated.

(4) Human Ages

In this scenario, students play themselves at different physical ages in their lives. They can begin by role-playing their behavior as small children at the age of two or three. Then they can be themselves in the near future, perhaps when they reach the age of twenty-one. Projecting into the future can continue as students experience middle and old age. The teacher should help the students imagine what the world will be like as they get older. The teacher should allow the students to describe their feelings as well as their intellectual views of what life will be like in the future.

Self-Concept Activities

A large body of material has been produced by a variety of people for examining self-concept. Knowing oneself is a legitimate future studies activity, since coping with change requires persons who are comfortable with themselves. Representative of the many books on developing a more positive self-concept is *100 Ways to Enhance Self-Concept in the Classroom* edited by Jack Canfield and Harold C. Wells. Two brief exercises from this book are reprinted here as examples of self-concept exercises.

TWENTY-ONE QUESTIONS

Hand out a sheet to each of your students with the following questions on it. Ask them to write the answers to any or all questions in whatever order they wish. When they have finished, have them discuss their answers in small groups, make "I learned . . ." statements, or discuss how the assignment made them feel. The students may want to record their responses in journals.

1. What would you like to do, have, accomplish?
2. What do you wish would happen?
3. What would you like to do better?
4. What do you wish you have more time for? More money for?
5. What more would you like to get out of life?
6. What are your unfulfilled ambitions?
7. What angered you recently?
8. What made you tense, anxious?
9. What have you complained about?
10. What misunderstandings did you have?
11. With whom would you like to get along better?
12. What changes for the worse or better do you sense in the attitudes of others?
13. What would you like to get others to do?
14. What changes will you have to introduce?
15. What takes too long?
16. What are you wasting?
17. What is too complicated?
18. What "bottlenecks" or blocks exists in your life?
19. In what ways are you inefficient?
20. What wears you out?
21. What would you like to organize better?

This is also a good time to introduce goal setting to your students as a technique for gaining control over their lives and achieving at least one of the goals mentioned previously.

FOUR DRAWINGS

Supply each student with a box of crayons and a large sheet of newsprint (if not availabe, use four sheets of 8½ by 11 in. paper instead). Ask the students to divide the paper into four equal sections and tell them that they are going to draw four pictures depicting the symbolic answers to four questions you are going to have them ask themselves.

Ask the students to close their eyes. You may also wish to have them become more relaxed by doing a deep-breathing exercise . . . or by simply taking a minute to stretch out any tension they may feel in their bodies. After they have had a minute or two to relax their bodies, ask them to let go of any emotions they may be feeling at the moment. Finally, ask them to quiet all the chatter of their minds so that they can become receptive to messages from their intuitive self, their true center. Tell them to imagine a blank movie screen in the middle of their forehead just above their nose. Tell them that you are going to give them a question to ask themselves, and that they should let an image be projected on their movie screen that will represent or symbolize the answer. As soon as they have seen the image (no matter what the image is, or how unrelated it may at first seem), they are to draw it in the upper left-hand section of their papers. The later drawings will go in the remaining sections. Have them number each picture in order.

The four questions are:

1. Where am I?
2. Where am I going?
3. What obstacles will I face?
4. What inner qualities will I need to develop to overcome these obstacles?

Allow about eight to ten minutes for each question and drawing. After they have completed all four drawings, ask them to share them in groups of three or four.

As you might have guessed, this exercise works best with students of high school age and older.

Writing Exercise

The class is divided into two groups. Each group receives one of the following paragraphs and is asked to complete the story. The students are given as much time as they need to finish the task. Neither group knows that the other group has received a different version of the story. The usual outcome is that the group with the future tense writes significantly less than the group with the past tense. This activity can be used to introduce future studies because it demonstrates how difficult it is for persons to deal with the future.

I

Mr. and Mrs. Jones live in a suburban neighborhood with their adopted Vietnamese daughter, Joyce, who is five years old. One afternoon, not too long ago, Mr. Jones heard some loud yelling outside the house. He went to the door to investigate, and saw Joyce and a group of other children in the front yard. Joyce was sobbing and her dress was torn. The other children stood near her, looking at her. Mr. Jones ran down the front steps and . . .

II

Mr. and Mrs. Jones live in a suburban neighborhood with their adopted Vietnamese daughter, Joyce, who is five years old. One afternoon, in the near future, Mr. Jones will hear some loud yelling outside the house. He will go to the door to investigate, and will see Joyce and a group of other children in the front yard. Joyce will be sobbing and her dress will be torn. The other children will be standing near her, looking at her. Mr. Jones will run down the front steps and . . .

SIMULATIONS

Chapter 7 provided an extensive list of simulation/games that are available for classroom use. Many of these games are relevant for teaching future studies. This section offers some additional resources. Two games are described along with information about where they may be obtained. Two complete simulations (written by the author) are also included for use in a future studies curriculum.

Food for Thought

This exercise is one of many available from Zero Population Growth, Inc. (located at 1601 Connecticut Ave. NW, Washington, DC 20009). It teaches the concepts of population distribution, density, and resource allocation. It can be used in middle and high schools. The exercise simulates the relative distribution of population in relation to food, per capita income, and protein.

The class is divided into six groups, which represent North America, Latin America, Europe, the U.S.S.R., Asia and Africa. The number of students in each group is proportional to the number of people in each of these regions. In the first part of the exercise, the class divides a loaf of bread in proportion to the distribution of food in the world. The North Americans receive a large share in relation to their numbers, whereas each other group receives a smaller share. The Asians, who vastly outnumber the North Americans, receive relatively little bread.

Hershey's Chocolate Kisses are used to represent per capita income. Once again the group representing North America receives a large number of pieces of candy, whereas other groups receive proportionately less. The groups must also decide how to divide the candy. The Europeans and North Americans must decide what they will do with the excess.

A similar task requires the distribution of unshelled peanuts that represent protein consumption. Each group learns how many peanuts are necessary to provide the minimum essential daily requirement of protein and then learns how many actual peanuts they will receive. Once again the North Americans and Europeans have enough whereas other regions have considerably less than an adequate amount.

Each group is led by an ambassador who has more power than the other members of the group and who decides how to allocate the various commodities received by the group.

The game is available from ZPG as a kit that contains all of the necessary data. The kit also contains a number of additional exercises that can be used by persons studying the future.

Future Decisions: The IQ Game

This game, which was developed by Betty Barclay Franks, is produced by The Simulation and Gaming Association, RR #2, Greentree Road, Lebanon, Ohio 45036. In the introduction to the game, the author states:

> Students must learn to think in terms of alternative futures and to examine the long-range consequences of the decisions that they make to solve today's problems. This does not mean that we abandon the study of the past nor that we study only the future. Future studies involves more than "escapism." Students must examine the past, think in terms of the long-range consequences of their decisions, and then return to the present in order to take action toward desirable futures.
>
> In so doing, students will discover that their present was not predetermined and unalterable—that choices existed in the past for in-

venting futures—and that, too often, our present problems result from "muddling through."

Future Decisions: The IQ Game is based on a future scenario in which an "IQ" drug has been discovered. The first part of the game asks students to join a hospital board to determine who should get the drug that will raise IQ. Players are not required to join the board, and those who do not become observers with an important function in the game. Provision is made for the possibility that no one will join the board (an unlikely occurrence). The first part of the game requires the board to decide who shall get the drug, which is in limited supply and expensive. This portion of the activity is a standard value clarification exercise.

Part II takes on a more futuristic tone. It asks students to deal with the long-range consequences of the decisions they have made. This segment demonstrates the need to respond to the implications of decisions. In Part Two, players listen to a radio program on tape that provides information about the consequences of using the IQ drug. As students react to these outcomes, they begin to see the effects of decisions on events in the future.

In the debriefing, students examine questions about the possibility of preventing, altering, or inventing futures. Players are asked to speculate about the kind of future, with regard to intelligence, they would like to create. Their conclusions are then applied to other future problems.

This simulation provides many materials for students to use including a newspaper that discusses the implications of the decisions made about the IQ drug. *Future Decisions: The IQ Game* is a sophisticated device that takes careful preparation and careful facilitating. When used properly, this game offers players considerable insight about anticipating the future.

The Energy Game

This exericse uses three interdisciplinary concepts to help players understand the nature of energy—now and in the future. The concepts—system, decision making, and model—are significant because they facilitate thinking about the future. The exercise examines a problem that will undoubtedly be a difficult one in the future by helping students learn to use important future-oriented terms.

The only material needed by the players is newsprint and crayons, which are used in Part Three of the exercise. The game is played in small groups of three or four persons. At the conclusion of the exercise, each group compares the model it has created. Debriefing consists of an examination of the values involved in deciding how the energy was expended and in a discussion of the viability of each solution.

Part I: Creating a System

The goal of your group is to design an allocation system for distributing energy. The term *energy* is used to represent all forms of power that are currently available or will be available in the future.
The energy needs are as follows:

1. There are ten housing units in the system. Under ideal conditions each unit will be maintained at a year-round temperature of 68 degrees. On an annual basis, five units of energy are needed to keep each house at 60 degrees. Each additional degree between 60 and 68 degrees requires one unit of energy per house.

2. All industrial units should have enough energy to produce enough goods to make a profit and stay in business. Each unit of industry needs five annual units of energy to break even. Each dollar of profit requires one-half unit of energy and a fair return requires two dollars of profit per industrial unit. There are ten industrial units.

3. The energy industry will need to maintain enough units on reserve to provide for emergencies such as unusual cold or other problems. You will need to decide how many units will be kept on hand.

4. Some units of energy will have to be spent in order to create new and additional sources of energy. You will need to decide how much energy to allocate for this purpose.

There are 200 units of energy available annually to meet the needs described. The first task of your group is to divide the 200 units in a way that maximizes the achievement of these needs.

Part II: Understanding Decision Making

After your group completes its allocations, analyze the factors you considered that led to the decisions you made. List as many factors as you can. After listing the factors on a sheet of paper, discuss the ways in which these factors might be different in a real as opposed to a simulated situation.

Part III: Constructing a Model

Using the newsprint and crayons that have been given to you, construct a model that represents the system you have created. Be prepared to describe your model to the other groups. (*Note:* Try and construct a working model. Do not use any form of graph but instead develop a model that represents the system in motion.)

Building a Future Community: A Simulation

Overview

This simulation enables participants to construct future communities using photographs of societal institutions. Pictures are placed upon a grid and labeled as desirable or undesirable aspects of future life.

In groups containing six roles, players choose a variety of components of a community (current and future ones) to include or exclude from the society they are building (e.g., schools, libraries, poverty, genetic engineering centers, and the like). The grid also contains blank spaces so that, by consensus, the players can add features to the community.

The game teaches concepts such as decision making while drawing upon geography and economics to provide a futurist perspective. It requires value clarification as players struggle with what should and should not be included.

Components

25 photographs   11 grid markers
5 blank cards   6 role cards

In order to play the game, 25 photographs are needed. These can be taken from magazines (and perhaps laminated to ensure their durability) or they can be taken with a camera. The institutions of which photographs needed are listed here in alphabetical order. Most are existing institutions that will be easy to find. A few, however (e.g., the genetic engineering center), are future institutions and so pictures must be found that can serve as representations of each institution. The alphabetical listing of needed pictures is as follows:

1. Automobile services (sales, repair, etc.)
2. Banking services
3. Computer center
4. Entertainment (movies, plays, etc.)
5. Factories (representing all forms of industry)
6. Fire department
7. Genetic engineering center
8. Highway system

9. Higher education
10. Housing (of all types including private homes, apartments, etc.)
11. Human management center (definition should be left open)
12. Libraries
13. Medical services
14. Museums
15. Nuclear energy (representing a primary but not exclusive form of energy in the future)
16. Park system
17. Police services
18. Pornography
19. Poverty
20. Religious institutions
21. Restaurants
22. Schools (K–12, public and private)
23. Shopping facilities (of all sorts including malls, convenience stores, and so on)
24. Space port (representing the primary mode of future long-distance transportation)
25. Sport facilities (representing spectator sports)

The six roles needed for the game include the following:

Role One: Laborer

Most manual labor has vanished in this future community. However, a need still exists for some persons to do work that requires physical exertion and little else. You are intelligent and believe that you have this unpleasant task because of circumstances beyond your control; you feel angry and bitter about your role in the society. Therefore you evaluate most events and proposed changes in very personal ways. It is difficult for you to negotiate with the other planners who are your social superiors. You believe you are as smart as they are and stronger both physically and emotionally.

Role Two: Academic

You are a professor in one of the community's finest universities. Both you and the school you teach in have great prestige. You believe that there has been an erosion of academic values in the recent past and one of your goals is to ensure that scholarly values are maintained in this future community. As a social elitist with very conservative political views, you do not like to mix with ordinary people. You believe that much is at stake in planning this community and you intend to have your way over these others whom you perceive as less able than you. The democratic notion that everyone should be heard offends you.

Role Three: Artist

You are a successful artist who works in the media of an advanced technological society. You have achieved much reknown for your creations; your goal is a society with strong support for the arts. You fear that as technological improvements continue to be achieved, the interest of the populace in the arts will diminish. As a person, you tend to be trusting and accepting of others almost to the point of being naive. You feel that the social reformer in the group best represents your point of view.

Role Four: Political Leader

You have become a successful politician in this society by knowing when to lead and when to follow. As a result, you have much political power and the admiration of a large number of people. Your success comes from being good at bringing people together and knowing how to compromise. As a young person you were considered a radical but time has mellowed you and now you see yourself as a political moderate sticking closely to the middle of the road. You are well liked by the others in the group and maintaining their goodwill is important to you.

Role Five: Apathetic Citizen

You are part of the great mass of average people who inhabit this society. You have a rather mundane job in one of the government bureaucracies and feel that very little of what goes on here will affect your life. As a result you have not much interest in or commitment to the process. On the other hand, you do not like to offend people or make them angry. Therefore you will try to participate as best you can and hope that whatever you do will be OK with everyone else in the group. You also hope that the process does not take too long because there is some shopping you need to do and you and your spouse have plans for the evening.

Role Six: Social Reformer

You believe that the current way things are done is usually wrong. The many changes in recent history seem, in your opinion, to violate the values of human dignity. You are pleased to be in this planning group because you feel, at last, that you are in a position to make a difference. As a political liberal with radical tendencies, you have little patience with those who do not see things as clearly as you do. You believe that in order for this process to work, the best approach should be slow and reasoned deliberation and you want to ensure that this happens. You see the artist as too naive to be effective and you do not wish to be identified with this person.

There are eleven grid cards, which can be made from 4 × 6 index cards. Six of the cards designate role numbers, and five cards designate position (STRONGLY FOR, FOR, NEUTRAL, AGAINST, STRONGLY AGAINST).

Rules

1. Using the grid cards, the facilitator lays out the following:

	Strongly For	For	Neutral	Against	Strongly Against
Role I					
Role II					
Role III					
Role IV					
Role V					
Role VI					

2. Players receive their specific roles from the facilitator. When there are more than six players, roles may be shared by two or more players. When this occurs, each group of players must elect a spokesperson. Players make choices based on their role descriptions.

3. After studying their roles, the players are ready to build the community.

4. The facilitator shuffles the photographs and blank cards together. S/he then presents the photographs and cards to the players one at a time.

5. The first person to ask for a photograph or card obtains it and places it on the grid. The players proceed through the photographs and cards until they have filled all the slots on the grid.

6. When all the pictures and blank cards have been placed on the grid, the players can rearrange the photographs and cards as they wish. However, democratic procedures must be followed in moving any pictures or cards. No card or picture may be moved until all the spaces on the grid are filled.

7. The group must also decide what to represent with the blank cards. They can use them to add desirable future institutions (placed in one of the positive slots—*strongly for* or *for*) or to prevent the existence of unwanted ones (placed in a negative slot—*against* or *strongly against*).

8. While the cards and photographs are being distributed, each role player controls the slots assigned to him or her. Once all the spaces are filled, however, the community of players owns the entire board and they must make decisions based on democratic group process.

9. Once the community is complete (at the point when no further agreements can be made regarding the rearrangement of photographs or cards) the facilitator conducts a post-game discussion in which players analyze the strengths and weaknesses of the community they have created, the process of decision making they engaged in, and the values represented by the community they have created. Attention should also be given to the nature of democratic group process followed in terms of its strengths and weaknesses for building a community.

SUMMARY

This chapter has examined the teaching of future studies. It began by discussing a number of curricular considerations including the need for information-gathering competence, critical thinking skills, the ability to communicate effectively, knowledge about the environment, knowledge about human institutions, and personal effectiveness. It then examined a scenario for a Third Wave school written by William C. Miller.

A section of the chapter introduced The World Future Society, an organization designed to help persons prepare for life in the future. Sample materials from the society's journal, *The Futurist*, were included.

Seven future studies activities were suggested that were drawn from a wide variety of sources. These activities were intended as samples of the many kinds of activities that can be used for studying the future. The chapter concluded with a section on simulation. Two simulation/games were described along with information on where to obtain them. Two complete games, ready for classroom use, completed this chapter on facilitating the teaching of future studies in the classroom.

NOTES

1. *The Futurist,* November–December, 1986, p. 55.

CHAPTER

11

Giftedness and Innovative Teaching Strategies

INTRODUCTION

True or False?

"Gifted and talented children receive considerable attention in America's public schools."

"It is not necessary to provide gifted and talented children with special focus because they will surely succeed without it."

"Gifted and talented children tend to have emotional problems."

"If special programs are provided for gifted and talented children, they will become elitist snobs."

"Helping the gifted and talented is not wise because they will become even more superior than they already are."

"Gifted and talented children will turn against less able persons if given a chance."

"Gifted and talented children become independent thinkers and lose their respect for authority."

"Gifted and talented children pose a threat to the traditional values of society. They are all radicals who wish to change the world."

All of these assertions represent the biases of many people toward the very able; they are all false.

Gifted and talented children often experience discrimination similar to the kind faced by other minority groups. This prejudice leads to the wastes of an important human resource. The difficult problems facing humankind need the talents of bright people whose intellect has been nurtured and who have a commitment to serving humanity.

The existence of a group of highly intelligent students presents American education with a dilemma. On the one hand, the ever more complex world requires that special attention be given to those who have unusual ability. On the other hand, schooling has been democratized; regardless of intellect, students are offered essentially the same curricula. During the course of American history, the focus of education has shifted from teaching the wealthy to teaching able learners to teaching everyone. The United States has achieved near universal secondary education and is moving toward post-secondary education for all as well.

Can a nation committed to universal education also be committed to the elite who are the gifted and talented? Clearly both goals are desirable but they can lead to conflict.

Joseph Renzulli, a major figure in the field of gifted and talented education, has argued that the dilemma can be resolved by developing gifted behaviors in everyone rather than by focusing on the very able. To the extent that this is possible, it is worthwhile. However, it fails to address the need to offer special programs for those who are identified as gifted and talented.

This book is about innovative teaching. The strategies described in this volume are useful ones for all students. The gifted and talented will find facilitating creative behavior, simulation/gaming, and the study of the future particularly motivating and interesting procedures. Part of the purpose of this chapter is to demonstrate their value in teaching the very able. These strategies also allow for the profitable interaction of the gifted and talented with less able students.

Interest in the gifted and talented has been cyclical, often heightening during great national crises. This occurred, for example, when the Russians launched the first *Sputnik*. In less demanding times, the gifted and talented have often been ignored. Fear of creating an elite group has existed—a process seen as inconsistent with the continuing democratization of the United States and its educational system. Furthermore, many believe that the gifted and talented can easily fend for themselves and need no special effort made on their behalf. Ironically, the most gifted, even under the best of circumstances, receive considerably less attention than the developmentally disabled. Certainly handicapped persons need help and support from the society, but so do the gifted and talented. Able students can repay the cost of their training by the tremendous contribution they can make to the nation.

Programs for the gifted and talented provide several benefits for society as a whole. Providing enrichment for the gifted and talented increases the availability of their talents to the society. These children offer the nation many high-level skills that are in scarce supply (including ability in mathematics, science, and leadership).

Schools benefit because programs for the gifted and talented provide these pupils with better opportunity to focus their energy. This is preferable to leaving them unchallenged. The bored but talented student can become a disruptive force in school, whereas a student who has been appropriately stimulated can be a major asset. Sometimes challenge can come from working with other, more typical students. This must be done carefully in order to avoid fostering arrogance, elitism, and snobbery. But when it is done intelligently, it can be a major benefit for all concerned.

The provision of specific programs for bright students can lessen the frustration of teachers as well as pupils. A competent instructor who faces a mixed classroom without a well-defined program may find it difficult to meet the needs of both traditional students and gifted ones. Formal programs in gifted and talented education can improve the effectiveness of the teacher.

These programs most directly aid the able learners themselves. Those with special ability have special needs as well. Their abundance of mental ability needs stimulation. A lack of challenge can result in painful frustration. Furthermore, these pupils gain by interacting with their intellectual peers. Their ability must be legitimized so that they can pursue the life of the mind without coming to feel that they are "freaks" or "nerds."

Gifted and talented education thus benefits the entire society, individual school districts as well as the talented children themselves.

DEFINITIONS

(1) Gifted and Talented

Congress passed a bill in 1978 that gave definition to the term "gifted and talented student." This definition, stated in Public Law 95-561 (November 1, 1978), reads:

> ...the term gifted and talented children means children and when applicable, youth, who are identified at preschool, elementary, or secondary level as possessing demonstrated or potential abilities that give evidence of high performance in capability in areas such as intellec-

tual, creative, specific academic, or leadership ability, or in the performing and visual arts, and who by reason thereof require service or activities not ordinarily provided by the school.

A distinction is sometimes made between students who are considered gifted and those who are talented. When this is done, *gifted* refers to cognitive ability, defined usually by a high IQ score. *Talented* refers to students with outstanding leadership skills or artistic or athletic ability. In practice, however, the two groups overlap. Students with high cognitive ability often are leaders and perform in a variety of aesthetic areas. They are usually physically adept and they participate in many kinds of organized sports. In this chapter, the two terms are used interchangeably or together and will sometimes be abbreviated as g/t.

(2) Enrichment

This occurs when gifted students receive additional and supplementary assignments and materials within a standard classroom.

(3) Acceleration

This is a process by which gifted and talented students move through classroom lessons at a faster pace than do traditional students. They may take the same algebra course as other ninth graders, for example, but over a shorter period of time. The course is compacted and this allows them to either finish school earlier (by skipping grades) or to use the extra time for enrichment activity.

(4) Homogeneous Grouping

This term means the placing of all g/t students into one group, class, or program in a way that segregates them from other students. Heterogeneous grouping refers to the opposite—integrating students of all ability levels into groups, classes, or programs.

(5) Divergent Thinking

This concept has already been discussed in the section on creativity theory. It means the ability to perceive the environment in an atypical manner, what creativity theorist W. J. J. Gordon calls "making the familiar strange." One characteristic of gifted and talented children is that they are good divergent thinkers, able to bring an innovative perspective to many things in the world.

COMPONENTS OF THE GIFTED AND TALENTED

When four factors exist together in a person, that person is identified as being gifted and talented. These factors include ability, creativity, motivation, and task commitment. The presence of any single component may be an indication of *potential* gifedness but by itself does not ensure it.

Ability is usually defined by a score on an achievement test or equated with IQ. The concept of intelligence quotient, however, has many limitations and should not be used as the sole determinant of the gifted and talented.

Students who perform well on standardized achievement tests are also demonstrating ability even if their IQ scores are not superior. (High correlations, however, do exist between IQ and achievement tests.) The entire question of native ability is a murky one replete with psychological, social, and even political issues. (e.g., can ability be nurtured or does it come only from nature? Do certain racial groups have superior gene pools with regard to ability?) A practical way to identify ability involves a combination of IQ, achievement test scores, and successful schoolwork.

Creativity has been defined earlier in this text as the ability to see the world in new ways. The creative person can "make the familiar strange." The innovator combines old experiences into new constructs and thus invents something new, at least for him- or herself.

Motivation is the third factor leading to the identification of the gifted and talented. Motivating talented pupils is sometimes difficult and schools often fail to do so. Whereas some activities can be engrossing for the gifted student, s/he also can easily be bored. The problem of motivation relates to the dilemma discussed earlier. If classrooms become places for the education of everyone, they can become settings where the intellectual elite are bored. On the other hand, providing only for g/t students can leave other, less gifted pupils stranded. Activities are needed that can appeal to both able learners and traditional students.

The strategies described in this book are ones that can often be used simultaneously by g/t students and other pupils. A good simulation/ game, for example, can be played at different levels of understanding. The gifted student pursues a complex strategy whereas the less able pupil uses a simpler one. Because games contain an element of chance, the less able player can sometimes defeat the more able one. This occurrence will be helpful to both of them—the gifted student because s/he will be motivated to try harder in the future, and the traditional student because s/he has won a contest against someone who usually defeats him or her (on competitive examinations, for example).

Finally, in order to be considered gifted and talented, one needs to have a strong sense of *task commitment*. In usual school programs, this is not always easy to achieve. Often the potential g/t pupil can do more than adequate work with minimal effort and commitment. Part of the reason for gifted and talented education comes from the need to create task commitment among the very able.

The strategies described in this book are ones that bring together the four components of giftedness: ability, creativity, motivation, and task commitment. All three strategies, of course, are appropriate for all students. The more able the student, the more s/he can obtain from any teaching technique. Students must be rewarded in proportion to their input. Such intellectual reward for effort is usually not a by-product of more traditional procedures (e.g., finishing all the math problems in a chapter assignment often leads to being given additional math problems—hardly an incentive for efficient work.) The student who recognizes this connection between effort and reward will often increase his or her mental productivity. Facilitating creative behavior, using simulation/games, and studying the future are all means of making the connection between effort and reward clearer—for gifted students and for traditional ones as well.

All three of the strategies lead to increased creative behavior. In fact, as has been pointed out before, they are synergistic. Participating in games makes one more creative, and innovative persons are able to play games more effectively. As a result of both procedures, persons increase their ability to cope with future shock and are more able to adjust to the future.

Effective participation in creative behavior, simulation/gaming, and the study of the future require intense involvement. Because all three strategies interact positively with other characteristics of the gifted and talented, they tend to be effective in achieving task commitment.

Thus, facilitating creative behavior, using games, and studying the future help bring about the development of mental ability, creativity, motivation, and task commitment. This leads to the nurturance of giftedness among those with great potential.

CHARACTERISTICS OF GIFTED AND TALENTED STUDENTS

Many characteristics define the gifted and talented student. These traits appear early in the life of the able child. A parent or preschool teacher who has been sensitized to these behaviors can identify the potentially able student at a young age. Unfortunately this identification is often not the case and many times the gifted child is seen as different or strange.

The young Thomas Edison was considered a stubborn and aloof child with little emotional response. Three months after he entered school he was forced to leave. School officials considered him to be "backward."

School officials also judged Albert Einstein's adjustment to school as very poor; they viewed him as unsocial and disturbed. At one point the young Einstein had an emotional breakdown and he too was removed from school. It was noted that he frequently withdrew into a fantasy world.

Will Rogers represents still another example of a gifted child who had great scholastic difficulty. The young Rogers had an intense dislike for schooling and was difficult to discipline. He was an habitual prankster and his activities led to the occasional damage of school property.

None of these three talented youngsters was seen by educators as having any potential. These examples could certainly be multiplied; historically, the gifted and talented have not fared very well in school environments.

One indicator of giftedness is the acquisition of language at an early age. The able child develops a large vocabulary while s/he is still young and becomes a chatterbox who speaks early and often. The gifted and talented child demonstrates great fluency, a trait that often indicates creative potential.

Closely linked with the acquisition of language is the development of intellectual skills. First among these is the ability to read. The gifted and talented read early and competently. Reading quickly becomes an integral part of their lives. Dashiell Hammett, creator of the hard-boiled private detective genre, was forced to end his formal schooling at the age of fourteen. In later life, however, he demonstrated an in-depth knowledge of classic literature—something he achieved by voracious reading on his own.

Another intellectual skill developed by these children is the ability to reason abstractly, which often leads to mathematical skill. Gifted children have fine memories and relatively long attention spans. They drive their parents and teachers nearly crazy by their continual question of why?

Self-confidence and independence are social characteristics found among the gifted and talented along with the development of empathy for others. The gifted child demonstrates organizational skills and is often the person who provides leadership. However, the self-confidence and independence can also sometimes irritate others and can cause a lessening of the ability to lead.

The gifted and talented child has a vivid imagination. S/he enjoys word games and also demonstrates a sense of humor. The able child often uses his or her toys in imaginative ways, demonstrating once more Gordon's process of "making the familiar strange."

Able children develop both fine and gross motor skills when they are young. On the average, the gifted child walks early and learns to run before other children do. At the same time the gifted child learns to competently use small objects—pencils, crayons, scissors. The gifted student arrives at school with many advanced skills.

Bright children combine a never-ending curiosity with persistence. It is difficult to dismiss him or her without a satisfactory answer to a question. The gifted child is perceptive, aware of much in the environment. S/he develops an early tendency to be self-critical and demands much from him- or herself and expects much from others as well.

The gifted child responds to complexity; s/he is able to follow involved directions more easily than others. Because of this ability, gifted children make exceptionally good game players. The gifted and talented accept new ideas readily and are often fallibilists who recognize that ideas and perspectives constantly change.

Gifted children tend to be more adventurous and self-confident, less defensive and insecure than other youngsters. They demonstrate a greater tolerance of frustration and enjoy working on projects by themselves.

Gifted and talented children become successful problem solvers early in life. They enjoy solving puzzles and are a good market for the "brain teasers" that are found in many publications. Because the mystery story has a puzzle-solving quality to it, gifted children often becomes readers of these novels. They also enjoy reading science fiction because this literature forces readers to speculate about problem-solving strategies and usually contain alternative views of the future.

Logic appeals to the g/t student who also seeks to understand cause-and-effect relationships. These children enjoy structure; they have a tendency to organize things in an orderly way. Sometimes, however, the order may be more apparent to them than to the outside world.

The gifted and talented have high energy levels, and demonstrate versatility and diversity of interests. They pursue many hobbies and often seem to have many simultaneous interests.

The following list of characteristics can serve as a summary of traits that are usually associated with gifted and talented children:

1. Gifted and talented children see the world as a magic place, full of awe and wonder.
2. Gifted and talented children are basically nonconformists who can sometimes go along with the crowd if the situation demands it.

3. These students tolerate greater amounts of ambiguity than others.
4. The gifted and talented see the familiar in new ways and in greater depth.
5. Divergent thinking methods appeal to these pupils; they tend to react against learning presented in an authoritarian manner.
6. The gifted and talented are able to learn through the use of fantasy.
7. The unconventional attracts able students.
8. Gifted and talented children depend more on self-evaluation than on the evaluation of others.
9. These children can be playful and sometimes their peers see them as silly.
10. The gifted and talented often make nonconventional life career choices.

CHARACTERISTICS OF TEACHERS

In developing programs for teaching the very able, careful attention must be paid not only to the nature of giftedness—those traits found in students that allow them to be classified as superior learners—but also to the nature of the teachers who work with students of high ability.

Those who teach the gifted should be gifted themselves. Persons sometimes are assigned to programs in g/t education because they have seniority and it is their turn to teach the "good kids." Actually, it is a mistake to assume that teaching very bright children is easy; experienced teachers know that instructing bright pupils can be very challenging.

Teachers of the gifted and talented must identify with very intelligent children and have a genuine desire to teach them. People enter teaching for many reasons, not all of which are altruistic. For some, teaching is a way to help children who are having a difficult time learning; for others, it represents a way to share a love of subject matter obtained in college. For still others, teaching can be the joy of working with talented children, and this latter group should be the teachers of the very able.

Joseph Renzulli has been the director of the Teachng the Talented Program at the University of Connecticut. In the November 1984 issue of *Curriculum Review,* Renzulli identified several other characteristics needed by those who would teach the gifted and talented.

First, Renzulli argues, teachers of the very able need to be capable of helping children focus upon their particular and specialized interests.

Being able to identify a particular talent at an early age can lead to the discovery of future Edisons and Einsteins.

Teachers of the gifted and talented, Renzulli argues further, must be able to help youngsters develop appropriate methodological skills. It is not sufficient, Renzulli says, to teach content, but rather the gifted child needs to know how to inquire—how to find answers to questions. The child must learn process and then be capable of creating his or her own product.

Another trait suggested by Renzulli is the ability to provide managerial assistance. Put another way, more than for any other kind of student, the teacher of the gifted and talented must serve as an enabler—a person who makes it possible for people to learn on their own.

The teacher of the gifted and talented must provide continual and appropriate feedback. Renzulli attributes this need to the public's concern about educational excellence. Learning theorists have long been aware of the importance of feedback. Renzulli makes the point that the skill of providing good feedback is particularly important for those who teach very able children.

Renzulli concludes his list by arguing that the teachers of the gifted and talented must be able to help children find appropriate outlets and audiences for their creative work. He says that this is important because able learners need a sense of efficacy with regard to the world outside the classroom.

DESIGN OF PROGRAMS

Three kinds of programs have been designed for the development of gifted and talented education. Each has its advantages and disadvantages.

The simplest design can be labeled *separation,* which leads to segregation. In this mode, gifted and talented students are placed in homogeneous classes which contain only other able pupils.

On the positive side, homogeneous grouping in a self-contained classroom with a teacher who has special training, empathy, and insight can provide the intellectual support of peers. It leads to the stimulation that occurs when bright people interact. The creative potential of such a group is high. In a segregated classroom the teacher can better provide individualized experiences since the range of abilities is smaller than those found in a mixed classroom.

On the negative side, separation can lead to feelings of elitism as well as to a sense of alienation and isolation. Gifted pupils need feedback from all kinds of people if they are to function effectively in the society as a whole. In the real world, when schooling is concluded, the g/t student will need to function with others who are not as capable as s/he is. Segregation may inhibit the learning skills that are necessary for this task. Another disadvantage is the loss—important in a democracy—that other students experience when they do not receive the benefits that come from exposure to these pupils. Finally, this pattern may create more administrative difficulties than alternative patterns—particularly in small school districts.

A second approach that may be labeled *semiseparate* consists of a mixed program. In an elementary school setting this means that g/t children are segregated for part of the day. Sometimes this occurs in particular subjects such as math and science. At other times it can be for a block of time in which children attend an enrichment program in a resource room. In secondary schools semiseparate programs take place when gifted and talented students study some subjects together—perhaps science, math, and English—and take other classes in a heterogeneous setting—e.g., social studies and physical education.

This pattern provides gifted and talented students with some of the benefits of separation described while minimizing some of the problems. G/t students spend considerable time with intellectual peers and some time with everyone. This approach provides both stimulation from other gifted students and the opportunity to develop the social skills for the real world outside of the school. The major disadvantages of this pattern come from the dilution of attention, focus, and resources available for the talented.

An *integrated* design also exists. In this form of organization, gifted and talented students take all of their work in a heterogeneous setting but receive special attention from the teacher through supplementary materials and assignments. This requires the instructor to provide a good deal of individualization of instruction as s/he attempts to administer two programs simultaneously. Integration allows all students to stay together in the same place, minimizing elitism and challenges to a democratic view of education—clearly an advantage. The system also has disadvantages; it is a cumbersome one to organize and it makes great demands on teachers. It also limits the kind of intellectual stimulation that occurs when gifted and talented students find themselves segregated together.

In general, the semiseparate approach appears to contain the best balance of pluses and minuses. However, the pattern chosen depends upon the circumstances existing in school districts seeking to create programs in gifted and talented education.

THEORISTS OF GIFTED AND TALENTED EDUCATION

Joseph Renzulli, whose work was referred to earlier, has combined research about and experience with gifted and talented children to develop his Enrichment Triad Model for curriculum development.
Renzulli's model is based on several assumptions about the gifted and talented. He assumes that gifted students demonstrate persistence to a higher degree than do others. He also believes that highly motivated, gifted, and talented students need opportunities to pursue genuine and meaningful problems in depth; they must also have the chance to present the results of their studies to real audiences.
As suggested by the title, The Enrichment Triad curriculum contains three types of enrichment. Type I consists of general exploration activities, which seek to motivate students and to help them discover areas in which they have a deep interest. Renzulli suggests interest centers, short discussions, films, and field trips as Type I procedures. These activities are designed to lead to more intensive involvement and further research if the student becomes engrossed in them.
Group training activities make up Type II enrichment. The pursuit of these activities allows for the development of specific skills so that students can deal effectively with content. These training experiences involve problem-solving strategies and creative thinking. They focus on areas defined by Guilford in the "structure of intellect" model (see Chapter 4). Type II activities involve skill-development exercises, games, and discussions.
Renzulli argues that experiences involving Type I and Type II enrichment should be available to all students, not just the gifted and talented. Type III, however, is designed primarily for motivated, able students. These activities Renzulli calls, "Individual and Small Group Investigations of Real Problems." Renzulli says about them:

> Type III Enrichment differs from presented exercises in several important ways. First, the child takes an active part in formulation of both the problem and of the methods by which the problem will be attacked. Second, there is no routine method of solution or recognized correct answer although there may be appropriate investigative techniques upon which to draw and criteria by which a product can be judged. Third, the area of investigation is a sincere interest to an individual (or small group) rather than a teacher-determined topic or activity. And, finally, the youngster engages in Type III activity with a producer's rather than a consumer's attitude and, in so doing, takes

the necessary steps to communicate his or her results in a professionally appropriate manner.[1]

At the conclusion of Type III enrichment, students move from learning to doing. They produce something new as they focus on a problem of real concern to them, treat it professionally, and present the findings in a professional way to an appropriate audience. Renzulli's Type III activities lead to many kinds of creative behavior.

A second important theorist of gifted and talented education is Frederick B. Tuttle—author, along with Laurence A. Becker, of *Program Design and Development for Gifted and Talented Students*.[2] Tuttle is the director of curriculum and instruction for the Wareham, Massachusetts, public schools.

Tuttle calls his theoretical model for teaching the gifted and talented the Advanced Skills Curriculum (ASC). He claims that whereas Renzulli's model provides for work outside the general curriculum, his model was designed to work in conjunction with it.

Tuttle lists five assumptions on which his model is based. These include the following:

1. Gifted students should receive appropriate differentiated instruction based on their particular learning characteristics.
2. A curriculum should provide continuous development in specified skills and concepts.
3. Instruction should be cohesive rather than fragmented.
4. Instruction should enhance a student's ability to produce quality projects or works.
5. Interaction with others is vital to the learning process.[3]

The Advanced Skills Curriculum contains four overlapping phases: *Introduction, Instruction, Culmination,* and *Evaluation.* In the introduction phase, the model is designed to motivate and interest students while introducing new concepts. In the instruction phase, ASC offers experience with advanced skills, instruction in content, and reinforcement of other skills. The culmination phase provides opportunities for students to work independently or in small groups to produce quality products. These demonstrate the ability to implement the advanced skills while also assessing the effectiveness of the instructional activities.

The purpose for overlapping the phases is to continually expose students to motivating experiences (even during the instruction phase) and to allow students to begin their culminating projects early while they still have time to acquire more information and skills so they can make appropriate revisions. Although such a sequence might work with nongifted students, Tuttle believes that the *overlapping* of the phases is what makes it particularly relevant to gifted and talented education. He concludes his description of the model by saying:

> The emphasis on instruction in specific skills and concepts during the instructional phase provides continuity and sequence throughout the program, an important criterion in any effective program. Within the instructional phase the teacher provides direct instruction in general skills such as critical thinking and problem solving and/or advanced content skills and concepts. Throughout the instruction and culmination phases students should receive periodic reaction to their work from both peers and teacher. Consequently, final evaluation is conducted separately, since by this phase the student product should be complete.[4]

In 1985, Ballantine Books published *Developing Talent in Young People,* edited by Benjamin S. Bloom, the learning theorist who is perhaps best known for his cognitive taxonomy. The book represents the findings of a long-term study on the nature of the gifted and talented.

Bloom found that the young child initially views the development of talent as recreation and play. A period of learning activity that involves much time and effort and meets high standards follows this beginning. The talented person ultimately engages in special learning experiences that transform the play into a calling or lifelong career.

The gifted and talented, Bloom states further, learn a strong work ethic from their parents, who also reinforce the belief that one ought to do one's best. Initially the work ethic is applied to home and school activity; later this value transfers to the chosen field of talent.

Parents strongly encouraged their children's development in areas where particular talent was shown and gave less support to other possible fields and activities. Bloom argues that no one ever reaches the limits of learning in a talent field on his or her own. Gifted and talented persons who excel in a particular field have the continual support of their families and teachers who have set the stage for exceptional achievement. The gifted and talented need clear evidence of achievement and progress over a long period of increasingly complex work in order to attain excellence.

Bloom's findings indicate that the development of talent is based on neither heredity alone nor environment alone but on the complex interaction that occurs between them. The strategies described in this volume can be viewed as procedures for maximizing the interaction of heredity and environment. This interaction can facilitate the development of all human beings, including the average and the very able. The application of these strategies to teaching the very able can be particularly rewarding because the gifted apply these procedures in ways that produce high levels of achievement. This chapter now turns to the use of these strategies with the gifted and talented.

THE THREE STRATEGIES AND GIFTEDNESS

Creativity

The acquisition of language at an early age indicated giftedness. In creativity theory, this relates to fluency and elaboration. The early acquisition of language supports these traits and hence g/t students have a head start toward developing creative behavior. At the same time, providing instructional opportunity for increasing fluency and elaboration supports both giftedness and creativity. Procedures for doing this were discussed in Chapter 5. Requiring gifted and talented students to engage in extensive amounts of writing can also be very useful in this regard.

Abstract reasoning, another trait of the gifted, can be supported by encouraging creative behavior. The abstract reasoning that comes from the creative condition of incompleteness results in challenge and provides the g/t student with a difficult task.

The self-confidence of gifted and talented children allows them to take the risks associated with creativity. In producing something new, the innovative person risks the alienation of others who do not seek new perspectives and who are threatened by innovation. In order to create, one must take these risks and the self-confidence of the very able supports this.

The imaginative nature of the gifted and talented child allows him or her to see familiar things in unfamiliar, strange ways. This is a seminal trait of creativity as well as of giftedness. Hence the use of procedures for facilitating creative behavior encourages the development of imagination in the gifted and talented student.

The persistence found among the gifted and talented children is still another trait that encourages creative behavior. Thomas Edison once remarked that invention requires 1 percent inspiration and 99 percent perspiration. The noncreative person gives up easily in the face of difficulty whereas the creative one persists to the end. The predisposition to persist is a trait shared by the gifted and the creative.

The short essay by Carol Carpenter that concludes this chapter points up a quality of giftedness that is also a central aspect of creativity. That quality is spontaneity that is the underlying energy for all creative behavior. All human beings are born spontaneous, but this trait tends to diminish and becomes inhibited as persons grow older. The creative person remains less restrained as s/he ages. Supporting spontaneity in gifted children (and in others as well) can increase creative behavior. Often the school serves as an agency that strengthens inhibition. The importance of this trait, however, cannot be overstated; as spontaneity increases, so does creativity.

Stimulation/Gaming

Many aspects of the gifted and talented can be related to simulation/ gaming, which offers players new experiences and increases their curiosity. Furthermore, gifted and talented children operate at high levels of abstraction and gaming abstracts metaphorically from real world events. Therefore good games meet the need of gifted children for abstract thought.

Game designers face the problem of reality orientation. This describes the extent to which a simulation/game conforms to actuality. All games (as well as all other media—including textbooks) are selective, leaving out many aspects of the world. Including too much can transform the game into the actual event; excluding too much distorts the process so badly as to render the exercise valueless. A game designer seeks to find a balance. In order to do this, complex directions often accompany simulation/games. Sometimes these are difficult for the average student to understand, but the complexity of directions adds to the enjoyment of the process for the gifted and talented. Furthermore, the complexity of the process provides g/t students with an opportunity to see the interaction of cause and effect, and also provides for an intellectual need of giftedness.

Able children accept new ideas readily. A good game provides new perspectives for players and often makes the familiar strange. In this way it offers ideas that stimulate the gifted while increasing their creative behavior as well. The gifted and talented have many interests along with an appropriate attention span for exploring them. Games of all sorts attract bright children. Chess has always fascinated them, providing an interesting, often exciting, contest. Quality instructional games have the same effect, capturing and holding attention.

Able children possess rich imaginations. Many simulations contain fantasy scenarios (not unlike commercial simulations such as *Dungeons and Dragons,* which also have wide appeal among the gifted and talented); students imagine themselves in other roles, times, and places. This feature of simulation/gaming matches well with the fanciful nature of able children.

Independent work characterizes the gifted and talented. Instructional games require the development of independent strategies, supporting the bright child's desire to work alone. Gifted and talented children need individualization of instruction just as other students do. Simulation/games provide for this, permitting and encouraging idiosyncratic strategies that can be played at varying levels of abstraction.

Future Studies

Helping gifted and talented students become futurists provides them with intellectual challenge and gives society the benefit of able persons who can cope with the transition to the Third Wave and with future shock.

Books describing major problems facing humankind—like those by Asimov, Brockman, and Naisbitt (discussed in chapter 9)—point up the primary need of tomorrow—the ability to solve problems. Gifted and talented students are ideal problem solvers and the challenge of tomorrow fits well with their need to face challenges.

Future studies seeks to enlarge and extend social perspectives, in part, by predicting and making forecasts about the future. This aspect of future studies is ideally suited to the gifted and talented who enjoy new perspectives and are fascinated by prediction and forecasting.

Futurists attempt to define as many possible futures as possible and recognize the limits of trying to identify a single scenario. This open-ended aspect of future studies appeals to the gifted and talented who enjoy speculation and who can produce a wide variety of alternative scenarios. Furthermore, the interdisciplinary nature of the process attracts the gifted and talented because synthesizing (a defining characteristic of interdisciplinary study) is something they do well. Approaching the future requires risks and gifted and talented students are ideal risk takers because they tend to approach new situations with great confidence.

The objectives for a future studies curriculum described in Chapter 10—information-gathering competence, critical thinking skills, the ability to communicate effectively, knowledge about the environment, knowledge about human institutions, and personal effectiveness—are all especially appealing to the gifted and talented.

The ability to prepare for life in the future improves for persons who are creative problem solvers and who are able to use the strategy of simulation/gaming. Careful development of these strategies with the very able will help them accommodate to tomorrow just as it helps traditional students prepare for the future.

SUMMARY

This chapter has examined the nature of gifted and talented education in relation to the innovative strategies described in this volume. It began by looking at the need for attention to the very able—one that arises because g/t students can make a major contribution toward the solution of society's most troubling problems. Gifted and talented students, teachers, schools, and society all benefit when the needs of the very able are addressed.

The chapter defined major terms relating to gifted and talented education and provided readers with the Congressional definition of the process. It demonstrated that four components—ability, creativity, motivation, and task commitment—are necessary for the identification of gifted and talented persons. Traits of the able were identified as well as characteristics of those who would teach them. Program design alternatives were described and theoretical issues were introduced. Finally, the chapter discussed the relationship between gifted and talented education, creativity, simulation/gaming, and future studies.

This chapter can be concluded on a lighter note with the following essay written by Carol Carpenter and published in *Curriculum Review* in April 1981.

WHO ARE THE GIFTED CHILDREN?

Gifted children never use just one sheet of paper, ask just one question, tell just one story, break just one pencil, hiccup just one time, tie just one knot in their gym shoes.

Gifted children can talk to kids behind them without moving their lips or turning around. They can also crack their toes and elbows, curl their tongues, and wiggle their ears—all while the teacher turns to pick up a book from the desk.

Gifted children dawdle on the way to school. They stop to watch a leaf float down the sewer, catch snowflakes on their tongues, drag sticks along cyclone fences, and pick up a paper someone else has dropped just in case it's a ransom note or a million dollar check.

Gifted children never forget to do their homework—it's just that their little sister ate it, or their big brother wrote an important phone number on it, or the dog got sick on it, or their mother threw it out because it was on the steps, or their father tore it up when he couldn't do the last problem, or a pelican swooped from the sky and stuffed it in his pouch.

Gifted children dare to color outside the lines and draw pictures on their friends' lunch bags.

Gifted children trade their squished, soggy cream cheese sandwiches for their friends' bags of potato chips, candy bars, and peanut butter and jelly crackers.

Gifted children want to know why subjects and verbs have to agree when governments don't, and why supplies provided by the school run out halfway through the first day.

Gifted children describe their teacher, classmates, and school day in such vivid detail that parents tiptoe into the room during Open House, glance apprehensively into the coat room, tell the teacher she's much younger than they thought, and ask about the poor child who got sleeping sickness.

Gifted children wave their hands while the teacher is giving directions for the reading assignment and ask if the seeds the class planted yesterday have started to grow yet.

Gifted children take their loose-leaf notebooks apart to figure out how they work, and when their fingers get caught in the metal rings, they study the blood flow to figure out how many gallons they've lost.

Gifted children drive parents crazy by keeping bottle cap collections in pants pockets, letting pet grasshoppers loose in the basement, climbing to the tops of trees, and asking why the man behind them in the line has such big feet.

Gifted children make teachers wish that desks were bolted to the floors, that gum had never been discovered, that spitballs couldn't be made out of spelling tests, and that children developed laryngitis during school hours.

Gifted children need teachers who "would gladly learn and gladly teach."

NOTES

1. Joseph Renzulli, *The Enrichment Triad Model* (New York: Creative Learning Press, 1977), p. 30.
2. Frederick B. Tuttle and Laurence A. Becker, *Program Design and Development for Gifted and Talented Students* (Washington, DC: National Education Association, 1983).
3. Ibid., p. 52.
4. Op Cit., Tuttle and Becker, p. 52.

CHAPTER

12

Classroom Management

INTRODUCTION

Teaching and learning require orderly classrooms. Unless order exists, nothing important can occur. This does not imply that every student must quietly sit at his or her desk. Many of the strategies described in this volume involve movement, interaction, communication, and sometimes even apparent disorder (when, for example, certain kinds of simulation/games are used). But no matter what technique the teacher uses with his or her students, classroom discipline must be present. The process of achieving this is called *classroom management,* which requires the teacher as manager to take charge of the setting and to use time efficiently so that the objectives of the lesson can be achieved.

Effective classroom management begins with effective teaching. Students will not participate in the classroom unless they have a sense of accomplishment. When students fail to see the point of the instruction, when they are bored and uninterested, when the teacher fails to demonstrate the connection between the lesson and life, pupils will respond in a negative manner. On the other hand, a setting in which students perceive the significance and relevance of their studies will lead to a minimum of classroom management problems.

This is not to suggest the existence of a panacea that can end all classroom management problems. No matter what teaching strategy is used and no matter what management techniques the teacher employs, there will always be some students—for reasons that the teacher may never know—who cannot be reached and who demonstrate negative behavior and attitudes. The goal of classroom management is to minimize these problems. In order to deal better with some students, the teacher will need outside support—from guidance counselors, school social workers, and administrators. The majority of pupils, however, will respond to effective teaching strategies, which minimizes the need for external control over the classroom. The teacher who uses innovative teaching strategies has a better chance of becoming an effective classroom manager.

Facilitating creative behavior in students calls for getting them involved in the teaching-learning process. This strategy reduces the need for specific classroom management techniques. The process of simulation/gaming always engrosses students. Game playing (as indicated in Chapters 6 and 7) is a basic part of culture and fun is an important need of human beings. Gaming results in teaching that makes limit-setting easier. This also results from the study of the future, which appeals to students because future shock is real to them and studying the future helps them to minimize the feeling of malaise that may be associated with it. The connection between future studies and the lives of students results in a reduced need for external classroom management techniques.

Effective organization of instruction can also be a classroom management strategy. Careful planning makes classroom instruction more effective and results in less student frustration and dissatisfaction.

An adage among football coaches states that the best defense is a good offense. This also applies to teaching since the teacher who is well prepared in the subject s/he teaches, who is in command of a variety of effective teaching strategies, and who has developed careful instructional plans, has already begun to be an effective classroom manager.

An intangible factor for setting limits on the behavior of students can be labeled "teacher presence," a sense of being in charge that the teacher communicates to the students. It is one of the most significant factors in classroom management, but also one of the most difficult to describe. Presence means that the teacher enters the classroom knowing that s/he is in charge and that the students will respond to him or her in a positive and constructive way. When teachers have this quality, discipline problems and the need for specific management techniques decrease. When teachers lack presence, other strategies for setting limits may also fail. Each teacher must learn to communicate presence in his or her own way based on his or her own personality. Presence does not derive from one's physical size or one's sex. Small men and women can communicate it to a room filled with students who are bigger than they, and men and women of large stature sometimes fail to communicate the feeling that they are in charge. Although how each individual achieves this feeling is difficult to say, it is facilitated for all through self-confidence which results from solid academic preparation, the use of effective teaching strategies, and the careful preparation of lesson plans.

Several approaches to classroom management can be identified. This chapter, which examines a number of them, begins by describing behavior modification, and then examines the work of Dr. William Glasser who advocates a process called reality therapy and who has recently begun to write about "control theory." Humanistic psychology also suggests methods of classroom management, which are also discussed in this chapter. A large body of anecdotal literature written by teachers in the classroom is available. These books and the advice they offer about classroom management are discussed. The chapter concludes with a list of specific suggestions that can help achieve the order necessary for implementing innovative teaching strategies.

BEHAVIOR MODIFICATION

Behavior modification comes from behavioral psychology, a perspective described in Chapter 2 that is briefly summarized here. Behavioral psychology stems from the work of Pavlov, Skinner, and others. Its basic concept is the stimulus-response or S-R bond which holds that all behavior can be understood in terms of responses to stimuli. A dog salivates when it hears a bell because it has been conditioned to believe that the bell represents something to eat. A pigeon presses a lever because it has learned that the lever will release a bit of food. A rat traces its way through a maze because it knows that food exists at the end of the maze.

Stimulus-response psychology introduces the concept of rewards—called *reinforcers*—for changing behavior. Reinforcers can shape behavior in particular directions. Behavior modification used for classroom management suggests that actions can be shaped and controlled through the use of appropriate rewards. Behavior that is not reinforced will be extinguished. Although not necessarily part of S-R psychology, the application of behavior modification often requires punishment. Appropriate behaviors are thus reinforced and inappropriate ones are punished.

Advocates of behavior modification for classroom management offer a variety of specific techniques that teachers can use to maintain order and set limits with students. The simplest reinforcer to modify behavior consists of verbal praise. Appropriate words from the teacher can reward appropriate student behaviors and increase the occurrence of such behavior. Teachers can offer positive responses to students by saying things such as "very good," "that's a very good point," "nice work," "terrific idea," and the like. For many students verbal reinforcers are sufficient reward because human beings need praise from those in authority; this type of reinforcement can shape behavior effectively. Teachers can offer nonverbal support as well. A simple smile, a sincere look of interest, and a nod of the head can also encourage desired behavior.

The use of grades on examinations and report cards are well-established expressions of praise. In elementary school this sometimes takes the form of a smiling face drawn on a returned paper. For many students, a good grade on an exam (this is relative—for some students this means an "A," for others a "C+" will do) can help shape their future behavior.

Unfortunately praise and grades are not effective rewards for all students. Some pupils do not respond to these traditional reinforcers because they fail to see any particular value in them. In order for behavior modification to be more universal, those who advocate its use have introduced other techniques.

A popular procedure for classroom management that uses behavior modification is the contingency contract—a formal agreement negotiated between the teacher and the student. The contract may apply to classroom work or to behavior that the teacher wishes to eliminate. The agreement spells out both the nature of the action and the proposed reward for that action. The student might agree to turn in all of his or her homework assignments on time for the next week and the teacher will then reward him or her with one class period of free time. Other kinds of rewards may also be used. For example, each assignment turned in on time can result in a candy bar, or chips can be accumulated and used to acquire a variety of objects in a "catalogue." These may include receiving an "A" on an exam without taking it, free books and magazines, or even a trip to a local amusement park. It is expected that students will modify their behavior in response to the specific and tangible rewards offered by the instructor.

An extension of this procedure is called *group contingency contracting,* which employs the same procedures as individual agreements but applies to groups of students rather than to individuals. This adds the use of peer pressure to the process.

Behavior modification also introduces the concept of *response cost.* This involves taking back a reward that was previously given to the student when s/he engages in undesired activity. It is a fine levied on the student in order to eliminate the negative activity.

Self-monitoring, another behavior modification technique, requires students to keep careful records of their activity in the classroom. The self-awareness that results from the use of this technique becomes a kind of reinforcer that strengthens positive behaviors and weakens negative ones.

Other kinds of behavior modification techniques also exist but the ones described are the most common. All of these techniques depend on the viability of the connection between stimulus, response, and reward. Behavior modification provides the teacher with specific concrete activity for classroom management; this is its major advantage. Many students do respond to praise—verbal and nonverbal. The use of grades is an established behavior modification device that is widely accepted. Some difficult students respond to contingency contracting, response cost, and self-monitoring some of the time. The popularity of behavior modification comes from its simplicity and the ease with which a teacher can learn its application.

Behavior modification, however, has several limitations. Many learning theorists (including Arthur Koestler, Eliot Eisner, William Glasser, and Leslie Hart) deny the existence of the S-R bond. If behaviorism is not valid, then classroom management based on it cannot be effective in the long run. Other limits are also apparent. Those students who respond best to praise are often those who are already motivated to achieve in school. The most difficult students are not so easily reached. Contingency contracting works with difficult students some of the time. However, the more real and tangible the reward (candy rather than free time), the better is the response. But teachers may not always be able to provide tangible rewards. Furthermore, the use of these kinds of reinforcers raises ethical questions about the honesty of buying compliance.

The limits of behaviorism have not diminished its popularity. Behavior modification will work for some teachers in some settings. Each teacher must decide whether this system appeals to him or her. At its best, behavior modification can be one of several classroom management strategies in the repertoire of the teacher.

WILLIAM GLASSER: REALITY THERAPY AND CONTROL THEORY

William Glasser, a psychiatrist who has sought nonbehavioral ways to deal with mental illness, turned to the study of school improvement in 1969 with a book called, *Schools Without Failure,* in which he applied his method of psychotherapy to the problem of classroom management.[1]

Glasser's treatment system, called *reality therapy,* is based on the assumption that most human problems come from the inability of persons to satisfy two basic needs: love and self-worth. Glasser says:

> From birth to old age we need to love and be loved. Throughout our lives our health and happiness depend on our ability to do so. . . .

When we cannot satisfy our total need for love, we will suffer and react with many psychological symptoms from mild discomfort through anxiety and depression to complete withdrawal from the world around us.

Equal in importance to the need for love is the need to feel that we are worthwhile both to ourselves and others. Although the two needs are separate, a person who loves and is loved will usually feel that he is a worthwhile person, and one who is worthwhile is usually someone who is loved and who can give love in return.[2]

For Glasser, love in the classroom translates into responsible helping and caring for one another by teachers and students. Glasser believes that schools fail because they do not foster the warm and constructive relationships that are essential for success. Another cause of failure is loneliness; this leads to anger, frustration, and withdrawal. These kinds of behaviors, found among schoolchildren, result in many of the classroom management problems faced by teachers.

Reality therapy includes an action component. It is not enough to provide persons with insight. In order for them to improve, persons must engage in activities that provide the components they are lacking.

Glasser introduces four concepts that lead to improved mental health for students and hence to improved classroom management by the teacher. These are: (1) reality, (2) responsibility, (3) morality, and (4) involvement.

Reality requires the determination of whether an action is realistic or not. To decide this, students must become aware of both the immediate and remote consequences of their behavior. They must understand these results in terms of their effects on themselves and on others. When students comprehend the nature of their actions, according to Glasser, they will most often choose realistic actions.

Glasser defines responsibility as "the ability to fulfill one's needs, and to do so in a way that does not deprive others of the ability to fulfill their needs."[3] Learning to be responsible helps pupils achieve a sense of self-worth. This occurs when they meet their obligations to others.

Unlike many psychotherapists, Glasser discusses the issue of right and wrong by introducing morality into reality therapy. In order to obtain a sense of self-worth, people must do what is right and avoid what is wrong. Pupils must have a standard of behavior and live in accordance with that standard.

For reality therapy to work, involvement must exist. In the classroom both the teacher and the student must become involved. This makes the setting real for the student. The teacher's concern, on an emotional level, with the question of whether or not the student succeeds becomes the equivalent of parental love. Involvement must be present for children and adults in order to minimize the feeling of loneliness.

Reality therapy requires that individuals understand their own failures and be personally accountable for their own successes. It is the student's responsibility to change his or her behavior and to comprehend the rightness or wrongness of it. The pupil must make a commitment to improvement that can be a written agreement. Reality therapy as a classroom management technique puts great emphasis on the ability of a student (with the support of a caring teacher) to recognize the limits of their current behaviors and to seek ways to improve them.

Glasser suggests ways to use reality therapy for classroom management. First, the teacher must be involved with each student in order to demonstrate that s/he cares about the students. This caring becomes the motivation for the pupils' desire to change. Second, the teacher must help the students identify their problem behaviors without passing judgment about them. Third, the students must be guided to assess the correctness of their own behavior; the teacher should not force this. Fourth, the teacher can suggest alternative actions to students; which will lead to improved behavior by the students. Fifth, the teacher must acknowledge and support these improvements. Finally, the students must accept the consequences of their own actions. Any failure to follow through or change by the students must be noted by the teacher, who then engages in appropriate response (lowered grades, detentions, and the like). At the same time the teacher does this, s/he should also be helping the student begin the process all over again.

Glasser describes a group procedure for classroom management that he labels "The Classroom Meeting." This gathering develops a caring social group, capable of fostering self-discipline and commitment. The classroom meeting is a time when teachers and students, perhaps on a daily basis, come together for an open-ended, nonevaluative discussion. The group can focus on behavior problems facing the class or be unstructured with no particular agenda. The classroom meeting can also be used to discuss a particular topic that is being studied.

The use of the classroom meeting for management follows the same procedures as reality therapy does when it is practiced with individuals; it asks the groups to face the same kinds of issues regarding reality, responsibility, morality, and involvement. The advantage of the group experience is that it provides peer support for behavior changes and helps to minimize loneliness.

In 1986, Glasser introduced another approach to classroom management in a book entitled, *Control Theory*.[4] This volume expands the ideas first formulated in *Reality Therapy* and in *Schools Without Failure*.

In his later book Glasser identifies several basic needs of human beings. He says:

> All living creatures are driven by the basic needs to attempt to stay alive and reproduce so that the species will continue. As creatures have evolved from simple to complex, the basic need to survive and reproduce has been augmented by additional needs... humans not only need (1) to survive and reproduce, but also (2) to belong and love, (3) *to gain power,* (4) to be free and (5) to have fun. All five needs are built into our genetic structures as instructions for how we must attempt to live our lives. All are equally important and must be reasonably satisfied if we are to fulfill our biological destiny. I italicize the need for power because, unlike the other four needs that are shared to some extent by many higher animals, the way we continually struggle for power in every aspect of our lives seems uniquely human.[5]

These needs must be met in school for productive learning to occur and in order for classroom management to be effective. Because of the importance of power to human beings, students must feel that they have it. Glasser argues that a feeling of powerlessness among students will lead to a lack of productivity in the classroom. Power is also important because most of what we do in life is either an attempt to control ourselves or to control others.

Glasser describes a teaching strategy for facilitating classroom management, which he calls the *learning team model.* Instruction, he argues, can and should often be organized for teams of students. (These should include high, middle, and low achievers.) This will facilitate learning for a number of reasons. First, students will obtain a sense of belonging by being part of a team. Second, membership on a team provides students with motivation. Third, the stronger students find it fulfilling to help the weaker ones because they desire the power that comes to a high-performing group. Fourth, the weaker students recognize that however small their input, they are providing for the well-being of the team. When working on their own, the contribution usually amounts to nothing. Fifth, students do not depend on the teacher as much as before and therefore become more dependent on each other.

Learning teams should be rotated from project to project so that each student has an opportunity to be on a high-scoring team. The team should be free to offer its own kind of evidence to the teacher that it has achieved its goals. Evaluation, therefore, should not depend only on examinations. Finally, Glasser believes that the learning teams approach can lead to greater depth in learning and avoid the superficiality that he feels often plagues schools.

The learning team approach, based on control theory, recognizes the basic needs of persons and allows students to feel a genuine sense of power. It provides a new role for the teacher—that of team facilitator. This can aid classroom management significantly because it offers the teacher more realistic ways to interact with students.

Glasser's approach has much to offer teachers. It provides specific ideas for controlling students while demonstrating that limit setting is complex and must occur in the context of total learning. Reality therapy and control theory are useful; they can be added to the teacher's tools for classroom management.

HUMANISTIC PSYCHOLOGY AND CLASSROOM MANAGEMENT

The basic tenet of humanistic psychology is that persons must be enabled to grow in whatever institution they find themselves—home, school, marriage, or workplace. Humanistic psychology has its roots in the existential philosophy of Jean-Paul Sartre with its constructs of freedom, choice, the need for self-definition, and the belief that the finite nature of life requires persons to define their own essence. The ultimate aim of humanistic psychology is self-actualization, which can be viewed as a protest against the overreliance on empiricism by other kinds of psychologists who study the human psyche.

Humanistic psychology seeks to extend the development of the "normal" limits of people. It has as a goal the creation of human beings who are healthy in mind and body and who are able to enjoy life to its fullest. It seeks the development of persons who can relate to others, solve problems—personal and societal—and adjust and adapt to new circumstances.

The ideas of Abraham Maslow (1916–1972) well represent the perspective of humanistic psychology. Maslow's ideas, which were described in Chapter 7, are briefly summarized here.

Maslow called humanistic psychology "the third force," by which he meant that it existed between behaviorism and psychoanalysis. The purpose of human life, according to Maslow, is to grow toward self-actualization—the point at which a person achieves all of his or her potential. Maslow knew that few people would ever accomplish this, but he saw it as an outcome toward which persons should strive.

The most important of Maslow's ideas is his hierarchy of needs. These relate to the necessities of living, and Maslow ranked them on a ladder of desires. Needs on the lower rungs must be satisfied before higher-order ones could be attempted. First on the hierarchy are the physiological requirements for air, water, food, shelter, sleep, and sex. Next on the ladder is the need for security and safety. After these needs are met, one seeks love and belonging, followed by the desire for self-esteem and the esteem of others. At the apex of one hierarchy is the drive for growth including meaningfulness, self-sufficiency, playfulness, order, justice, perfection, individuality, aliveness, beauty, goodness, and truth.

From time to time, Maslow argues, persons have "peak experiences," which are rare moments of feeling self-actualized. Characteristics of self-actualization are listed in Chapter 7 and the reader might turn back to review them.

Humanistic psychology offers a perspective on classroom management that can aid teachers—particularly when viewed as one of several psychological perspectives for helping the teacher establish and maintain control in the classroom.

In a classroom managed by humanistic principles, freedom will be maximized. This does not mean anarchy or lack of control. From a humanistic perspective control and freedom are not incompatible. A teacher following humanistic practice must decide, within the limits of school district policy, what rules are necessary for the efficient operation of the classroom and which are superfluous. Is a compulsory seating chart necessary or can students choose their own places? Is the prohibition against gum chewing critical to the operation of the classroom or can this be another area of student freedom? Are dress codes essential to the successful operation of the school? Every teacher and every school district must make their own policies about these issues, but the humanistic perspective suggests that freedom be maximized in the classroom. Fewer restraints may actually lead to better management.

A second principle of humanistic management practice is the maximization of choice. Teachers can often find ways to offer choices to their pupils. Not every student must read the same book for every reading assignment; sometimes students can select from a list of authors. Students can choose units of study for themselves or for the entire class. Teachers can provide a wide variety of alternatives to pupils. This will not weaken control but may increase it as students take responsibility for their own actions and hence for themselves.

The humanistic classroom teacher can help students function more effectively in the classroom through the use of role play as a classroom management technique. Many students will function better in the classroom when they learn more productive roles. Teachers can structure role-playing activities that allow students to experience new behaviors. Coupled with freedom and choice, the use of role play to learn new ways of acting can significantly improve classroom control and management.

Humanistic psychology suggests that students obtain strong emotional support from teachers. Pupils should be addressed in a positive manner with a minimum of criticism and negative remarks. This is not to say that anything goes but only that evaluation should be constructive building on the need for self-esteem rather than denying it. Teachers must draw on the most positive aspects of a student's personality and support it instead of responding to the most negative aspects of the pupil.

Teaching activity should be designed to encourage self-actualization. It should offer the possibility for the development of creativity and spontaneity and minimize the use of fear as a motivating device. It should allow students to make decisions and to live with the consequences of those decisions.

The humanistic view of the classroom is quite different from other perspectives. Its major advantage is that it can foster a classroom atmosphere that is more pleasant for the teacher and for the student. Its disadvantage is that when taken to an extreme, humanistic procedures can lead to chaos and a lack of order. Humanistic psychology requires a balance; the application of these principles can lead to more effectively managed classrooms.

ADVICE FROM PRACTITIONERS

There is a large body of anecdotal literature about classroom management written by teachers who have described their experiences in the schools. Much of this material offers insights about classroom management from teachers who have faced the problem in actual settings.

During the 1960s—a period of great change in education—a number of books about the specific experiences in the schools were published. Many of the authors of these books later became educational reformers and continue to write about and influence schools today.

One of the most significant of these books was *Death at an Early Age* by Jonathan Kozol, who wrote about his teaching experiences in the Boston public schools.[6] He described the experience of a retarded boy whose knuckles were beaten bloody as a punishment. Kozol argued that the punishment was pointless because the child was incapable of understanding the connection between it and his behavior. Kozol has continued to be interested in educational reform, turning his attention most recently to the problem of illiteracy in the United States.

Another of the young reformers of the 1960s was Herbert Kohl, whose book, *36 Children,* described the difficulties involved in teaching in Harlem.[7] Kohl, who became an advocate of the open classroom in the 1970s, also continues to write about educational reform. His most recent book, *Basic Skills,* is a call for a sensible and balanced approach to basic education.[8]

One of the most interesting writers of the 1960s was James Herndon, who wrote about his experience as a teacher in a school district in California—a book entitled *The Way It Spozed to Be.*[9] In this book, Herndon described his struggle to find meaningful activity for all the students in his elementary schoolroom. Finally, near the end of the school year, a day came when he provided important activity for each student. All around his classroom, pupils were engaged in a variety of projects including the production of a play and the creation of a newspaper. Herndon was feeling a great sense of satisfaction when an administrator walked into the room. What seemed like success to Herndon looked like chaos to the supervisor. Herndon lost his job.

As a result of writing *The Way It Spozed to Be* Herndon was able to find another teaching job in another California school district, where, because his book had given him a certain amount of notoriety, he found a supportive environment and an administration that gave him the freedom to teach in his own way. Herndon, however, had problems in this setting as well. Although the school supported academic development, Herndon found that it also sought to create winners and losers among the students. This led to a great deal of pressure and tension for the pupils. Herndon described these experiences in a second book called *How to Survive in Your Native Land.*[10]

Herndon has recently published *Notes from a Schoolteacher* based on his most current experiences as a teacher.[11] In this book Herndon describes the conflict that exists between prescribed classroom management and the perspective of the practitioner who must improvise and who can not always rely on the strict prescriptions of the school administration.

In 1972, best-selling author Pat Conroy published *The Water Is Wide* which describes his experiences as a teacher in Beaufort, South Carolina, where he taught poor, rural black children.[12] The book was later made into a moving and sensitive film, *Conrack,* with Jon Voigt in the title role. Conroy describes his success in reaching children by finding many kinds of activities for them that resulted in their intense involvement. Conroy, like Herndon, was fired despite his apparent success and in spite of the attempts of parents of his students to have him retained.

In 1986, Stuart B. Palonsky, an education professor, wrote a book he called *900 Shows a Year* about his experience as a teacher in a New

Jersey high school.[13] Palonsky's book described the two years that he took off from a state university to return to high school teaching, Palonsky reached a number of conclusions about schools in the 1980s. First, he found that teaching remains a difficult and demanding job. A good deal of time is required for reading papers and grading exams and less time is available for reading current literature about the subject or the nature of teaching. Teachers feel unsupported and vulnerable a good deal of the time. Palonsky believes that schools are modeled on the factor—a mass-production enterprise in which students march along in assembly-line fashion, moving every period at the sound of a bell. Palonsky also discovered that he could introduce an element of creative teaching into his classroom. He found students receptive to this and he learned that if he were careful not to make waves, he could gain the support of the administration in his attempts at innovation.

These books are representative of many anecdotal descriptions of classroom management by teachers who have day-to-day experience in the field. These accounts are both entertaining and enlightening. Persons seeking to improve their classroom management skills will find reading this literature helpful and interesting.

A number of conclusions about classroom management can be drawn from this literature. First, all of these teachers viewed their students compassionately, seeking to teach in humane ways. They all argue for empathy in working with difficult students. Without compassion and empathy, bad situations can only become worse ones.

A second conclusion from this material is that teachers need to accept the students as they find them. Only by accepting the students on their own terms can teachers ever hope to reach them. Rejecting pupils for their lack of knowledge, their lack of motivation, or their lack of good manners will make any attempt to teach them futile.

Third, teachers must use procedures that will result in a high level of involvement. Activities that are meaningless to students will not work; those that are meaningful will lead to learning and to increased participation in the process.

This literature also leads to the conclusion that teachers must be flexible about the curriculum and about their expectations of children. Instructors must be slow to judge children in negative ways and they must not reject the culture they find in the school setting. More can be accomplished with less judgment about the culture and with more focus on helping students meet their human needs.

A final conclusion that can be made from this literature is that teachers must learn to communicate with those in authority who can be helpful to them. Teachers often need strong support from the administration if they are to be effective classroom managers.

CONCLUSIONS

This chapter has examined classroom management by offering perspectives derived from a number of different sources including behaviorism, reality therapy, humanistic psychology, and practitioners in the field. It concludes by listing a number of generalizations drawn from all of these sources, which can help teachers maintain order so that the innovative strategies presented in this book can be effectively used.

1. *Classroom management is facilitated by effective teaching.* Students who are engrossed in a lesson and who are taught in meaningful ways are less likely to be disruptive.
2. *Effective organization of instruction leads to successful management.* Well-prepared teachers will find students more responsive than teachers who are not organized or who seek to simply fill time.
3. *The teacher must develop classroom presence.* Students who understand that the teacher is in charge will be less likely to create problems in the classroom. Classroom presence results, in part, from knowledge of the subject and from effective organization of instruction.
4. *The teacher should use praise generously.* Sincere praise can be used to reinforce all kinds of positive behavior; this can make classroom management easier to achieve.
5. *The criteria for grading should be as clear as possible.* Student who know how they are being evaluated and how to increase their chances for good grades will tend to be more cooperative than those who do not.
6. *Classroom management is facilitated when students are made to feel a sense of self-worth.* Teachers must relate to students in ways that do not diminish the pupils' sense of self. Praise is much more useful than criticism. Sarcasm and anger seldom result in effective classroom management.
7. *Students must be held responsible for the consequences of their actions.* Increasing choice in the classroom facilitates responsibility.
8. *The use of group process is important in classroom management.* Groups can be used for instructional purposes as they are in games or with learning teams. They can also help students focus on discipline problems.
9. *A sense of freedom is important; it should be extended as far as possible.* Rules without purpose should not exist. Fewer rules are easier to enforce than many.

10. *Teachers should offer maximum support to their students.* This includes intellectual as well as emotional support. Students need to feel that the teacher is on their side and is not an adversary.
11. *Teachers need to be flexible.* Things seldom proceed on the schedule the teacher has set or in the manner the teacher has envisioned. Instructors need to go with the flow and avoid becoming upset when things do not occur in the prearranged order.
12. *Finally, when all else fails, teachers must know when to go for help.* It is not a sign of weakness to recognize that one is unable to cope with a situation. Knowing when to go for help is a sign of strength. Outside support exists in all school districts and must be used when appropriate.

NOTES

1. William Glasser, *Schools without Failure* (New York: Harper & Row, 1969).
2. William Glasser, *Reality Therapy* (New York: Harper & Row, 1965), pp. 9–10.
3. Ibid., p. 13.
4. William Glasser, *Control Theory* (New York: Harper & Row, 1986).
5. Ibid., p. 23.
6. Jonathan Kozol, *Death at an Early Age* (Boston: Houghton Mifflin, 1967).
7. Herbert Kohl, *36 Children* (New York: New American Library, 1967).
8. Herbert Kohl, *Basic Skills* (Boston: Little Brown, 1982).
9. James Herndon, *The Way It Spozed to Be* (New York: Simon and Schuster, 1968).
10. James Herndon, *How to Survive in Your Native Land* (New York: Simon and Schuster, 1971).
11. James Herndon, *Notes from a Schoolteacher* (New York: Simon and Schuster, 1985).
12. Pat Conroy, *The Water Is Wide* (Boston: Houghton Mifflin, 1972).
13. Stuart B. Palonsky, *900 Shows a Year* (New York: Random House, 1986).

EPILOGUE

Implications and Conclusions

Jessica Barnes loves teaching American history to eighth-grade students at the Lyndon B. Johnson Middle School in a suburb of Minneapolis. She is particularly knowledgeable about the American Revolution, having done her master's thesis on this period. One morning she had intended to describe the positions of each of the states at the Constitutional Convention to her class. She had planned to ask her students to analyze the Constitution to determine the effectiveness of each of the states in achieving its purpose. However, that day Ms. Barnes had laryngitis. She could not speak much above a whisper. But the lesson was not lost. Ms. Barnes then prepared data cards listing the demands of each state. She organized an activity in which the students played the roles of the states at the meeting. With this alternative technique, she provided the necessary data. Ms. Barnes accomplished her objective in an innovative and interesting manner. The successful teacher must have both subject matter expertise and competence in the use of teaching strategies.

This book describes innovative teaching strategies that increase instructional options. No technique can replace a thorough knowledge of subject matter, yet the strategies described in this volume can improve teaching effectiveness because they provide the teacher with a wide range of possibilities for achieving desired objectives. This is also important in the context of recent research about the brain. Understanding the structure and the functions of the brain enables educators to understand learning better than ever before.

Leslie Hart, a writer and researcher in education, has coined the term "brain compatible education."[1] He has applied knowledge about the brain to teaching methods. Hart offers an interesting metaphor: a person can easily bend his or her fingers forward to touch the palm of the hand; however, no one can bend his or her fingers backward to touch the back of the hand. The first action is compatible with human physiology whereas the second is not. This analogy applies to education; some teaching strategies are compatible with human learning and others are not.

An understanding of the triune nature of the brain can help make this clear. This concept was first described by medical doctor Paul MacLean.[2] During the course of evolution, human brains developed with three vertical sections. The first of these parts MacLean calls the *reptilian* brain. This segment supports routine behavior and it is the part of the brain that becomes upset when routine is broken. It is based on the reptile's dependence on habitual behavior or survival. A more recently evolved segment of the brain is the *paleomammalian* (also called the *limbic* system). Its function is to require animals to be responsible for their young (rather than to eat them, as animals lacking this segment are prone to do). This portion of the brain also accounts for emotion. It is the section of the mind that causes animals to flee or fight, telling the creature to run from more powerful opponents or attack those who are weaker. The third segment of the brain—the *neomammalian*—is found in the higher primates and in human beings; it is the location of reason and also provides for the ability to read and to write.

The following example demonstrates the importance of the concept of brain-compatible learning. When a human being feels threatened, the limbic system—the paleomammalian brain—comes to the fore; it overrides the rest of the brain until the feeling of threat subsides. Teaching based on traditional strategies relies heavily on threats of all kinds. Students may fear punishment, poor grades, failure, and the possibility of losing face in the estimation of their peers. When the threat is serious enough, the limbic system takes control and the huge gray matter of the neomammalian brain is temporarily rendered useless. The use of threat in the classroom often results in teaching that inhibits learning.

Knowledge about the hemispheres of the brain also can add to an understanding of brain-compatible learning. The human brain consists of two hemispheres connected by a large cable of nerve fibers called the *corpus callosum* whose function is to transmit the separate processes of each hemisphere to each other. During the late 1950s and early 1960s a psychologist, Roger W. Sperry, first described the nature of the two lobes of the brain. He received the Nobel prize for medicine in 1981 for his work on the brain. Sperry's basic hypothesis was that although both sides of the brain are involved in high-level cognitive work, each specializes in its own style of thinking and each has its own capabilities. In effect, the two hemispheres use different modes of information processing.

The left hemisphere in most persons specializes in analytical thinking. It is the source of reason and logic and is the verbal side of the brain. The left hemisphere is also the source of conceptual ability; it is the part of the brain that names and categorizes. The left lobe thinks linearly; it puts things in order and expects first things to come first. Using a term devised by Edward T. Hall, whose work was described in Chapter 1, the left hemisphere supports monochronic culture.

For most persons, the right hemisphere functions in nonverbal, spatial, and intuitive ways. It is the location of perception and its way of processing information is nonlinear and nonsequential. Instead of dealing with one thing at a time, the right hemisphere deals with many things simultaneously. In Hall's terms, it is the part of the brain that supports polychronic culture.

Early research on the hemispheres of the brain tended to rigidly divide their functions. The conclusion reached was that the two sides of the brain were independent lobes with differentiated purposes. The separateness of the two sides has not been supported by later research. Neuropsychologist Karl Pribram—among others—has described the holographic nature of the brain. Pribram uses the hologram, a method of photography using laser light to create three-dimensional pictures, as a metaphor for the brain. He argues that, like a hologram which can reconstruct a picture from any part, the brain distributes information across its entire surface. Memory, for example, is stored over the entire area of the brain. Individuals who have lost 50 percent of the brain still retain almost 100 percent of their memories. Other functions of the brain also exist holographically.

The holographic nature of the brain weakens the notion that the two hemispheres function independently. Rather it appears to be the case that the two sides of the brain specialize in different functions even though each is capable of doing the work of the other.

Betty Edwards, in a book called *Drawing on the Artist Within,* refers to the specialization of the left hemisphere as the "L-mode" and labels the capabilities of the other hemisphere as the "R-mode."[3] For Edwards, an art teacher, it is the R-mode that contains the unconscious part of creativity called *incubation,* a process that occurs while the conscious mind is engaged elsewhere. Using Edwards's conceptualization, the rigid division of the two hemispheres can be modified. One can view the two modes as capabilities of the brain occurring in the separate hemispheres but not necessarily limited to them. Thus one can conclude that the brain can do analytical, sequential, conscious, monochronic work (its L-mode activity) while it also has intuitive, spatial, nonlinear, unconscious polychronic ability (its R-mode function).

The strategies described in this book, with their emphasis on developing human potential and with their concern for engaging learning in many ways, are brain-compatible strategies. They provide for the creation of environments in which students function in ways that utilize their mental ability securely and effectively. They use activities that engage both modes of the brain.

That the innovative teaching strategies described in this book are brain compatible is the first conclusion that can be made. The remainder of this epilogue lists and discusses several other conclusions about innovative teaching strategies.

1. *Innovative teaching strategies are needed to increase the problem-solving capacity of students.* The increasing complexity of human life continues to generate enormous problems for humankind. These require the attainment of new perspectives. The strategies described in this column are ones that lead to the development of new outlooks.

2. *The strategies of facilitating creative behavior, simulation/gaming, and the study of the future support a variety of learning styles.* Human beings learn in many different ways. Not only does variation exist between human beings but an individual's style of learning may vary depending on what she or he is being asked to accomplish. The strategies described in this volume can be used with many different kinds of learning styles.

3. *The most effective use of the strategies described in this book will occur when careful organization of instruction takes place.* Competent organization of instruction requires careful selection of objectives. Furthermore, it requires an understanding of the components of planning and their interrelationship. Effective planning is facilitated when the teacher has an in-depth knowledge about the subject being taught.

4. *Human beings have the capacity to establish new perspectives; this enables them to be creative.* The ability to create is found in all human beings. It can be seen in small children who learn to fashion new ways to use their environments. Teachers can learn to facilitate creative behavior in students of all ages.

5. *An understanding of creativity can be achieved in many different ways.* Innovation can be understood by examining studies of creative people, processes, products, and environments. No matter how one approaches the study, similar conclusions about the creative process tend to emerge.

6. *The process of creativity contains a number of components.* Among the more significant are fluency, flexibility, originality, elaboration, and redefinition.

7. *Creativity has been studied by theorists studying consciousness and by those interested in the unconscious.* J. P. Guilford and E. Paul Torrance have analyzed the nature of innovation from the perspective of consciousness. Sigmund Freud and William J. J. Gordon are theorists who have been interested in creativity as an unconscious process. Both perspectives have led to similar conclusions.

8. *The process of simulation/gaming is a powerful one that results in a highly effective teaching strategy.* Part of its effectiveness comes from its ability to involve students. Part of its significance relates to the central role of gaming in all cultures.

9. *Simulation/gaming helps people learn how to learn; it is one of the most brain-compatible teaching devices in existence.* Simulations provide students with direct rather than vicarious experiences. This makes the activity meaningful. The process offers students direct and immediate feedback.

10. *Gaming is an interdisciplinary technique.* Gaming can simulate problems in any teaching field; this adds to its value as a strategy.

11. *Simulation/gaming facilitates group process.* The reliance of simulation/gaming on group interaction makes it a valuable technique that enhances the teacher's ability to use groups for succcessful classroom management.

12. *Simulation/gaming supports Dewey's construct of experiential education.* Dewey urged that teaching involves real as well as vicarious experience. A simulation/game is a vicarious experience to the extent that it mirrors a real world event in an abbreviated fashion. But the playing of the game is also an actual event that occurs in the here and now.

13. *Simulation/gaming can facilitate the development of human potential.* John Dewey and Abraham Maslow helped to develop humanistic psychology. The process of simulation/gaming leads to the kind of growth advocated by this perspective on learning. Simulation/gaming demands decision making, which also facilitates human growth. The need to make decisions in an exciting game becomes important to the player.

14. *The role-playing aspects of gaming foster the development of improved mental health.* Transactional analysis and psychodrama, systems used for therapy, achieve their effectiveness, in part, by using and understanding role-play. The process of gaming relates to these therapies since a good game is often a sociodrama—a nontherapeutic application of TA and Psychodrama.

15. *Simulation/gaming is a futures language.* This adds to its importance as an innovative teaching strategy and it supports its use for studying the future.

16. *The need to anticipate the future in a manner that allows for accommodation to rapid change reinforces the need for future studies.* The writings of a number of futurists including Asimov, Naisbitt, and Toffler support this conclusion. The study of the future, although frightening, is also necessary.

17. *The primary purpose of future studies is to extend and enlarge social perspectives about the time to come.* Studying the future in the classroom helps students become problem solvers and problem anticipators. This ability to anticipate difficulties is critical in a world affected by future shock.

18. *The strategies of facilitating creative behavior, simulation/ gaming, and future studies are synergistic.* Creative persons are better gamers. Learning to be an effective simulation/gamer can make one more creative. Both of these strategies provide persons with skills that prepare them for more effective life in the future.

19. *The study of the future can be accomplished in separate courses or by the addition of future studies to other courses in the curriculum.* Specific kinds of curricular outcomes facilitate the study of the future. These include: (1) information-gathering competence, (2) critical thinking skills, (3) the ability to communicate effectively, (4) knowledge about the environment, (5) knowledge about human institutions, and (6) personal effectiveness.

20. *The innovative strategies described in this book can facilitate the development of gifted and talented students.* The complexity of problems facing humankind need the attention of the most able student. These pupils often find facilitating creative behavior, simulation/gaming, and the study of the future very challenging. The strategies are also useful because they can be used with g/t students and more typical students simultaneously. Persons of differing abilities can participate in these activities at different levels of sophistication.

21. *Classroom management is facilitated by effective teaching strategies.* No matter what approach to limit setting the teacher chooses, s/he will find that when students are fully involved in the teaching-learning process, they will be less likely to create discipline problems. The use of innovative teaching strategies increases student involvement and reduces the need for negative approaches to classroom management.

Teaching is a complex and demanding profession. It can often be rewarding but it can also be frustrating. A teacher finds him or herself called upon to play many roles. A teacher can maximize his or her effectiveness by the possession of a large repertoire of instructional techniques. This volume offers a variety of innovative teaching strategies, and also includes a great variety of complete exercises. The reader is urged to try these techniques in the classroom. Following the use of these techniques, the reader can then obtain the additional exercises described in the three chapters of the text that discuss teaching procedures.

NOTES

1. Leslie A. Hart, *How the Brain Works* (New York: Basic Books, Inc., 1975).
2. Paul MacLean, "Man and His Animal Brains," in *Modern Medicine,* March 2, 1964.
3. Betty Edwards, *Drawing on the Artist Within* (New York: Simon and Schuster, 1986).

ADDITIONAL READING

Asimov, Isaac. *Exploring the Earth and the Cosmos.* New York: Crown Publishers, 1982.

Asimov, Isaac, ed., *Living in the Future.* New York: Beaufort Books, 1985.

Barell, John. *Playgrounds of Our Minds.* New York: Teachers College Press, 1980.

Bramble, William J., et al. *Computers in Schools.* New York: McGraw-Hill, 1985.

Clarke, Arthur C. *Profiles of the Future.* New York: Warner Books, 1985.

deBono, Edward. *Future Positive.* London: Maurice Temple Smith Ltd., 1979.

deBono, Edward. *Lateral Thinking.* New York: Harper & Row, 1970.

De Koven, Bernard. *The Well-Played Game.* New York: Anchor Books, 1978.

Edwards, Betty. *Drawing on the Right Side of the Brain.* Los Angeles: J. P. Tarcher, 1979.

Eisner, Elliot. *The Educational Imagination.* New York: Macmillan Publishing Company, 1985.

Gordon, William J. J. *Synectics.* New York: Collier Books, 1961.

Grady, Michael P. *Teaching and Brain Research.* New York: Longman, 1984.

Hart, Leslie A. *Guide to School Change.* New York: Brain Age Publishers, 1985.

Hart, Leslie A. *Human Brain and Human Learning.* New York: Longman, 1983.

James, Muriel, and Dorothy Jongeward. *Born to Win.* Reading, MA: Addison-Wesley Publishing Co., 1971.

Raudsepp, Eugene. *More Creative Growth Games.* New York: Perigee Books, 1980.

Samples, Bob. *The Metaphoric Mind.* Reading, MA: Addison-Wesley Publishing Company, 1976.

Sanders, Donald A., and Judith A. Sanders. *Teaching Creativity Through Metaphor.* New York: Longman, 1984.

Swartz, Ronald M., et al. *Knowledge and Fallibilism.* New York: New York University Press, 1980.

INDEX

Abt Associates, Inc., 125
Advanced Skills Curriculum, 209
Analogy Game, 71
Anderson, Alan R., 95
Arieti, Silvano, 43, 104, 167
Asimov, Isaac, 74, 213
  and extraterrestrial civilizations, 158
  and the need for future studies, 152
Auction, 138
Autotelic activity, 93

Bafa Bafa, 5, 139
Barron, Frank, 41
Beat Detroit, 139
Becker, Laurence A., 209
Behavioral psychology, 18, 219
Behavior modification, 219–221
Berne, Eric, 96, 119, 165
Bettelheim, Bruno, 60
Binet, Alfred, 7, 52–53
Bloom, Benjamin, 29, 210
Bloom's taxonomy, 29–30
Brain compatible education, 233
Brainstorming, 72
  and group process, 107
  and synectics, 41
Brockman, John, 153, 213
Bruner, Jerome, 22, 77
Building the Future's Community, 27, 151, 191–195
Burdick, Eugene, 9

Carleton Video Tape Project, 114
Carpenter, Carol, 211, 214

Cartooning, 73
Chester, Michael, 5, 131
Christie, Agatha, 96
Classroom management:
  advice from practitioners, 227–230
  conclusions about, 230–231
Cleaves, Anne, 125
Cognitive-field psychology, 21
Command: The Norm Game, 130
Components of instruction:
  content, 16
  evaluation, 17
  instructional techniques, 16
  materials of instruction, 17
  objectives, 15
  reference materials for teachers, 17
Computer gaming, 107–108
Computerize, 139
Concepts, 20–21
  advantages of teaching, 23
Conceptualizing the future, 158
Conroy, Pat, 228
Control theory, 219, 223–225
Creativity:
  and bisociation, 38
  central premise, 35
  and classroom management, 218
  definition, 6, 36–39, 56
  components of, 45
  conscious orientation, 46, 51
  and endocepts, 42–44
  generalizations about, 39
  and giftedness, 211–212
  and incubation, 41

241

Creativity (continued)
  and IQ, 7
  and Janusian thinking, 42–44
  questions about, 44
  and the study of the unconscious, 51
  unconscious orientation, 47
Creativogenic societies, 167
Csikszentmihalyi, Mihalyi, 94
Culture Contact, 5, 104, 121, 140
Curriculum Review, 205, 214

DeBono, Edward, 166
Decision theory, 99
Democracy, 140
Desert Island, 73
Dewey, John, 47
  and activity in education, 69
  and democracy in education, 114
  and experience, 70, 114
  and experiential education, 116
  and meaningful activity, 48
  and simulation/gaming, 114–116
  and student involvement, 114
  and work, play, and leisure, 115
  as a third force psychologist, 118
Diary and journal keeping, 74
Dickson, Paul, 11
Discovering the Apple, 74
Discussion, 31–32
Duke, Richard, 121, 157
Dungeons and Dragons, 212

Edison, Thomas, 48, 203
Edwards, Betty, 235
Einstein, Albert, 48, 203
Eisner, Eliot, 221
Elaboration, 46
The Energy Game, 189–191
Energy X, 141
Enrichment Triad Model, 208
Expressway, 141

Failsafe, 9, 10, 141
Fairy tale enactment, 76
Film, as future studies activity, 180–181
Flexibility, 45

Flight, 142
Fluency, 46
Food for Thought, 187
Franks, Betty Barclay, 188
Freeway Planning Game, 5, 131–133
Freud, Sigmund, 8, 59–60, 116
  and daydreams and fantasies, 60
  definition of creativity, 47
Future Decisions: The IQ Game, 142, 188–189
Future planning games, 181–182
Future shock, 1, 157, 160–163
Future languages, 157
Future studies:
  and classroom management, 218
  and creativity theorists, 163
  curriculum outcomes, 172–174
  curricular considerations, 171
  and giftedness, 213
  history of, 10
  interdisciplinary nature of, 157
  nature of, 156
  need for, 151–156
  scenario for a third wave school, 174–177
  scenarios, 183–184
  simulations, 187–195
  writing exercise, 186–187
Futurism and population, 182–183
Futurist, The, 178
Futurist Bookstore, 179

Galton, Sir Francis, 6, 10
Game, defined, 10, 95
The Game of Farming, 142
The Games Preserve, 125
Generalizations, 21
Gifted and talented:
  characteristics, 202–205
  components of, 201–202
  definition, 199–200
  and discrimination, 198
Gifted and talented education:
  benefits of, 198–199
  characteristics of teachers, 205–206
  design of programs for, 206–207
Glasser, William, 219, 221–225
Goertzel, Mildred, 41

Goertzel, Victor, 40
Gordon, Alice Kaplan, 100, 123
Gordon, William J. J., 8
   and the beginning of synectics, 62–67
   and the components of the creative act, 64–65
   and facilitating creative behavior, 103
   and *The New Art of the Possible,* 66–67
   and settings for synectics, 42
   and the uses of metaphor, 65
Gould, Stephen Jay, 52
Guided fantasy, 76
Guilford, J. P., 7
   and components of creativity, 45
   conscious orientation to creativity, 47
   and divergent thinking, 57
   and primary mental abilities, 54
   and structure of intellect, 54–57
   and traits associated with creativity, 164–165

Hall, Edward T., 2–6, 235
Hammett, Dashiell, 203
Hart, Leslie, 221, 233–234
Hausman, Carl R., 40
Herndon, James, 228
High School Geography Project, 5, 98, 142
Horn, Robert, 5, 120, 122, 125
Humanistic psychology, and classroom management, 225–227

Information Resources, Inc., 125
Inner City Housing, 143
Innovative teaching strategies, conclusions about, 236–239
Intelligence quotient, 7
Interact, 125
Interdepartmental Decision Making, 5, 143
Inventory of Hunches about Simulations as Educational Tools, 111

Kaufman, Draper, 158
Koestler, Arthur, 221
   and bisociation, 38
   and the concept of holon, 101–102
   and the human brain, 167–168
Kohl, Herbert, 228
Kohler, Wolfgang, 21
Kommisar, 143
Kozol, Jonathan, 227
Kriegspiel, 98
Kubie, Lawrence, 61

Lasch, Christopher, 160
Lateral thinking, 166–167
Learning team model, 224
Lesson planning:
   behavioral, 18–19, 26–29
   conceptual, 20–26
   long-range, 32
   and psychodrama, 70
Lewin, Kurt, 106
Lifeline, 77
Lifestyles, 144
Livingston, Samuel, 143
Logic puzzles, 78–80
Lost on the Moon, 80–81

MacKinnon, D. W., 40
MacLean, Paul, 234
Mager, Robert, 18
Magic shop, 82
Mankala, 144
Maslow, Abraham, 36
   and classroom management, 225
   and hierarchy of needs, 117, 225
   and peak experience, 117
   and psychotherapy with healthy persons, 165
   and self-actualization, 37, 116–118, 226
   and third force psychology, 117
Mastermind, 103, 144
May, Rollo, 37, 160
   and the courage to create, 164
   and the definition of creativity, 38
McConatha, P. Douglas, 133
Metfab, 5
Micro Time, 2–4
Miller, William C., 174
Milton, Ohmer, 143
Models, 82–83

Monochronic time, 2–4
Monopoly, 10
Moore, Omar Khayham, 95
Moreno, J. L., 120, 166
Mozart, 39
Mystery Puzzle, 83

Naisbitt, John, 154, 172, 213
National Game Center and Laboratory, 125
Newmann, Fred M., 145
Nonverbal brainstorming, 73
Nostalgia, 145

Objectives:
  behavioral, 18–19
  conceptual, 22
  global, 13
  and organization of instruction, 15
  as part of the simulation/gaming process, 103
Oliver, Donald, 145
Originality, 46
Osborne, A. F., 41

Palonsky, Stuart B., 228–229
Parnes, Sidney J., 58–59
Participative Decision Making, 5, 120, 122
Pavlov, Ivan P., 18, 219
Penetration, 46
Personal identification, 84–85
Polychronic time, 2–4
Pribram, Karl, 235
Prince, George, 61
The Propaganda Game, 145
Psychodrama, 119, 120, 166
Puppetry, 85

Questioning, 29
Quick City: A Societal Simulation, 135

The Railroad Game, 145
Raser, John, 97, 98
Reading:
  for facilitating creativity, 85
  as future studies activity, 179–180

Reality therapy, 221–223
Redefinition, 46
Reinforcers, 219
Renzulli, Joseph, 198, 205, 208
Rogers, Carl:
  and creative environments, 42
  and creativity as growth, 37
  and conditions for emerging creativity, 105
  and innovation, 38
Rogers, Will, 48, 203
Role-play, 105
Role-training, 164
Rothenberg, Albert, 40, 43

Sartre, Jean-Paul, 225
Science fiction, 11, 88
Self-concept activities, 185–186
Sensitivity to problems, 46
Shaver, James, 145
Shirts, Garry, 111
Simile II, 126
Simulation/gaming:
  advantages of, 93
  as autotelic folk models, 95
  and cause and effect, 96
  and classroom management, 218
  and computers, 99
  and closure, 97
  and creative environments, 104
  and creativity, 101, 102–103
  debriefing, 127
  definition of, 94
  design of, 128–130
  evaluation of, 127–129
  and extensions, 5
  and facilitating creative behavior, 99–100
  as future's languages, 121–122
  and gestalt, 113
  and giftedness, 212–213
  and group process, 106–107
  history of, 9, 97–99
  how to use, 126
  and human potential, 118
  and interdisciplinary learning, 101
  and interpersonal synchrony, 5

and meaningful work, 116
outcomes of, 93
and peak experiences, 118
and polychronic time, 4
and psychodrama, 120
psychological aspects of, 119
and the role of teachers, 97
and socialization, 10
Skinner, B. F., 18, 116, 219
Small group experimentation, 99
Smuin, Stephen K., 83, 182
Social Science Education Consortium, Inc., 126
Sociodrama, 86
Sperry, Roger W., 234
Spontaneity exercises, 86–87
Starpower, 5, 146
Stern, W., 53
Stoll, Clarice Stasz, 143
Structure of intellect, 7, 54–56
 theoretical model, 55
Sync time, 2–4
Synectics, 8
 and brainstorming, 41
 definition of, 64
 exercises, 87
 and group process, 107
 and simulation/gaming, 104
Systems theory, 99

Taba, Hilda, 22
Teacher presence, 218
Techniques for facilitating creative behavior, 71–91
Terman, Lewis, 53
Third force psychology, 116, 225
Third wave, 115, 161
Thurstone, L. L., 54
Toffler, Alvin, 1, 11, 115, 157, 160

Top Management Decisions, 98
Torrance, E. Paul, 7
 and components of creative thinking, 58, 59
 and components of creativity, 45
 and the conscious orientation to creativity, 47
 and creativity associated with vocational success, 165
 definition of creativity, 103
 and environments for creative persons, 57
 and incompleteness, 49
 and school settings, 42
Torrance Tests of Creative Thinking, 58
Totem, 91
Transactional analysis, 37, 96, 119, 121
Transfer, 23
Triune brain, 234
Tuttle, Frederick B., 209

Urban Gaming/Simulation Conference, 126

Videotape productions, 91–92
Voyage of the Mimi, 146

Wallas, Graham, 41, 43
War gaming, 98
What Would You Do?, 147
"Who Are the Gifted Children?", 214–215
Wiener, Norbert, 154
World Future Society, 144, 171, 178–179
Writing, 92

Zero Population Growth, Inc., 187